Literature and Ethics

LIVERPOOL HOPE UNIVERSITY STUDIES IN ETHICS SERIES
SERIES EDITOR: DR. DAVID TOREVELL
SERIES DEPUTY EDITOR: DR. JACQUI MILLER

VOLUME ONE:
ENGAGING RELIGIOUS EDUCATION
Editors: Joy Schmack, Matthew Thompson and David Torevell with Camilla Cole

VOLUME TWO:
RESERVOIRS OF HOPE: SUSTAINING SPIRITUALITY IN SCHOOL LEADERS
Author: Alan Flintham

VOLUME THREE:
LITERATURE AND ETHICS: FROM THE GREEN KNIGHT TO THE DARK KNIGHT
Editors: Steve Brie and William T. Rossiter

Literature and Ethics:
From the Green Knight to the Dark Knight

Edited by

Steve Brie and William T. Rossiter

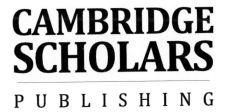

CAMBRIDGE
SCHOLARS
PUBLISHING

Literature and Ethics: From the Green Knight to the Dark Knight,
Edited by Steve Brie and William T. Rossiter

This book first published 2010

Cambridge Scholars Publishing

12 Back Chapman Street, Newcastle upon Tyne, NE6 2XX, UK

British Library Cataloguing in Publication Data
A catalogue record for this book is available from the British Library

ISBN (10): 1-4438-2288-4, ISBN (13): 978-1-4438-2288-6

CONTENTS

INTRODUCTION:
"DISTINCT AND SEPARATE"?

STEVE BRIE AND WILLIAM T. ROSSITER

Writing to the *St James Gazette* on 25 June 1890 in response to a review of *The Picture of Dorian Gray*, Oscar Wilde claimed that "[t]he sphere of art and the sphere of ethics are absolutely distinct and separate" (Beckson, 1974: 67). The essays in the present volume refute this assertion in their examination of the complex interrelationships which exist between literature and ethics. There have of course been previous studies of literature and ethics, but they have often been circumscribed in terms of their chronology and focus. Andrew Newton's *Narrative Ethics* (1995) is a highly informative book but limited to narrative, whereas the present volume also incorporates poetry and the graphic novel, amongst other forms. Also, in terms of chronology, Newton's book is restricted to the nineteenth century and beyond. Likewise, Hadfield, Rainsford and Woods' *The Ethics in Literature* (1999), with a few exceptions, focuses primarily upon the twentieth century.[1] The present volume spans the entire history of English literature. The volume edited by Adamson, Freadman and Parker, *Renegotiating Ethics in Literature, Philosophy and Theory* (1998), whilst illuminating, does not focus upon literature alone, and as such may be seen to have too wide a remit for the undergraduate literature scholar, at whom the present volume is pitched. Louis P. Pojman and Lewis Vaughn's *The Moral Life: An Introductory Reader in Ethics and Literature* (1999) is useful and reliable as an anthology of literary and philosophical texts, but it is nevertheless an anthology, as is *The Moral of the Story: An Anthology of Ethics through Literature* (2004), edited by Peter and Renata Singer.

Whilst the present volume is primarily aimed at an undergraduate readership, the intellectual rigour of the essays, and their impact upon contemporary research, guarantees that the volume will appeal to a wider academic readership. The scholars who have contributed to this volume are established or ascendant figures in their respective fields. These fields are sufficiently varied in their scope to enable an interdisciplinary approach without losing focus upon the relationship between literature and ethics.

This focus is predicated upon a very basic question: does reading literature make one a better person? The fact that this question is so simple has the converse effect of making it very difficult to answer, as it is littered with variables. In the first instance, the term "literature" needs refining— what kinds of literature are we talking about? The Classics? *Heat* magazine or *National Enquirer*? Or the "best that has been thought and said in the world", as Matthew Arnold (1932: 6) once posited? Indeed, the term "literature" is fraught with connotations which could leave one stranded in a sea of post-structural relativity, or which would reignite the debate between highbrow and lowbrow, or fire up T. S. Eliot's canon once more.[2] For the purpose of this volume, a provisional definition of literature has been adopted, referring to those works which either have held up consistently under critical examination, works which manage to convey the mindset of a given historical period, or more recent works which have managed to balance critical and popular acclaim. These definitions are far from perfect, but to prevent the discussion from collapsing into generality parameters are necessary.

The second variable is "better", which might be understood as morally better. This necessitates a fixed definition of what constitutes being morally virtuous. However, ethical codes do not transcend their historical moment, but are produced by them. For example, the ethics discussed by Aristotle in the *Nichomachean Ethics* are not the same codes and practices as those discussed by Kant in his *Groundwork on the Metaphysics of Morals*, which are different again from Alan Badiou's recent prescription, discussed below. Yet because ethical predicates change across time, it does not follow that there are no continuities. The same might be said for literature: literary tastes, styles and modes change, but some things—as Ben Jonson said of Shakespeare—are "not of an age, but for all time" (Jonson, 1996: 264 [line 43]). There is the danger here of lapsing into New Critical liberal humanism, but this volume does not claim the existence of a temporally transcendent human nature, which is free from taint by such vulgar things as society, history, gender, race or class. In fact, this is the key to one of the problems this volume is addressing: can there exist a literary ethics—what might be termed an ethical hermeneutics—which comes after the radical relativism of postmodern literary theory, and which does not retreat back into the moral certainties of Leavisite liberal humanism, which privileged white, middle class, Western European and American male values?[3] This question will be addressed below, and in doing so return to the original question of whether reading literature makes us better people. Firstly, however, the volume's scope must be clarified.

The subtitle to the *Literature and Ethics* volume illustrates its chronology: *from the Green Knight to the Dark Knight*. The Green Knight refers to the central character in an anonymously authored fourteenth-century alliterative poem called *Sir Gawain and the Green Knight*. This poem tells of how a giant Green Knight enters the court of King Arthur "upon Krystmasse" (Anderson, 1996: 168; line 37), and throws down a challenge to the brave and renowned Knights of the Round Table.[4] If one of them would be so bold as to step forward and deliver a blow with an axe upon the Green Knight, then the Green Knight will return the blow in a "twelmonyth and a day" (*SGGK*, 298). The message is clear: the Green Knight is asking the court of Camelot to live up to the stories which have been told about it. However, none of the famous knights is brave enough to take the challenge.[5] The implications for the court are dire; with its honour besmirched, the Round Table is morally redundant. A young, inexperienced figure named Gawain takes the honour of the Round Table upon his slender shoulders, a task which should have been fulfilled by a more experienced knight.[6] Gawain strikes the blow, removing the Green Knight's head in the process. The Green Knight, however, calmly picks up his head, and tells Gawain that he must receive a return blow from the axe "at this tyme twelmonyth" (*SGGK*, 383), when Gawain has sought him out. Gawain thus takes on the responsibility for his society's honour. Camelot, which represents the ideal of medieval romance, is a community with its own ethical code. This chivalric code is predicated upon honour and duty. Gawain has been brought up to believe in that code—when it is threatened, he seeks to preserve it. In doing so he becomes a hero, but also an outcast; whilst others claim to honour the ethics of the chivalric code, it is he who transmutes ethical principles into moral conduct. The poem ends with Gawain being celebrated by the court, but feeling utterly alone: at the close of the poem it says that he "groned with gref and grame" (*SGGK*, 2502).[7] This is the cost of his ethical actions.

Whilst the story of Gawain might seem removed from the figure who concludes the volume, the similarities between the modern and medieval texts are in fact multiple. Batman, the Dark Knight, like Gawain, preserves the ethical code of his community, the cost of which is his effective alienation from that community. *Sir Gawain and the Green Knight*, *Batman: The Dark Knight Returns* and *Batman: The Killing Joke* are concerned with the ethical codes and moral conduct of a given society. Aristotle, whose concept of ethics is directly informed by the Greek *polis*, or more specifically the Athenian city-state, indirectly illustrates the point that each community, each society, formulates its own ethical criteria, yet they rarely start from scratch. For example, Aristotle—like his teacher Plato—frequently uses Homer as an example in his writings, when the ethics of the Homeric poems are in many ways very different from those of the Athenian city-state. Homeric ethics are informed by functionality, what makes a good king, a good sailor, a good farmer. The ethics of the city-state, on the other hand, are concerned with what makes a good *person*, which is linked to the good of the whole society; a good person is a good citizen. As Alasdair MacIntyre noted:

> The Homeric chieftain's personal values, the values of the courageous, cunning, and aggressive king, are now, if exercised by the individual in the city-state, antisocial. [...] The social order in which his qualities were an essential part of a stable society has given way to one in which the same qualities are necessarily disruptive. [...] Different cities observe different customs and different laws. Does and should justice differ from city to city? Does justice hold only within a given community between citizens? Or should it hold also between cities? (MacIntyre, 1967: 11-12)

Ethical codes change not only between places but between times—the ethical codes which are enabled by and inform Gawain's Camelot are not those which are enabled by and inform Batman's Gotham City. Yet, the ethical practices within each community are similar—the way in which Batman acts is similar to the way in which Gawain acts. Both seek to preserve the code, despite its personal cost. As MacIntyre points out, "there are continuities as well as breaks in the history of moral concepts" (1967: 2).

In his *Ethics: An Essay on the Understanding of Evil*, Alain Badiou argues that:

> According to the way it is generally used today, the term 'ethics' relates above all to the domain of human rights, 'the rights of man'—or, by derivation, the rights of living beings.
> We are supposed to assume the existence of a universally recognizable human subject possessing 'rights' that are in some sense natural [...]. These rights are held to be self-evident, and the result of a wide consensus. 'Ethics' is a matter of busying ourselves with these rights, or making sure that they are respected. (Badiou, 2001: 5)

As Badiou's tone suggests, he is not an advocate of this concept of ethics, for him it is "a vague way [...] backed up by official institutions", which has "inspired a violently reactionary movement" (2001: 2-5).[8] In response to this "vague way" Badiou posits "the enduring maxim of *singular processes* [...] the destiny of *truths*, in the plural" (2001: 3). The problem Badiou has with this formulation of ethics is evident: it is predicated upon non-existent universal assumptions, such as an unchanging, one-size-fits-all human condition and a conviction that natural rights exist, without having to clarify in what they exist, and how. However, Badiou's preference for "*truths*, in the plural" opens the door to complete moral relativism. Indeed, we are reminded of Bacon's essay "Of Truth" (1625):

> *What is truth?* said jesting Pilate, and would not stay for an answer. Certainly there be [those] that delight in giddiness, and count it a bondage to fix a belief; affecting free-will in thinking, as well as in acting. (Bacon, 1985: 61)

Unlike his French predecessor, Montaigne, Bacon believed in a fixed truth, although he perhaps uses the term in a circumscribed way—it roughly equates to keeping faith with others, as in late medieval *troth*[9]—and his definition of truth is predicated upon the availability of a universal Real: "truth is a naked and open daylight, that doth not show the masques and mummeries and triumphs of the world half so stately and daintily as candlelights" (Bacon, 1985: 61). Masques and mummeries are literary-dramatic forms, and Bacon notes in the same essay that poetry is a pleasurable lie. It is the purpose of this volume to establish the extent to which literature, far from being little more than a pleasurable untruth, establishes or illustrates ethical truths which are neither so relative as to render ethics redundant, nor which claim complete universality whilst being circumscribed *de facto* by the values of a privileged few. Literature, embedded in history, looks to "*truths*, in the plural", without dissipating the value of those truths. The history of literature is the history of ethical codes as they are inscribed within the wider cultural moment.

These cultural moments are traced by *Literature and Ethics*. If there exists an ethical hermeneutics, informed by an inherent morality within the reading of literature, then it is intertextual, not the product of an individual work, but of what Hans Robert Jauss terms the reader's *Erwartungshorizont*, or "horizon of expectations", which is constructed out of the reader's hermeneutic history (1982: 44). It is this intertextuality which perhaps distinguishes the post-postmodern study of literature and ethics: certain ethical codes and practices recur in literature because new works of literature are informed by their reading of older works of literature. Frank Miller might not have read *Sir Gawain and the Green Knight*, but he surely knew *The Lord of the Rings*, not to mention the earlier Batman incarnations. As such, *Literature and Ethics* considers not only how the ethical considerations of texts are informed by the society and history in which they were produced, but also looks at how intertextuality enables continuity across chronological boundaries. As society changes so does its ethics, and those who hold dear the ethics of the previous shift are apt to defend their codes in the face of this change. It is in fact the continuities that are so often overlooked, yet which it is hoped will become apparent through a cursory outline of the chapters in the volume.

*   *   *

The volume opens with a chapter which emphasizes those continuities by means of a comparative discussion of *Sir Gawain and the Green Knight* and Frances Hodgson Burnett's *The Secret Garden*. Gillian Rudd, the author of the chapter, is a leading ecocritic who specializes in medieval and Victorian literature. As such, her chapter analyzes the eco-ethics of two works, written five hundred years apart, which stress the relationship between humanity and the environment. The second chapter, by Will Rossiter, is a discussion of Renaissance humanism and its claims that literature can make us better people. Beginning with the debate between Plato's *Republic* and Aristotle's *Poetics*, and drawing upon Aristotle's *Nichomachean Ethics*, it proceeds to analyse late medieval and early modern defences of poetry and drama, before culminating in a discussion of Shakespeare's repudiation of the belief that literature can foster a moral code in his play *Titus Andronicus*. The chapter's emphasis upon literature and moral instruction highlights the thematic framework of the volume. Whilst *Literature and Ethics* is predicated upon the question of whether literature has the capacity to make one a morally better person, it is underpinned by three interrelated themes: instruction, judgment, and justice. These themes recur throughout the chapters in diverse manifestations. The two chapters which follow look at further aspects of Shakespearean morality. Unhae Langis examines Hamlet's moral justification for revenge, and the fact that Hamlet's moral code—which is informed by Aristotelian ethics—will not permit him simply to kill his uncle. In a heroic society, vengeance is fuelled by anger towards a violation of one's honour. However, Hamlet, a student of (Christian) humanism, strives for moderation, the rational guidance of passions towards virtuous ends. Jim Casey widens this focus on Shakespearean ethics by exploring the ethical requirements of early modern bodies and the moral judgements tied to them. In Shakespeare's plays, gendered bodies have ethical freight, foreign bodies have moral limitations, and deformed bodies have monstrous associations. By examining the sociocultural expectations that were yoked to early modern bodies, postmodern readers may reassess Shakespeare's plays and re-examine assumptions regarding Elizabethan and Jacobean corporeality. Jim Daems' chapter continues the focus on gendered ethics by examining the prevalence of rape narratives as prologues to freedom in Milton's work, as a prompt for us to consider the ethics of violence in literature, and whether, as Stephanie Jed argues, rape narratives legitimize both republican laws and institutions as well as the conditions of sexual violence in Milton's thought. Li-Hui Tsai maintains the theme of gendered ethics, but transfers the focus from male to female authors. Her chapter on writing women's lives examines the complex relationship between literature and ethics in a wider historical and literary context: it explores, for instance, how women's life stories function as a method for a philosophical ethics among eighteenth-century and Romantic-era writers, critics and reviewers. This emphasis upon the Romantic era leads into Louis Markos's discussion of the dark side of Romantic inspiration; poetic inspiration, it is argued, is not automatically morally beneficent, but is neutral, and shaped by the recipient of that inspiration, as is shown by Coleridge's fragment, "Kubla Khan", and its paratext. In this neutrality, Romantic inspiration is akin to the moral goodness which is found in Renaissance humanist discussions of literature's moral effect being dependent upon disposition.

In his essay on Charles Dickens and human rights, Robert McParland discusses questions such as: can stories prompt us toward ethical reasoning, or perhaps encourage ethical conduct? Some critics argue that ethical judgments about stories are merely subjective opinion. So what can we say about literature's presumed salutary effects upon the reader? Drawing upon recent critical debate, the chapter shows how the readers of Dickens' time believed in Dickens' texts for their ethical power. This chapter is followed by Becky McLaughin's response to the question of whether literature can teach us to be better people. For her, the answer is—resoundingly—yes. McLaughlin, drawing upon the writings of Sartre, conceives of reading as a Passion in the Christian sense of the word, a situation in which the reader freely assents to the tale being told, putting him or herself "into a state of passivity to obtain a certain transcendent affect by this sacrifice", a situation in which the reader takes responsibility for the world that s/he and the writer jointly create through a dialectical process involving production and revelation. Following this, Susan Fischer returns to the subject of gender in her discussion of intersectionality in contemporary women's fiction. Drawing upon feminist political and ethical discourses, contemporary women's fiction often envisions a more just world. The chapter examines the kind of feminist ethics that emerges in contemporary women's fiction and the extent to which such writing draws upon an ethics of intersectionality—the recognition of the non-hierarchal nature of oppression and the need to oppose it in all its forms—and presents the possibility of justice. The chapter by Lawrence Phillips which follows maintains the focus upon contemporary fiction by discussing ethical atavism in J. G. Ballard's sub/urban nightmares. If broadly interpreted as a search of 'the life worth living' or 'satisfaction' rather than reductively as 'good conduct' or 'virtue', in the face of the persistent pressure of modern social spaces to constrain both physically and psychologically, the ethical 'core' of humanity seems to be placed before the reader for debate. Tantalisingly, Phillips argues, this also seems to be associated with the atavistic energies of revolution. In Ballard's writing it is certainly the relentless pressure placed on the individual that releases the energy of revolution, but that energy seems to contain within it the equal potential for evil as well as release. Self-awareness or self realisation seems to have been lost in the equation of modern society as Ballard reads it. The volume concludes with Steve Brie's "Spandex Parables", which examines justice, criminality and the ethics of vigilantism in Frank Miller's *Batman: The Dark Knight Returns* and Alan Moore's *Batman: The Killing Joke*. Utilising theoretical ideas developed by philosophers such as Althusser, Kant, Kierkegaard, Kohlberg, Mill, Nietzsche and Plato, this chapter will explore and interrogate the moral and ethical relationship between Batman and the Joker as documented in *The Dark Knight Returns* and *The Killing Joke*. In analysing the underlying psychological context in which superheroes and supervillains such as Batman and the Joker operate, the chapter suggests that, in terms of moral and ethical contexts, there are as many similarities as there are differences between the two characters.

Underpinning the question of whether literature can make us better people is a debate concerning the meaning of a text, the extent to which that meaning is clear, and therefore fixed, and the degree to which the reader can access that meaning. Roland Barthes famously declared the Death of the Author back in the 1960s:

> We know now that a text is not a line of words releasing a single 'theological' meaning (the 'message' of the Author-God) but a multi-dimensional space in which a variety of writings, none of them original, blend and clash. The text is a tissue of quotations drawn from the innumerable centres of culture. [...] Once the Author is removed, the claim to decipher a text becomes quite futile. To give a text an Author is to impose a limit on that text, to furnish it with a final signified, to close the

writing. [...] Classic criticism has never paid any attention to the reader; for it, the writer is the only person in literature. We are now beginning to let ourselves be fooled no longer by the arrogant antiphrastical recriminations of good society in favour of the very thing it sets aside, ignores, smothers, or destroys; we know that to give writing its future, it is necessary to overthrow the myth: the birth of the reader must be at the cost of the death of the Author. (Barthes, 1977: 146-48)

According to Barthes, the attempt to determine a specific, fixed meaning is futile; the creation of meaning is dependent upon the reader, not upon an Author-God, an omnipotent determiner of semantic parameters who declares that the text definitely means *this* and definitely *not* that. However, if meaning is not fixed then how can any text convey a moral message, given that the message of the text is entirely determined by the reader? The answer to this question lies in addressing Barthes's assertion that "[c]lassic criticism has never paid any attention to the reader", as this is simply not true.

The earliest work of literary criticism is *entirely* dependent upon the reader, or rather the audience (both terms in any case refer to the recipient of the text). Aristotle, in his *Poetics*, states that through pity and fear the audience of a tragedy will effect the proper purgation of those emotions through the process of *katharsis*. *Katharsis* is thus the *telos* of tragedy, its purpose. Classical tragedy cleanses us spiritually or emotionally by allowing us to feel pity and fear in their correct magnitude. By experiencing these emotions during the drama we give them an outlet; were we not to do this, those emotions might disturb our sense of well-being, and be expressed at an inappropriate time. To watch a tragedy, then, is to operate an emotional pressure valve: it does one good. And if it does one good, then one must consider what this good means.

As such, we have to ask ourselves if meaning is as impossible in practice as Barthes would have it be. We might debate the specifics, but overall an idea of what a text would appear to mean can become apparent. For example, the majority of English undergraduates do not read *King Lear* as a delightful romantic comedy, despite the fact that Barthes posits the possibility of such radical semantic discretion within each text. Barthes is of course basing his argument upon a radical indeterminacy which post-structural critics claim as being inherent within language as a semiotics. If meaning within such a semiotics is dependent upon the other elements which together constitute it, then ultimate meaning—the Logos—is endlessly deferred, in a process which Jacques Derrida (1976) called *différance*. Like jam in *Alice in Wonderland*, meaning is always tomorrow and yesterday, but never today.[10] Yet language still *works*, for the most part, as a means of communication; the individual word's potential for ambiguity and misinterpretation still exists, but in general we do not read cat as meaning dog, and we do not mistake a raven for a writing desk. *Katharsis* can thus be effected.

It is worthwhile revisiting earlier models of interpretation in order to emphasize this point. In the medieval commentary tradition it was the job of the commentator to provide the exegesis or allegoresis of a given work, to decode, decipher, and clarify the meaning of the text. The post-structuralist argument claims that the commentator's task is impossible, as no one ultimate meaning exists. Were this argument or *disputatio* to be placed before the medieval commentator, it is likely he would disagree, but would perhaps acknowledge the need for plurality of interpretation in determining meaning. A plurality of readings will produce a plurality of interpretations; the commentator, drawing upon previous commentaries upon the text, can identify common responses and thereby decipher what was called the *intentio auctoris*, the intention of the author, which has been described by A. J. Minnis:

> *Intentio auctoris* (*intentio scribentis*). The intention of the author.
> Here the commentator explained the didactic and edifying purpose of the author in producing the text in question. [...] there was rarely any attempt (at least, not until very late in the Middle Ages) to relate a person's purpose in writing to his historical context, to describe an author's personal prejudices, eccentricities and limitations. The commentators were more interested in relating the work to an abstract truth than in discovering the subjective goals and wishes of the individual author. The *intentio auctoris* [...] was considered more important than the medium through which the message was expressed. (Minnis, 1988: 20-21)

This concept of the *intentio auctoris* would of course be dismissed by Barthes as the theological meaning of the Author-God; it is not impossible to ascertain, but the idea that meaning is limited to such an intention is anathema to post-structuralist sensibility. However, Minnis notes that the *intentio auctoris* is linked to an "abstract truth" rather than "the subjective goals and wishes of the individual author". The author is a conduit for meaning, not a semantic arbiter—in other words, the medieval author is not the Author-God.[11] Umberto Eco (1992) has identified two further intentions: the *intentio lectoris* and the *intentio operis*. The *intentio lectoris* is the intention of the reader, which corresponds with Barthes's concept of the birth of the reader (1997: 148). This, however, despite the reader's intention being determined in part by what Stanley Fish (1990) called interpretive communities, smacks too much of solipsism, or what W. K. Wimsatt and Monroe Beardsley termed the affective fallacy (1972

[1949]). For example, one might be convinced that the sky is green, but that does not make it so, no matter how deeply that conviction is held.[12] The *intentio operis* is more interesting, as this is the intention of the work itself, and is "what the text says by virtue of its textual coherence and of an original underlying signification system [...]. The text's intention is not displayed by the textual surface" (Eco, 1992: 64). This intention might not correspond with that of the author or that of the reader, but is produced textually, contextually and intertextually, by the text pointing to itself ("its textual coherence") and elsewhere, beyond itself ("an original underlying signification system").

It is at this point, with the identification of *intentio operis*, that one can allow the ethical considerations of literature to re-emerge. Again, the previous school of criticism that founded its reading upon literature's capacity for moral amelioration—those critics who subscribed to the ideas of F. R. Leavis—is now viewed with suspicion. In his popular guide to literary theory for undergraduates, *Beginning Theory*, Peter Barry argues that one of "Leavis's faults as a critic [...] [is that] his approach to literature is overwhelmingly moral; its purpose is to teach us about life, to transmit humane values" (2009: 16). The problem here is not necessarily that reading literature for moral lessons is wrong—although Barry's tone suggests that it is distasteful—but that Leavis did not qualify or define his terms with sufficient precision: how does one define "life" or "humane values"? If all literature were concerned with a kind of moral didacticism then it would cease to teach through delight: we would find ourselves asking, like Alice, if everything must have a moral (Carroll, 2001: 94-6). Literature which serves primarily as a vehicle for the author's implicit moral design upon us is rarely popular, and rarely read. In our present culture such designs are often met with suspicion, if not hostility, despite the popularity of self-help books and lifestyle gurus. The *intentio operis*, however, enables an ethical hermeneutics not based upon the views of the author or the ego of the reader, but which channels —through a fusion of text, context and intertext—the ethical code of the society in which it is produced; recalling that ethical codes do not remain static, but alter across time. The intention of the text is thus a means of gauging the ethical moment of the text's production.

For example, were we to take a number of popular texts written in the same period—such as Zadie Smith's *White Teeth* (2000), the Harry Potter series (1997-2007), the Twilight novels (2005-2008), and Mark Haddon's *The Curious Instance of the Dog in the Night-Time* (2003)—then we would be able to extrapolate the ethical code for early twenty-first century Britain and America, despite generic and qualitative difference. This code, on the basis of these texts, would most likely consist of the rights of the individual, and the willingness to accept—and celebrate—cultural differences relative to mainstream normativity, without upsetting the *status quo* (it is the ethical model which Badiou inveighs against, in fact).[13] These codes are not necessarily inscribed as deliberate moral lessons being taught by the author, but reveal the *intentio operis* as being produced by wider socio-political currents. What is also evident is the degree to which the ethical code which underpins these works is in fact very traditional, despite the different approaches of the texts. In Harry Potter we find recycled figures from Lewis Carroll, J. R. R. Tolkien, and C. S. Lewis; all writers who engage with questions of individual and social morality. Zadie Smith frequently channels E. M. Forster.[14] The Twilight novels extend the vampire tradition—itself an industrial age's fantasy of feudal order—to the emo and ME generation, whilst Mark Haddon's novel takes its title from a Sherlock Holmes story. The meanings of each of these texts is produced intertextually and contextually, but without giving way to the radical semantic slippage which Barthes promulgated; each transposes traditional ethical concerns to the present day, without leaving us feeling overly "lectured" (and of course the word "lecture" in the modern idiom carries with it a wealth of negative associations).

Indeed, the inherent hostility towards moral guidance within popular culture entails that literary morality must operate in the same way as advertising—obliquely. The society which refuses to be told how to live its life, ironically, is told how to live its life much more than any previous generation—it is told by fashion designers, by car manufacturers, by supermarkets, by gossip magazines, by computer programmers, by the blogosphere, by social networking sites which interpret our online profiles and send us advertisements which reinforce what we believe to be true of ourselves. But we are not "lectured", so it is ok. We read the hyperreal simulacra of modern life every single day and follow their ethical (or unethical) narratives, but they are not metanarratives, or grand narratives, as they are not explicit, nor do they seek to explain, rather they only represent: as Lyotard wrote, "I define *postmodern* as incredulity toward metanarratives [...] The narrative function is losing its functors, its great hero, its great dangers, its great goal" (Lyotard, 1984: xxiv). The hyperreal texts of post-postmodern culture represent (or misrepresent) ourselves to ourselves, they provide us with the texts of ourselves, which we can either refute or read as gospel.

What is indisputable is that texts need readers, as the reader is necessary for literature to be capable of effecting moral improvement. To address this point we might turn again to Aristotle, who stresses the importance of personal disposition to ethics (Aristotle, 1976: 98). According to this view, the effect, and hence the meaning, of each text is made morally multiform in accordance with ethical hermeneutics, despite there being an ethical code which can be identified by reading a series of texts produced during the same historical moment. The *intentio operis* is not in competition with the *intentio lectoris* so much as it is with what we might term the *dispositio lectoris*—the disposition of the reader, which is, like the intention of the text, shaped by its socio-cultural context. The books by Smith, Rowling, Meyer and Haddon mentioned above all reinforce the *dispositio lectoris*, as they have been shaped by the same context, by what was once called the *zeitgeist* or the Spirit of the Age, or by Fish's interpretive community.

Why is this theoretical argument important? It is important because it is not theory for its own sake—quite the opposite. It is in fact an attempt to reassert reading as something which has practical application, as it had been for centuries. The study of literature is in danger of being made irrelevant precisely at a time when local book groups are oversubscribed and book sales are—we are repeatedly told—at an all time high. Whether hardline theorists like it or not, people tend to read for (a) escapism, for (b) a reinforcement of what they already know or enjoy, for (c) a kind of legitimized voyeurism, for (d) the opportunity to experience a different perspective, and finally (e) to learn something new.[15] Each of these reasons is attended by an ethical consideration: (a) escapism implies something intolerable or displeasing about the reality of one's everyday life, we do not wish to escape from that which we enjoy (b) reinforcement of what one knows or enjoys suggests that what one knows or enjoys is somehow under threat (c) voyeurism has become deeply ingrained within our society, with the proliferation of CCTVs manifesting the panopticon of ideology (d) a different perspective presupposes a willingness to engage with others' opinions. Even (e), learning something new, carries with it the Aristotelian perspective that knowledge is intrinsically good. But there are other reasons too, there are organizations which arrange reading groups for people with depression or other mental illnesses, for people recovering from drug addiction and alcoholism, and it helps them to improve, or at least stave off the progression of the illness.[16] This surely constitutes literature's 'impact'. If we allow the legacy of postmodern theory to persist in making all interpretation relative and thereby make meaning impossible or futile, then we run the risk of making the study of literature completely irrelevant at a time when people are hungrier than ever for the written word. Indeed, we run the risk of forgetting that joy which led to us reading books for a living, and of ignoring the fact that literature is one of the main conduits for the ethical code of a society that is frequently accused of not having one.

Notes

[1] These exceptions are the essays by Ortwin de Graef, David P. Haney and Janis McLarren Caldwell, on Shakespeare's *Coriolanus*, Coleridge and Mary Shelley's *Frankenstein*, respectively.

[2] See Michel Foucault's "What is an Author?" (1977: 113-38) for a discussion as to what one should include under the remit of literature. Foucault's influence upon the expansion of what we consider to be literature has been considerable, notably in relation to new historicism.

[3] These might be better termed moral uncertainties, if one recalls Leavis's famous refusal to accept Rene Wellek's challenge to define his critical terms (in the March 1937 edition of Leavis's journal *Scrutiny*). The present volume does not reject theory either, far from it; see the fascinating discussion of theory and ethics by Becky McLaughlin.

[4] Hereafter cited as *SGGK* and line number.

[5] Arthur, through shame—"The blod schot for scham into his schyre face" (*SGGK*, 317)—accepts the challenge, but Gawain pleads that he be allowed to take it up (339-65).

[6] However, the Green Knight claims that the knights are all adolescents: "Hit arn aboute on this bench bot berdles chylder" (*SGGK*, 280). J. R. R. Tolkien, who edited *Sir Gawain and the Green Knight* in 1925, and translated it into modern English later in his life, might have had this act of bravery and honour in mind when he had Frodo Baggins, a simple hobbit, take on the task of destroying the ring of power when the experienced Elves, Dwarves and Men of the Council of Elrond were not brave enough to do so in his work *The Lord of the Rings*.

[7] Gawain feels foolish after being duped by Bertilak, who bears the true identity of the Green Knight, and his wife, who repeatedly attempts to seduce Gawain as a means of testing his chivalric honour.

[8] Badiou makes it clear through his paraphrasing of the Declaration of Independence ("We hold these truths to be self-evident, that all men were created equal"), that his view of the dominant modern concept of ethics is informed by what has been termed American cultural imperialism. Badiou sees modern ethics as characterized by what he terms "an immense 'return to Kant'" (2001: 8). One might supplement this claim with a concomitant return to Rousseau ("Man was born free, and he is everywhere in chains. [...] common liberty is a consequence of man's nature" [Rousseau, 1968: 49-50]), or a return to Paine. However, Badiou's obvious anti-American bias perhaps limits his conception of ethics.

[9] See for example Chaucer's "Truth".

[10] Carroll's jam is a linguistic pun on the Latin adverb *iam* (which was often written with a descender on the first letter), which is used in the future and past tenses but is substituted by *nunc* in the present tense. See Carroll (2001: 206 n.3).

[11] Unsurprisingly, for the medieval commentator, God is the Author-God, the *deus artifex*, who makes the author a conduit for the abstract truth of which Minnis speaks.

[12] However, see *The Taming of the Shrew* (4.6).

[13] As Peter Hallward writes in his Translator's Introduction to Badiou's *Ethics*, "nothing is more orthodox today than a generalized reverence for the other *qua* other" (Badiou, 2001: xxii).

[14] See Smith (2003).

[15] This is not conjecture; these are the most recurrent responses given by first-year undergraduate students to the question: 'why do we read books?'

[16] See Blake Morrison's *Guardian* article (January 2008) on "The Reading Cure": <http://www.guardian.co.uk/books/2008/jan/05/fiction.scienceandnature> [accessed 23 May 2010]

References

Adamson, Jane, Richard Freadman and David Parker (eds). 1998. *Renegotiating Ethics in Literature, Philosophy, and Theory*. Cambridge: Cambridge University Press.

Anderson, J. J. (ed.) 1996. *Sir Gawain and the Green Knight; Pearl; Cleanness; Patience*. London: Dent.

Aristotle. 1976. *Ethics*. Trans. J. A. K. Thomson. Rev. Hugh Tredennick. London: Penguin.

Arnold, Matthew. 1932 [1869]. *Culture and Anarchy*. Ed. J. Dover Wilson. Cambridge: Cambridge University Press.

Bacon, Francis. 1985 [1625]. *Essays*. Ed. John Pitcher. London: Penguin.

Badiou, Alan. 2001 [1993]. *Ethics: An Essay on the Understanding of Evil*. Trans. Peter Hallward. London: Verso.

Barry, Peter. 2009. *Beginning Theory*: An Introduction to Literary and Cultural Theory. 3rd Edn. Manchester: Manchester University Press.

Barthes, Roland. 1977. *Image-Music-Text*. Trans. Stephen Heath. London: Fontana.

Beckson, Karl (ed.) 1974. *Oscar Wilde: The Critical Heritage*. London and New York: Routledge.

Carroll, Lewis. 2001 [1865, 1871]. *The Annotated Alice—The Definitive Edition: Alice's Adventures in Wonderland and Through the Looking Glass*. Ed. Martin Gardner. Rev. edn. London: Penguin.

Derrida, Jacques. 1976 [1967]. *Of Grammatology*. Trans. Gayatri Chakravorty Spivak. Baltimore: Johns Hopkins University Press.

Eco, Umberto. 1992. *Interpretation and Overinterpretation*. Ed. Stefan Collini. Cambridge: Cambridge University Press.

Fish, Stanley. 1990. *Is there a Text in this Class? The Authority of Interpretive Communities*. Cambridge, MA: Harvard University Press.

Foucault, Michel. 1977. *Language, Counter-Memory, Practice: Selected Essays and Interviews*. Ed. and Trans. Donald F. Bouchard and Sherry Simon. Oxford: Blackwell.

Hadfield, Andrew, Dominic Rainsford and Tim Woods (eds) 1999. *The Ethics in Literature*. London: Palgrave Macmillan.

Jauss, Hans Robert. 1982. *Toward an Aesthetic of Reception*. Trans. Timothy Bahti. Brighton: Harvester.

Jonson, Ben. 1996. *The Complete Poems*. Ed. George Parfitt. Rev. edn. London: Penguin.

Lyotard, Jean-François. 1984 [1979]. *The Postmodern Condition: A Report on Knowledge*. Manchester: Manchester University Press.

MacIntyre, Alasdair. 1967. *A Short History of Ethics: A History of Moral Philosophy from the Homeric Age to the Twentieth Century*. London: Routledge and Kegan Paul.

Minnis, A. J. 1988. *Medieval Theory of Authorship: Scholastic Literary Attitudes of the Later Middle Ages*. 2nd edn. Philadelphia, PA: University of Pennsylvania Press.

Morrison, B. 2008. "The Reading Cure". *Guardian*, 5 January 2008 <http://www.guardian.co.uk/books/2008/jan/05/fiction.scienceandnature> [accessed 23 May 2010]

Newton, Andrew Zachary. 1995. *Narrative Ethics*. Cambridge, MA: Harvard University Press.

Pojman, Louis P., and Lewis Vaughn. 1999. *The Moral Life: An Introductory Reader in Ethics and Literature*. Oxford: Oxford University Press.

Rousseau, Jean-Jacques. 1968 [1762]. *The Social Contract*. Trans. Maurice Cranston. London: Penguin.

Singer, Peter, and Renata Singer (eds) 2004. *The Moral of the Story: An Anthology of Ethics through Literature*. Oxford: Blackwell, 2005.

Smith, Z. "Love, actually". *Guardian*, 1 November 2003 <http://www.guardian.co.uk/books/2003/nov/01/classics.zadiesmith/print> [accessed 13 July 2010]

Tolkien, J. R. R., E. V. Gordon and Norman Davis (eds) 1967. *Sir Gawain and the Green Knight*. 2nd edn. Oxford: Oxford University Press.

—. (trans.) 1975. *Sir Gawain and the Green Knight, Pearl and Sir Orfeo*. Ed. Christopher Tolkien. London: Allen & Unwin.

Wimsatt, W. K., Jr, and Monroe Beardsley. 1972 [1949]. "The Affective Fallacy", in David Lodge (ed.), *20th Century Literary Criticism: A Reader*. London: Longman. 345-58.

"SUBSTITUTING EARTH FOR GOD"? ETHICS AND THE RECOGNITION OF SPECIFIC PLACE IN *SIR GAWAIN AND THE GREEN KNIGHT* AND *THE SECRET GARDEN*

GILLIAN RUDD

In her essay on T. S. Eliot, Louise Glück asserts that "the impulse of our century has been to substitute earth for god as an object of reverence" (Glück, 1994: 21). The implication is that such substitution is possible, not because the two terms are synonymous, but because they now evoke similar combinations of response: "reverence" implies respect, awe, and the sense that the entity revered has the power to heal and to avenge, which further implies a right of judgement. Reverence is in turn an indication of ethical outlook, which confers on the revered being (god/earth) the role of touchstone: how we react, collectively and individually, is taken as an indicator of our moral worth. Those who cannot recognise the value of the revered object are not worthy, or not operating within the pertaining ethical systems, so the process indicates how we regard ourselves in relation to the object of reverence (god or earth) both as individuals and as species. Glück's "impulse" then becomes a compulsion to prove ourselves, our identity and capabilities and so ensure our place in the world as species, but also as individuals within our communities. The texts discussed here offer in Sir Gawain and Mary Lennox two protagonists who enact precisely this complex process as they take it upon themselves to find and then enter specific locations. For Gawain that place is a "green chapel", which he is bound to seek in fulfilment of a challenge issued to the whole of Arthur's court by an anonymous Green Knight during one New Year's festivities. In taking up that challenge Gawain also takes on the mantle of representative of Camelot and the codes it embodies. For Mary the place is the "secret garden" of the book's title. In her case the quest seems more personal as this lonely girl seeks a "bit of earth" (70) to call her own, but as the book goes on her search for belonging becomes a healing process for the whole household at Misslethwaite Manor. The direct encounters with the natural world (earth) experienced by these two protagonists probe the value systems of Camelot and Edwardian England, leaving readers reflecting on their own ethics as well as those upheld by the stories they have just read.

The anonymous poem *Sir Gawain and the Green Knight* survives in one manuscript which was compiled around 1380; Frances Hodgson Burnett's *The Secret Garden* was first published as a book in August 1911, having been serialised during the previous year in *The American Magazine*. Where *Sir Gawain* is a late medieval courtly romance whose audience is invited into the Arthurian world of knights, quests, tests and magical events, *The Secret Garden* offers its readership of American and British middle class families a tale of childhood loneliness and friendship set in contemporary Edwardian England. Such differences are immediately apparent; a moment's reflection makes the similarities just as evident. In Gawain and Mary Lennox, each text introduces a character with whom the audience readily identifies, regardless of how different each reader's actual experience may be. The series of events experienced by each protagonist tests and changes their characters, but also offers room for the reader to evaluate the codes of conduct which guide Gawain and Mary's actions. The quest motif which is explicit in *Sir Gawain* and sends Gawain off alone to find a green chapel to fulfil his bargain with the giant Green Knight who gate-crashed Arthur's Christmas at the start of the poem, is also present in *The Secret Garden*, as Mary is first isolated from her immediate family by an outbreak of cholera in India and then removed from India to England, where she finds herself again largely left to her own devices in Misselthwaite Manor, a large and isolated mansion set in the Yorkshire moors. There she takes it upon herself to discover the secret garden, the equivalent of Gawain's green chapel, in a way reminiscent of Wilson's study of the shared patterns of medieval romance and fairy stories (Wilson, 1976; 1983).

Further parallels are offered in the way each protagonist is initially overlooked by their community. Gawain may be Arthur's nephew, but when the poem opens there is no indication that he is a particularly significant member of Arthur's court. Indeed his request to be allowed to take up the Green Knight's challenge is based on the fact that he, Gawain, is not important, being in his words, the weakest, least clever and so most expendable of Arthur's knights (*SGGK* 354-55). Mary Lennox has been so peripheral in her initial community of English in India that she has been utterly forgotten during the outbreak of cholera which kills or scatters the entire household, leaving her an orphan. She is then sent "home" to her nearest relative, an uncle-in-law, where she finds herself equally marginalised if not equally neglected in Misselthwaite Manor. For the reader, these two marginalised figures become representatives of their respective communities (for today's readers of their respective eras also) and the adventures that occur draw out not only the protagonists' individual characters but also reveal the kinds of character produced by the societies they represent.

It is significant that the places sought by Gawain and Mary are both revealed to be places where nature has taken its course. Although the terms "chapel" and "garden" both presuppose human construction, the function and indeed the magic of these two venues are rooted in their identities as places where human intervention has either been non-existent (the green chapel) or has long since been abandoned (the secret garden). Christianity provides the framework for both texts, but within that framework both texts also share a common reliance on an embedded belief in the restorative powers of the earth. This is clearly articulated in *The Secret Garden* as Mary frequently refers to the "Magic" which makes the bulbs send up shoots, the flowers bloom, and the leaves unfurl, and which also leads her to discovering the door to the secret garden. In *Sir Gawain* the magic is at first unambiguously exemplified in the Green Knight who cheerily survives decapitation, gleefully retrieving his head from being kicked around the floor and then holding it up to address the dais apparently totally unaffected by having that head no longer attached to his body (427-56). Later this magic becomes blended with religious miracle as Gawain sees a castle just after he has prayed in desperation for somewhere to shelter and hear Mass at Christmas (763-70). Each text thus imbues the natural world with a sense of the sacred and at the same time tacitly acknowledges that in order for a place to be sacred it must literally admit human presence. *Sir Gawain* and *The Secret Garden* reveal that the substitution identified by Glück rests on a longstanding mixture of wonder and appreciation (reverence) which typifies our human responses towards earth and its natural forces. Simultaneously, they recognise that running through such responses is a deep and paradoxical sense of being in close relation to, but separate from, the object revered.

In Glück's description of the consequences of substituting earth as an object of reverence for god, that paradoxical relation is described as consequence of the "hunger for meaning and disposition to awe" found in "the religious mind" which "transforms" "the anecdotes of natural process" into "myth" (Glück, 1994: 21). It is an appealing argument, particularly when our two texts contain characters who invite being read as personifications of such mythic transformations of natural processes. In the Green Knight and Dickon we are presented with figures who are clearly at one with the nonhuman world. The Green Knight's very appearance invokes the Green Man of legend (Basford, 2002) with all his connotations of winter death and spring renewal, of Pagan rituals and seasonal cycles, while his alter ego, Bertilak, expresses in his hale and hearty love of hunting and outdoor pursuits a vibrant and confident version of the relationship between human and animal worlds (Marvin, 2006: 143-157). Dickon, in contrast, offers the more romantic notion of the boy whose empathy with animals is so strong he is never without a wild animal companion. He is explicitly linked to Pan, and while Burnett never exploits the wilder aspects of Pan in her book, Dickon retains in benign form elements of the untamed forces Pan represents. Both texts imply that these nature figures inhabit the wilder reaches of the outdoors world: in *Sir Gawain* that is initially whatever lies beyond the bounds of Camelot, later becoming specifically the wilderness of the North West in which the green chapel lies; in the *The Secret Garden* it is the equally untamed Yorkshire moors, which Mary sees but never ventures into, passing through them only when accompanied by Martha (Dickon's sister and Mary's maid) on a visit to the Sowerby's home. Yet, despite their apparently wild abodes, both Dickon and the Green Knight inhabit human homes. Dickon lives in a moorland cottage, one of the large Sowerby family, while the Green Knight, as Bertilak, lives in Hautdesert, a complete castle household of nobles and servants. Yet for each text it is this figure who seems to have the right understanding of the best relation of human to nonhuman worlds and so can be regarded as the embodiment of Glück's "instinct" of the twentieth century. That is, the Green Knight and Dickon do not dictate what is right or wrong so much as elicit responses from other characters which are indicative of the value systems at work in the societies they represent and the texts they inhabit. The Green Knight inspires fear and admiration, where Dickon elicits trust and affection, each reflecting the attitudes towards the natural world at the foundations of their respective texts. However, the critical moments of "myth-making" within these texts lie not in the deployment of these figures, but in the direct encounters with the environment that Gawain and Mary experience when they first discover the specific locations they set out to find.

The single most marked difference between the medieval poet's green chapel and Burnett's walled garden is that where the garden is a cultivated space now derelict and running wild, the "chapel" is nothing but wild landscape. The poem makes explicit the fact that it is only because Gawain has been assured that the chapel he seeks is here (albeit by a guide whose parting directions amount to "keep straight on and it's on your left; you can't miss it") that he is able to make a chapel out of the rocky landscape he is looking at. It is useful to trace the process of recognition here. First

Gawain halts, sitting on his horse and looking about him, "the chapel to seche: / He segh [saw] non suche in no side, and selly [strange] hym thoght" (2169-70). There is a slight ambiguity here as Gawain may be thinking the landscape itself "selly", as well as finding it odd that there is no building. He then notices a rocky outcrop with a river bubbling through it, dismounts and explores on foot. There is a hole at one end and two further ones at either side, the top is overgrown with moss and grass: it is, the narrative surmises (now surely ventriloquising Gawain's thoughts) "nobot an olde caue" (2182)—nothing but an old cave. It is only after much deliberation that he can contemplate even the possibility that this wild crevice can be the appointed "grene chapel" and even then he has to couch the possibility as a question because it looks more like a place the devil might say his morning prayers: "'We, Lorde,' quoth the gentyle knight, / 'Whether this be the grene chapelle?'" (2185-6). A sharper contrast to Burnett's garden it is hard to imagine; both are presented as wild, overgrown places, but one is the natural result of water on rock, while the other is a once carefully constructed and tended space run riot. Nevertheless finding the way in to each place requires a level of attention to the detail of the landscape that we rarely bestow on our surroundings.

Mary's equivalent to Gawain's slow scrutiny from the saddle and subsequent careful exploration on foot is her repeated study of the walls of the orchard which she knows must adjoin the locked garden. Chapter 5 sees her visiting one part of the Manor's grounds more often than any other and even noticing that a section of the walk seems more neglected than the rest: "Mary stopped to notice this and wondered why it was so. She had just paused and was looking up at a long spray of ivy swinging in the wind when she saw a gleam of scarlet and heard a brilliant chirp" (28), which is of course the robin. It is a further two chapters before Mary discovers the key while watching the robin pecking for worms, hopping over and then stopping on "a small pile of freshly turned up earth" (40). Looking at this pile, Mary catches sight of the ring of the key, newly dug up (the narrative tells the reader but not Mary) by the dual forces of a mole and a dog (40). Impelled by this discovery Mary again searches for the door, but again draws a blank, despite getting nearer with her awareness that "the ivy was the baffling thing" (41). Here, as in *Sir Gawain*, the narrative reflects its protagonist's thoughts and in doing so notes the increased attention the human is paying to the plants. No longer just "ivy" as in Chapter 5, the creeper now has "thickly-growing, glossy, dark green leaves" and it is when Mary is again by the wall with the untrained ivy that she sees a door knob briefly uncovered by a gust of wind. Although the focus on the natural surroundings is less explicit here than in *Sir Gawain* it is nonetheless similar in that Mary finds the doorknob only because she is paying very particular attention to what is going on around her. As if to highlight the point, each text marks the moment of discovery/recognition with a pause in the narrative: Gawain identifies the chapel at the end of one stanza and then begins the next with speech on its desolation; Mary enters the garden at the end of Chapter 8 with the description of it following at the start of Chapter 9.

Mary's reaction is a complete contrast to Gawain's—he sees desolation and ugliness where she sees sweet neglect—but both feel that their respective places are cut off from the rest of the world and both promptly redefine the spaces they have found. For Mary this abandoned garden is now "a world all her own" (47) and her continued attention to it allows her to see the tips of emerging bulbs and smell the scent of oncoming spring. For Gawain what was previously "nobut an olde caue, / Or a creuisse of an olde cragge" (2182-3) speedily becomes a devilish place, fit for the fiend, "a chapel of meschaunce" (2195). Although this shift in definition may seem extreme (from natural to fiendish in one easy jump) it is less a change of perception than of terminology. Gawain's world view here accords with that summarized by Gregory Stone: "whatever is human is *not* natural and whatever is natural is *not* human" (Stone, 1998: 3), so all the nonhuman can be lumped together and regarded with suspicion. Regarding the crevasse as either natural or devilish means that whatever it may be, it is not an example of human architecture, which is what the word "chapel" normally connotes. He has overlooked the importance of the adjective "grene" that has tended to accompany "chapel" in this poem and in doing so has effectively relegated the natural world to mere backdrop. His recognition allows that backdrop to become central, but the moment passes quickly as, pat upon his realisation that this is indeed the "grene chapel" he has sought, comes the sound of the Green Knight sharpening his axe. A different apprehension takes over as Gawain in effect opts to deal with a figure who, as a knight, belongs to a familiar human social construct rather than continue the disconcerting encounter with a landscape that has called into question his understanding of the world.

Without recognising their surroundings for what they are neither Gawain nor Mary could have entered the place they set out to find, successful entry into which is a sign of worth in both *Sir Gawain* and *The Secret Garden*. Gawain has proved his ability to keep his word by finding the green chapel on the appointed day and goes on to make good his promise to abide a return blow from the giant Green Knight. In his text Gawain is the only unambiguously human character to gain this access;

the guide he was given deserts him through fear at the top of the valley, while the Green Knight having proved his magical powers at the start of the poem by surviving decapitation, then describes himself as a kind of spirit of the place when he declares "The Knyght of the Grene Chapel men knowen me mony" (454). Mary's entry into the garden is proof of her ability to care about and engage with others. In contrast to *Sir Gawain* it is not just Mary who proves her character by perceiving the natural world directly, and thus gains access into the desired space. Colin studies minutely the samples from the outdoors world that are brought to his sick chamber before he is taken to see the garden himself and Mr Craven, Colin's father, experiences a moment of insight when he is struck by "one lovely mass of blue forget-me-nots" on the Austrian Tyrol (164). Dickon, that Pan-like figure, is presented as being thoroughly at one with the processes of nature, having spent all his eleven years doing little other than notice them while his mother, Mrs Sowerby has similarly been established as someone alive to the wonders of the world. Ben Weatherstaff's plantsman's knowledge which inspires Mary's desire for "a little bit of earth" of her own likewise qualifies him for entry. The fact that all these characters are brought into the garden can be seen as confirmation not only of their individual ethical correctness, but also of Mary's ability to recognise their respective virtues, indeed according to Gretchen V. Rector they gain entry only because Mary permits it (Rector, 2006: 198). Nonetheless, it is only Mary herself who actually finds the garden; only once she has opened the door is it possible for these others to follow her. The order of events is similar to that of *Sir Gawain*, where Gawain's identification of the dell as the green chapel triggers the Green Knight's entrance.

Finding these places and recognising them for what they are is thus crucial to both texts, and so it is only fitting that the green chapel and the garden are both simultaneously known to and hidden from the seeker within the text and indeed the reader of it. For Burnett's readers the garden is identified immediately in the title of the book but it is only when we read that we discover that it is Mary who designates the garden "secret". Everyone else at Misselthwaite Manor knows exactly where the garden is, but they also know why it has been locked up for ten years, so they do not seek it out. In *Sir Gawain* the case is different. The title (bestowed by editors) focuses on the two main players in the poem, Sir Gawain and the mysterious Knight who rides into Camelot and proposes a game of exchange of blows. It is the Green Knight who mentions the "grene chapel", designating it the venue for his return blow to Gawain, to be delivered the following year. Unlike the secret garden, this chapel is an oddly elusive place. On the one hand it is, according to the Green Knight, so well known that it lends its identity to the giant knight himself: "The Knyght of the Grene Chapel men knowen me mony" (454). Furthermore finding both chapel and knight will be merely a matter of asking: "Forthi me for to fynde, if thou fraystez, faylez thou neuer" (455). However, those alert to conventions of folktale may detect some hint of trickery in the parenthetical "if thou fraystez" (if you ask) which perhaps implies that those who do not ask will fail to find it. This is borne out by Gawain's experience. Initially he draws a blank to his numerous enquiries during his travels in quest of the Green Chapel, it is only when he enters Hautdesert, the castle that appears almost as literal answer to his prayer for shelter over Christmas, that he finds himself surrounded by people who do indeed know of the chapel and the Green Knight. It is not just asking, it transpires, but asking the right people, that is a condition of successfully finding what you seek. Moreover, the seeking must be done personally and according to one's own belief and hope as to where the place or person is most likely to be found. Such at least is the meaning of the Green Knight's words to Gawain, "thou schal seche me thiself, whereso thou hopes / I may be funde vpon folde" (395-6).

There is some similarity here to the way that Mary Lennox discovers first the buried key and then the door to the secret garden. She has heard of the locked up garden from Martha and is thinking about it as she explores the grounds on her own. Like Gawain, she has no companion or human helping her, and although it is usual to say that the robin shows her the way, the order of events shows that this is not wholly the case. Mary has already worked out where the hidden garden must be by noticing that the wall of the orchard "did not seem to end with the orchard but to extend beyond it as if it enclosed a place at the other side" (23). It is as she looks at the tops of the trees above the wall and, crucially "when she stood still" that she sees the robin who helps reveal the garden's key and door (23). Importantly, Mary has begun the search herself and when she continues she does so by seeking the door to the garden where she believes it must be, following her own instincts much as the Green Knight tells Gawain he must follow his. This strategy is only partly voluntary, her attempt to make the gardener, Ben Weatherstaff, tell her where the garden is fails as he asserts there is no door, an assertion which he qualifies with the significant phrase "None as any one can find" (27). Like Gawain, then, Mary has a paradoxical quest before her: to find a place that is known to many, but whose entrance is apparently non-existent.

Mary's situation is simply one of a lonely, neglected child finding something to do and some way to fit in to her new surroundings. Gawain's is rather more serious; if he does not find his way to his appointed place he will be a recreant and, by implication, a coward and the reputation of Arthur's court will be in tatters. The Green Knight's instructions boil down to saying he is sure to find the chapel as long as he is seeking it; not the most comforting set of directions, yet those rather mystical lines of information contain two crucial elements of advice buried in the phrases "whereso thou hopes" and "if thou fraystez". Each clause reinforces the notion that as long as Gawain has the right aspirations he cannot help but find what he seeks. All this clearly signals that the Green Knight's "game" is more a test of character than of brute strength. Like Mary, Gawain will be able to find and enter the green chapel only if he is the right kind of person, in the right frame of mind. As with Mary, part of the proof that he is capable of being that person is the simple fact of undertaking to seek out the place to start with.

Burnett's garden inevitably recalls the garden of Eden, which is often imagined as a walled garden, from early medieval illustrations forward. These connotations are only enhanced by details of the story through which the garden, originally created for the young and beautiful Mrs Craven is also the place she suffered her fatal fall. Such details add Biblical connotations to Mary's name as she works to bring this garden back to life after years of neglect, and then introduces others to it. Thus as Dickon, Colin, Ben Weatherstaff, Mrs Sowerby and finally Archibald Craven enter the garden in turn they each suddenly understand what their task is. Dickon must aid Mary and Colin in finding health and a proper appreciation of the world around them, both human and natural. Colin discovers his identity as the tall and fit son of the house and Ben finds a proper new young master to serve in place of the mistress he loved and whose roses he tended until rheumatism prevented him. Mrs Sowerby realises that she is the one who must recall Mr Craven to his house and his duty as a father, and Mr Craven finds his own recovery from mourning confirmed and his role as proper father to his now fit and able son already begun as Colin hurtles into his arms. Recognition, of oneself, of one's role and of the values one will subscribe to and seek to maintain, is thus integral to the right reaction to place *The Secret Garden* presents, just as it is in *Sir Gawain*.

Rector sees the garden as becoming Mary's home, the only home she has in the book and one which other characters can enter only through her agency (Rector, 2006: 198). The implication of this reading is that Mary is the only one who truly enters the garden; the others merely visit and then depart, and indeed all but Mary leave it at the end of the book. While this is persuasive it imbues Mary with more power than I think is the case, despite those Marian allusions, and ignores the effect of the garden on all the characters who enter it. It is as if Mary's identity is now so involved with that of her garden that she is no longer part of the human, familial, world of the Cravens, or even the Sowerbys. Rather, like the deceased Mrs Craven, she becomes a kind of spirit of the place, someone so in tune with the nonhuman world that they never fully leave it. This points to one of the salient differences between the natural cave in Gawain's world and the garden in Mary's. Gardens may have contrary associations as places of temptation and sin as much as innocence and enjoyment, but they are also necessarily connected to culture and cultivation with all the punning connotations those words imply. In *The Secret Garden* the garden is allowed to be predominantly good not only because that is how Mary decides to define it, but also because of the presence of the moors, which allow for wild nature to be admired but held at one remove. We hear of the moors, and know that Dickon and Martha love them, but direct engagement with them is deferred to beyond the bounds of the book. Gawain does not have that option; he has had to travel across wilderness to arrive at the chapel and will have to cross it again to return home, but there is no court garden mentioned at either Hautdesert or Camelot to offer him the kind of interim space occupied by Mary. Nevertheless, in the reactions of both Mary and Gawain to the spaces that define them we have seen traces of that "impulse" which Glück wishes to locate in the twentieth century alone. Their conclusions may be different, but the impulse stems from the same source—that of using the nonhuman as a kind of ethical barometer.

This might suggest that earth as represented by cave or garden is not replacing God so much as acting for him. That is fully in keeping with a medieval view of Nature as God's regent and taps into the association of all gardens with God's initial and perfect creation of the Garden of Eden. It also makes sense of Glück's use of "impulse", implying an innate compulsive reaction which survives religious scepticism by transferring its attention to another object without substantially changing its essence. Where before we trusted to an ineffable Divine to guide and correct, ultimately to take care of Creation, now it appears we place trust in earth itself as the superhuman force which will right the wrongs we commit and in doing so tell us whether as individuals we are praiseworthy or contemptible. Read like this, Glück's words suggest similarities with Lovelock's concept of Gaia—earth as complete system which obeys rules unfathomable by humans but which acts to keep the planet in balance (Lovelock, 1987; Joseph, 1990). However, there is a further layer to Glück's comment, revealed in the paragraph preceding her assertion about "our current impulse." She is describing T. S. Eliot's relation to the material and eternal worlds and states: "Only through the closing of that gap between the actual and the ideal could the physical world attain meaning, authority" (Glück, 1994: 20). In Mary and Gawain's reactions to their specific places in their texts we see just such a closing of the gap, but we also see how very different the results can be. Mary unites the ideal world of health, companionship and cultivation in her adopted garden. In Burnett's world such direct physical engagement with nature can be only good and so it is left to less certain readers to detect the more discomforting implications of seeing Mary left to keep company with the dead Mrs Craven in a walled garden, which seems to have served its purpose now that the old master is home and the young master healthy. Gawain, in contrast, sees all too clearly that uniting actual and ideal landscapes opens the way to god and devil alike and more particularly that such unity denies the possibility of maintaining a sense of distance between the human and nonhuman worlds. Unlike Mary, he resists being absorbed by the place that instigated his moment of insight and so he lives to ride home, leaving the Green Knight-Bertilak in possession of the field.

Thus, although a general moral drawn by both texts is that one is part of a larger social whole, not apart from it, the reactions of our two heroes to this moral is very different. At the end of his text Gawain is left disgruntled, unfulfilled, albeit alive, and deeply unhappy at being hailed as a hero by a Camelot which refuses to hear his version of his story. Gawain is simply not allowed to be the individual he desires to be. Just as the Green Knight refused to accept that Gawain's act of accepting the girdle from Bertilak's wife was a mark of cowardice and instead insisted on it being a sign that Gawain is a human like anyone else (itself a bitter blow to someone wishing to be an individual hero) so Arthur's court refuses to either regard him as a failed knight or to allow him sole possession of the triumph they insist upon cheering. This narrative is perhaps telling us we should not strive to be exceptional, being simply a good example of the general will do.

Mary is likewise finally denied a central place by her story, but only arguably more happily so. Having begun the story as an isolated and disliked child who "has to struggle all the way to achieve a true heroine's status" (Rowe Townsend, 1990: 65) she ends as part of the somewhat bizarre but newly reinvigorated Misselthwaite household. More specifically and interestingly the end of the book leaves her alone in the secret garden as the now healthy Colin and his newly-returned father enter the house in triumph. Although readers may have misgivings about the implications of this ending, Mary can be seen as happy to remain in her garden, a sharp contrast to Gawain who cannot get away from Bertilak, the green chapel and Hautdesert fast enough. Comparison of the endings of the two texts thus offers Mary a contrasting position in the narrative. No longer the equivalent of Gawain, she can be associated instead with the Green Knight. Like him, she is aligned with the natural world and particularly with the earth, and the bulbs which she tended with innate care when she first entered the garden and worked without Dickon's expert help. That care echoes the association of children with nature found in many nineteenth-century children's stories (Hines, 2004), but here takes on an additional aspect. Those bulbs were the flowers of early spring, the "crocuses an' snowdrops an' daffydowndillys" whose green spikes are promised by Ben Weatherstaff and noticed by Mary during her first tour of the garden (39, 47). By the end of the book Colin is a fit, tall boy, his father has returned and the bulbs are over, replaced by the roses which are explicitly associated with Colin's mother and through her with Archibald Craven, Colin and even Ben Weatherstaff. While Colin races back to the house, secure in his newly gained health and the attention of his father, and while Ben breaks the news to the whole of the household staff, Mary is silently left behind, arguably no longer in need of the individual attention and attendant hue and cry that Colin relishes and Gawain desires. Rather, like Bertilak who in his guise of Green Knight is left to go wherever he wishes ("Whidewarde-so-euer he wolde", 2478), Mary's whereabouts become somewhat mysterious as, almost like one of those spring bulbs, she is absorbed into the garden which has given the book its name and ethical force.

This returns us to Glück's comments on Eliot's relation to the material and eternal worlds which in Glück's rhetoric, and perhaps Eliot's too, are utterly distinct. Glück focuses on the bringing together of "the actual and the ideal" through which "the physical world attain[s] meaning, authority" (Glück, 1994: 20). Here, with that inclusion of authority, we see the kind of relation to the physical world that underpins both *Sir Gawain* and *The Secret Garden* and also a good deal of current environmental awareness and green literary criticism, particularly the reception of Lovelock's Gaia thesis (Garrard, 2004: 102, 172-75). The yolking together of meaning and authority effected by Glück here is similar to the attitude that allows "green" to be automatically regarded as "ethical" so much so that the two terms are frequently (and mistakenly) assumed to be synonymous. This confusion rests on two basic, complementary, errors: the assumption that what is regarded as best for the planet and thus the environment (hence green) is necessarily best also for people and that every action that can be termed "ethical" is good for the environment (whereas frequently it is concerned with right dealings with other people and takes no notice of the non-human world at all). It all rather depends on where humans either en masse or individually figure within a given ethical stance. That however, is matter for a very different debate; here we are concerned with two literary texts which clearly regard humans and how they act both as individuals and as part of a community as vitally important. Ideals matter in such a system and, as with Eliot (if we follow Glück) the physical world is the place where the actual and ideal may, possibly, meet.

I think we see this happening in the moments of recognition that I have highlighted within each text. These are not the big set pieces which display the courage of each protagonist, not, in other words, the moments when Gawain steps forward to take up the challenge and deliver the first blow, nor when he again steps forward to receive its return. Not when Mary defies the tantrums of Colin and the fears of the household, matching his temper with hers in an explosion that proves cathartic for both of them, nor in her growing admiration of the moors or even her careful nurture of the garden itself. Rather in each case the pivotal point is one of recognition— the moment when they see that the real landscape about them is indeed the ideal one they have been seeking. Through that recognition they are admitted into the settings that prove their characters and seal their futures. In broad terms, then, these two texts invite us to reassess our reliance on purely human codes and knowledge and instead to take more account of the world around us. Importantly, such reassessment is possible not when we interact with nature figures, to crudely characterise the Green Knight and Dickon, but when we stand alone and simply pay attention to the precise physical space around us. It is at these moments that our own personal understanding of where we as individuals and as species stand in the world becomes apparent. The author of *Sir Gawain and the Green Knight* knew that we might not like what we see and prefer to strive to keep the human and the nonhuman worlds distinct. Burnett, on the other hand, cannot acknowledge this, preferring to believe in a nature that is always beneficial, even if her own plot relies upon an incident that denies this (Mrs Craven's fatal fall was the result of a bough breaking, an event that occurs prior to the events traced in the book, allowing it to be the *felix culpa* of *The Secret Garden*'s world). Just as the reactions offered by each text can be regarded as indicative of their own times, so our own latter day reactions may go far to illuminate our personal attitudes towards how nature is defined and the kinds of relations with it we seek to endorse in the anxious climate of the twenty-first century.

References

Anderson, J. J. 2005. *Language and Imagination in the "Gawain"-Poet*. Manchester: Manchester University Press.

Basford, K. 2002. *The Green Man*. Woodbridge: D. S. Brewer.

Burnett, F. 2006. *The Secret Garden*. Ed. G. Gerzina. New York: Norton & Co.

Garrard, G. 2004. *Ecocriticism* London and New York: Routledge.

Glück, L. 1994. *Proofs and Theories: Essays on Poetry*. New Jersey: Ecco Press.

Hines, M. 2004. "'He made *us* very much like flowers': Human/Nature in Nineteenth-Century Anglo-American Children's Literature", in *Wild Things: Children's Culture and Ecocriticism*. Eds S. Dobrin and K. Kidd. Detroit: Wayne State University Press. 16-30.

Joseph, L. 1990. *Gaia: The Growth of an Idea*. New York: St Martin's Press.

Lovelock, J. 1987. *Gaia: A New Look at Life on Earth*. Oxford: Oxford University Press.

Marvin, W. 2006. *Hunting Law and Ritual in Medieval English Literature*. Cambridge: D. S. Brewer.

Rector, G. 2006. "Digging in the Garden: The Manuscript of *The Secret Garden* by Frances Hodgson Burnett", in *The Secret Garden*. Ed. G. H. Gerzina. New York: Norton & Co. 186-99.

Rowe Townsend, J. 1990. *Written for Children: An Outline of English-language Children's Literature*. 5th edition. London: Bodley Head.

Stone, G. 1998. *The Ethics of Nature in the Middle Ages: On Boccaccio's Metaphysics*. Basingstoke and London: Macmillan.

Tolkien, J. R. R. and E. V. Gordon (eds). 1967. *Sir Gawain and the Green Knight*. Rev. N. Davis. Oxford: Clarendon Press.

Wilson, A. 1976. *Traditional Romance and Tale: How Stories Mean*. Ipswich: Brewer.

—. 1983. *Magical Thought in Creative Writing: The Distinctive Roles of Fantasy and Imagination in Fiction*. Stroud: Thimble Press.

THE ETHICS OF RENAISSANCE HUMANISM: LITERATURE, HISTORY AND THE MORAL HIGH GROUND

WILLIAM T. ROSSITER

In canto XI of the *Inferno* (ca. 1314), during his explanation of the structure of Hell, Virgil recalls to the Pilgrim a piece of Aristotelian morality:

> Non ti rimembra di quelle parole
> con le quai la tua Etica pertratta
> le tre disposizion che 'l ciel non vole,
> incontenenza, malizia e la matta
> bestialitade?

> Do you not remember the words with which your *Ethics* treats so fully the three dispositions that Heaven refuses, incontinence, malice, and mad bestiality? (XI. 79-83)[1]

Virgil is here making reference to book VII of the *Nichomachean Ethics*, wherein Aristotle confirms "that there are three kinds of states of character to be avoided, viz. vice [*kakia*], incontinence [*akrasia*], and brutishness [*thēriotēs*]" (Aristotle, 1976: 226).[2] Dante's reference to Heaven ("'l ciel") illustrates Aristotle's appropriation by late medieval Christian scholasticism and the commentary tradition. Indeed, it was most likely the commentary of St Thomas Aquinas upon the *Ethics* which was Dante's source.[3] However, Aristotle's original statement also corresponds with later humanist concepts of man's dignity (*dignitas hominis*): "mortals become gods through superlative goodness, [so] the state opposed to brutishness would clearly be of this kind" (Aristotle, 1976: 226). Renaissance humanism was still a Christian ethos, but Dante's Thomistic conception of a forbidding Heaven ("'l ciel non vole") is somewhat different both from what is to be shunned in respect of moral character and the godlike elevation of the virtuous, and stands apart from the Christian humanist conception of the ethical.[4]

This chapter will then examine the ethical considerations which underpin Renaissance humanism and its conception of literature's role in developing and adhering to a moral code. The chapter will discuss the ways in which humanist apologists respond to classical discussions of poetry and ethics, such as those found in Aristotle and Plato, and in doing so formulate an ethical hermeneutics which is differentiated from the previous, scholastic model of interpretation. It will also discuss how humanism's emphasis on literature's capacity for moral prescription is ultimately interrogated by authors who recognize both the benefits and the pitfalls of classical exemplarity. To paraphrase Louis Montrose's famous chiasmus, this chapter examines the textuality of the ethical, and the ethics of text.[5] In doing so it follows a trajectory from Dante, Petrarch and Boccaccio through to Sidney, Jonson and Shakespeare, the latter of whom may be seen to query humanism's ethical project by pointing to the bloody spectacles disinterred by Renaissance philology. Coincident with this trajectory will be a comparative analysis of how literature's ethical imperative differs from that of historical exemplarity as a means of fostering a moral code.

It would perhaps help to begin with a working definition of early modern or Renaissance humanism. Humanism, as it is understood in this chapter, involves the reading of classical texts through a non-exegetical or non-scholastic hermeneutics. That is, classical texts are to be understood on their own terms, for their intrinsic value and not primarily in terms of Scriptural revelation.[6] Humanism also advocates the active search for lost classical texts, and the stylistic imitation of those extant. Yet the humanist ethic does not exclude Christian theology. Indeed, the notion of the Dignity of Man, or rather of the Individual, is formed around the central belief in the Word made flesh (*verbum caro factum*), and a shift in emphasis away from the objective metaphysics of scholasticism to the subjective ethical dilemmas faced by the individual Christian.

To return to our point of departure, it is worth noting that Dante's Heaven does not only refuse "incontenenza, malizia e matta / bestialitade" but also Aristotle himself on account of his being a pagan. The Philosopher—as he was known—is rather to be found in the first circle of Hell (IV. 133-35):

> Poi ch'innalzai un poco più le ciglia,
> vidi 'l maestro di color che sanno
> seder tra filosofica famiglia.
>   Tutto lo miran, tutto onor li fanno:
> quivi vid' ïo Socrate e Platone,
> che 'nnanzi a li altri più presso li stanno

When I lifted my brow a little higher, I saw the master of those who know, sitting among a philosophical company.

All gaze at him, all do him honour: there I saw Socrates and Plato, standing closer to him, in front of the others. (Alighieri, 1996: 76-77)

Dante here inverts the order of priority by making Plato subordinate to Aristotle, who had in fact been Plato's student. Dante would not have known Plato's work directly—aside from the partial translation of the *Timaeus* by Calcidius—but would have encountered him for the most part via Augustinian Neoplatonism. As Durling points out, however, Dante's Aristotle "was more Platonic than not, since, in common with his time, Dante ascribed to him several works by late followers of Plato and read him in a Neoplatonic key" (1996: 84). Indeed, it would be facile to ascribe to Dante an entirely Aristotelian perspective as his knowledge of "'l maestro di color che sanno" was filtered through commentaries by Aquinas, Avicenna and Averroes, amongst others, many of whom subscribed to Neoplatonic ideas. Nevertheless, there appears a distinctly anti-Platonic bias within the *Commedia* which serves to place Dante at odds with the early Italian humanists, despite critical arguments for Dantean proto-humanism (see Weiss, 1969).

Interestingly, Aristotle's *Ethics*, stripped of its scholastic paratext, appears not so very far removed from humanist ideas:

Every art and every investigation, and similarly every action and pursuit, is considered to aim at some good. [...] Does it not follow, then, that a knowledge of the Good is of great importance to us for the conduct of our lives? [...] we are studying not to know what goodness is, but how to become good men, since otherwise it would be useless. (1976: 63-64, 93)

Aristotle's statement is by no means alien to early modern humanists. It is recalled, for example, by Sir Philip Sidney in his *Defence of Poesy* (1595): "as Aristotle saith, it is not *gnosis* but *praxis* must be the fruit [...] to be moved to do that which we know, or to be moved with desire to know" (2002: 226). Following his discussion of astronomy and mathematics, Sidney notes that the liberal arts are "serving sciences", which are "all directed to the highest end of the mistress-knowledge, by the Greeks called *architektonike*", which consists of "knowledge of a man's self, in the ethic and politic consideration, *with the end of well-doing and not of well-knowing only* [...] *the ending of all earthly learning being virtuous action*" (2002: 219-20, emphasis added).[7]

Aristotle's *Ethics* was also a work that Petrarch, one of the architects of humanism, knew well and cited often (see Trinkaus, 1979: 15-16), which might seem somewhat surprising in light of his fervent anti-scholasticism.[8] However, Aristotle's prescription for acting virtuously as being the *telos* of the knowledge of goodness is not realized in the work, according to Petrarch:

> I often complained to myself and sometimes to others that the goal announced by the philosopher in Book One of his *Ethics* is not realized in fact—namely, that we study this branch of philosophy not in order to know, but in order to become good. I see how brilliantly he defines and distinguishes virtue, and how shrewdly he analyzes it together with the properties of vice and virtue. Having learned this, I know slightly more than I did before. But my mind is the same as it was; my will is the same; and I am the same. [...] it is better to will what is good than to know what is true. (2005: 315-19)

It is one thing to understand what makes a person morally virtuous; it is another thing to be morally virtuous. One way of achieving goodness, or rather of moving others to virtuous acts, is literature. As N. S. Thompson explains, "[Petrarch] raises the very question for literature [...] What is the point of the mere presentation of vice, without any overt moral from the author?" (1996: 34-35). In his 1355 *Invective contra medicum* (*Invectives against a Physician*), Petrarch writes in response to an attack on poetry that poets "strive to adorn the truths of the world with beautiful veils [...] for perceptive and diligent readers it [truth] is just as delightful to discover as it is difficult to find". In doing so poets "treat ailing souls" (2005: 29, 31). The struggle to find truth and thereby become good is consonant with Aristotle's view in the *Ethics* that "the harder course is always the concern of both art and virtue, because success is better in the face of difficulty" (1976: 96-97). Boccaccio likewise, in his famous defence of poetry in book XIV of *De genealogia deorum gentilium* (1350-74), argues that the poet seeks "to make truths which would otherwise cheapen by exposure the object of strong intellectual effort and various interpretation, that in ultimate discovery they shall seem more precious" (Osgood, 1956: 60). Sir Philip Sidney continues this tradition by arguing that "under the veil of fables, to give us all knowledge [...] there are many mysteries contained in poetry" (2002: 249). In the humanist critical tradition, therefore, poetry combines hard-earned knowledge of truth with the instillation of willing towards moral goodness, as the former without the latter is morally defunct: "it is better to will what is good than to know what is true".

Petrarch's *Invective contra medicum* and *De sui ipsius et multorum ignorantia*, book XIV of Boccaccio's *De genealogia deorum gentilium*, and Sidney's *Defence of Poesy* all respond to attacks on poetry's alleged immorality, falsehood and lack of utility. They are all also linked in that Boccaccio, who names Petrarch as "my reverend teacher, father, and master" (Osgood, 1956: 115), draws upon the *Invective contra medicum* for many of the arguments in *De genealogia*, and Sidney in turn draws upon Boccaccio's *De genealogia*—amongst other works—in his *Defence*. Ironically, the ultimate defence of poetry against specifically Aristotelian or scholastic charges is Aristotle's *Poetics*, which Petrarch cites in response to the physician who verbally attacked him:

> The Muses belong to the poets, and no one doubts it. Philosophy called the Muses "her own" [in Boethius's *De consolatione philosophiae*], but you fail to consider this, madman. [...] If this were not the case, Aristotle—a less important philosopher than you!—would not have published his book on poetics, which I surmise you have not seen, and which I know you have not understood, and could never understand. (Petrarch, 2005: 97)

Indeed, if we turn to the *Poetics* we can see even an even greater similarity between Aristotle's thought and the concepts underpinning early modern humanism, which again might seem somewhat surprising given humanism's anti-scholastic impetus:

> The distinction between historian and poet is not in the one writing prose and the other verse [...] it consists really in this, that the one describes the thing that has been, and the other a kind of thing that might be. Hence poetry is something more philosophic and of graver import than history, since its statements are of the nature rather of universals, whereas those of history are singulars. By a universal statement I mean one as to what such or such a kind of man will probably or necessarily say or do—which is the aim of poetry, though it affixes proper names to the characters; by a singular statement, one as to what, say, Alcibiades did or had done to him. (Aristotle, 1984b: 2333)

Sidney cites this passage almost verbatim when making his case for poetry in the *Defence* (2002: 223), again arguing that it supersedes history by virtue of its universality, as opposed to being bound to the specific. The benefit of this universality is not only that it will extend a specific illustration of moral virtue beyond its immediate point of reference, but that it allows for amelioration of the historical illustration with a view to increasing the moral effect upon the reader or audience, what we might term ethical hermeneutics. For Aristotle, poetry is more philosophical than history, and Petrarch follows Aristotle in uniting philosophy and poetry. Poetry's moral force lies in its universality, although Petrarch's conception of history as a moral compass is not so far removed—both are dependent upon hermeneutics and reception. Sidney goes further, as we shall see, in placing poetry above both history and philosophy in terms of its ability to inspire people to moral virtue.

How then does poetry inspire moral virtue? In the first instance its rhetorical force has the power to move its audience. According to Boccaccio, poetry can "awake the idle, stimulate the dull, restrain the rash, subdue the criminal, and distinguish excellent men with their proper meed of praise" (Osgood, 1956: 39-40). We can see poetry's rhetorical force in the proemical sonnet that opens Petrarch's sequence, the *Rerum vulgarium fragmenta* (*Fragments of Vernacular Things*):

> Voi ch'ascoltate in rime sparse il suono
> di quei sospiri ond'io nudriva 'l core
> in sul mio primo giovenile errore
> quand'era in parte altr'uom da quell ch'i'sono,
>
> del vario stile in ch'io piango et ragiono
> fra le vane speranze e 'l van dolore,
> ove sia chi per prova intenda amore,
> spero trovar pietà, nonché perdono. (Bettarini, 2005: 5 [*RVF* I. 1-8])

> You who hear in scattered rhymes the sound of those sighs with which I nourished my heart during my first youthful error, when I was in part another man from what I am now:
>
> for the varied style in which I weep and speak between vain hopes and vain sorrow, where there is anyone who understands love through experience, I hope to find pity, not only pardon. (Durling, 1976: 36)

The vocative plural "Voi" which opens the poem establishes the implied reader (see Iser, 1974) as being part of an audience, an audience which is to be moved to pity ("pieta")—Aristotle's *pathos* (1984b: 2320)—by the poet speaker's "scattered rhymes ("rime sparse") and "varied style" ("vario stile"), operating upon their own experiences of love.

However, poetry is distinct from rhetoric by virtue of mimesis and allegory, as Boccaccio notes, "among the disguises of fiction rhetoric has no part, for whatever is composed under a veil, and thus exquisitely wrought, is poetry and poetry alone" (Osgood, 1956: 42). Boccaccio is here drawing on Petrarch's arguments in the *Invective contra medicum*, discussed earlier, whereby truth is unveiled through delightful difficulty. These veils or *integumenta* differentiate poetry from rhetoric as they emphasize the figurative, as in Horace's dictum that a poem should be like a picture ("ut pictura poesis" [1926: 72]). It is through *figura* (see

Auerbach, 1984: 11-76) that poetry approaches theology in its ability to teach through moral illustration, as Boccaccio notes, "what the poet calls fable or fiction our theologians have named figure" (Osgood, 1956: 49). Petrarch likewise claims in a letter to his brother Gherardo (*Familiares* X. 10) that "theology is the poetry of God" (1982: 69), whilst Sidney calls the Psalms "heavenly poesy" (2002: 215). All three point to Scripture as an example of poetic fable and religious instruction being intertwined (Petrarch, 2005: 29; Osgood, 1956: 87; Sidney, 2002: 223). Indeed, both Petrarch and Boccaccio claim that the first poets (*prisci poetae*) were theologians (Petrarca, 2005: 115; Osgood, 1956: 121-23; see also Trinkaus, 1970: 689-97). The use of figurative language is the source of poetry's ability to instruct through delight, which itself comes of pleasure taken in mimesis (Aristotle, 1984b: 2318). Indeed, Sidney predicates his defence of poetry upon this fusion: "[Poets] imitate to delight and teach; and delight, to move men to take that goodness in hand, which without delight they would fly as from a stranger; and teach, to make them know that goodness whereunto they are moved" (2002: 218). The moral force of poetry thus lies in its rhetorical energy and figurative, allegorical language, which— once understood—teaches through delight. It does not merely establish the knowledge of what constitutes virtue, but instils in the reader or audience a desire to act in accordance with that knowledge.

And yet, as the detractors to whom Petrarch, Boccaccio, Sidney and Jonson are responding claim, poetry has the potential to be morally corruptive. The source of this allegation is of course Plato's *Republic*, and the various humanist apologies for poetry might be seen as responding, directly or indirectly, to Plato's call for such a defence at the close of his dialogue, after he had banished poetry from his ideal commonwealth:

> It is fair, then, that before returning from exile poetry should publish her defence in lyric verse or some other measure; and I suppose we should allow her champions who love poetry but are not poets to plead for her in prose, that she is no mere source of pleasure but a benefit to society and to human life. [...] We shall reiterate that such poetry [dramatic poetry] has no serious claim to be valued as an apprehension of truth. One who lends an ear to it should rather beware of endangering the order established in his soul [...] it is a choice between becoming a good man or a bad. (Cornford, 1941: 332)

Plato's banishment of poets from his republic is well known, yet it cannot be understood independently of its context. As such, we must identify the ethical reason why Plato exiles poets and how this exile is dependent upon his wider philosophical concepts. Plato's theory of Forms is essential to understanding why poets are deemed to be pernicious. As is known, Plato identifies two planes of existence, the realm of Being and the realm of Becoming. We exist in the latter, the material world, whilst the former is populated by the unchanging Forms. That which exists in the realm of Becoming is a shadow or reflection of that which exists in the realm of Being, and as such is at a remove from true existence, in that everything within it is an imitation of that which exists in the realm of the Forms. Plato famously illustrates this concept via the parable of the cave (Cornford, 1941: 222-30). In this parable, we are told of people chained together in a cave, behind whom are a fire and a puppet show; these together cast shadows upon the walls of the cave, which the prisoners take to be reality, having never known the sunlight outside of the cave. Were someone to escape, s/he would gradually become accustomed to sunlight, and real objects. Yet were s/he to return to the cave to tell others of the 'real' world beyond, s/he would cause great resentment and be killed—if the other prisoners could break free of their shackles. Thus Plato says in the *Republic* (514a-521b). From this distinction between Being and Becoming it becomes clear why poets cannot remain within Plato's society. The world in which we live is itself already at a remove from true reality (the realm of the Forms); poetry, in presenting a *mimesis* of the world in which we live, is then an imitation of an imitation, leading people—and specifically Plato's young philosopher kings, whose education is in question—away from the truth.

However, a further distinction is being made here. Plato specifically means to exclude dramatic poets, as Petrarch notes:

> The so-called dramatic poets are placed in the last rank of poets. [...] Plato himself declared their nature in his *Republic* when they wrote that they should be banished from his city. [...] Yet Plato's judgment, rather than harming epic poets and others, was of great benefit to them. [...] When did any illustrious poets dedicate themselves to stage plays, including Homer among the Greeks, or Virgil among the Latins? Absolutely never. Instead, with their marvellous style, which I would labour in vain to explain to you, they treated the nature of people and the world, the virtues, and human perfection. (2005: 101-3)

Boccaccio follows Petrarch in this distinction between the moral virtues of epic and comic or dramatic poetry, noting how Plato cites Homer frequently (Osgood, 1956: 89-90). In fact, Boccaccio goes much further than Petrarch in his vehement attack upon comic poets:

> Comic poets [...] defiled the bright glory of poetry with their filthy creations. [...] Whether from innate foulness of mind, or greed for money,

or desire of popularity, they wrote dirty stories and presented them on the
stage, and thus prompted lascivious men to crime, unsettled those who
were established in virtue, and weakened the moral order of the whole
state. [...] Indeed, I think that they ought to be not expelled, but
exterminated. (Osgood, 1956: 93-94)

There is a typological implication here pertaining to the effect of immoral
mimesis upon specific dispositions, to the effect which those possessing
"innate foulness of mind" can have upon those who are "established in
virtue", a point which will be discussed subsequently. Sidney likewise
distinguishes the English comic poets, or rather the comic aspects of
tragedy, as being morally reprehensible: "in that comical part of our
tragedy, we have nothing but scurrility, unworthy of any chaste ears, or
some extreme show of doltishness" (2002: 244). However, Sidney does
not go so far as to call for the extermination of comic poets, but rather
argues that comic poetry, when done properly, can serve as a moral
stimulus:

> The comedy is an imitation of the common errors of our life, which [the
> Comic poet] representeth in the most ridiculous and scornful sort that may
> be, so as it is impossible that any beholder can be content to be such a one.
> [...] And little reason hath any man to say that men learn the evil by seeing
> it so set out, since, as I said before, there is no man living but, by the force
> truth hath in nature, no sooner seeth these men play their parts, but wisheth
> them *in pistrinum* [...] So that the right use of comedy will (I think) by
> nobody be blamed. (2002: 229-30)

Sidney draws on the Platonic distinction between forms of poetry (epic
and dramatic or comic), to which both Petrarch and Boccaccio adhere and
use to defend poetry against its detractors, but extends that distinction to
comic poetry itself—comedy, when composed and performed in
accordance with virtue, can have a beneficial effect upon the ethical
hermeneutic; when it is composed and performed in discord with virtue its
effect is "scurrility", to the degree that it threatens the moral order of the
state. The Elizabethans were certainly aware of the threat posed by the
stage; in 1581 the office of the Master of the Revels was patented, the
holder Edmund Tilney ensuring that plays avoided political and religious
controversy. This was followed in 1606 by the Act to Restrain Abuses of
Players (see Chambers, 1923: IV: 285-7, 339). The normative moral order
was thus bound up with loyalty to the state, as politics and ethics are in
many ways inseparable, as Alasdair MacIntyre notes, "moral concepts
change as social life changes" (1966: 1).

Sidney's reference to "the right use of comedy" points to a possible discrepancy in Boccaccio's thinking, or rather an alteration of it. Many of the humorous *novelle* in Boccaccio's *Decameron* (1349-51) could be charged with scurrility, as Boccaccio was no doubt aware. As such, he writes in the *conclusione dell'autore* which follows the collection of one hundred tales, that "[a]ll things have their own special purpose, but when they are wrongly used a great deal of harm may result, and the same applies to my stories" (1995: 800). Boccaccio is here echoing Aristotle's assertion in book II of the *Ethics* that "[t]hings that have a use can be used both well and badly" (1976: 142), and indeed the discrepancy between Boccaccio's two positions on the subject of comedy and morality may be unified through reference to Aristotelian disposition. Boccaccio refers to "innate foulness of mind" in *De genealogia*, and in the *conclusione* of the *Decameron* argues that "[n]o word, however pure, was ever wholesomely construed by a mind that was corrupt" (1995: 799). According to this argument, there *is* such a thing as an inherently moral poet and an inherently immoral reader, and *vice versa*. Does it then follow that if an immoral reader can pervert the meaning of a moral text, that a moral reader can ameliorate the meaning of an immoral text? This is not to say that meaning is fixed within each text, rather it is a matter of what Boccaccio called "various interpretation". However, the medieval exegetical practice of *intentio auctoris*—whereby the exegete confirms the intention of the author—would suggest that meaning was more stable then than it is for the postmodern reader writing in the wake of the Death of the Author (see Minnis, 1988: 20-21; Barthes, 1977: 142-48), albeit not completely fixed. It would appear, somewhat paradoxically, that a text can be read morally or immorally, and that the moral interpretation is somehow the "right" interpretation, although this does not negate each text's inherent polysemia and its potential conjunction with an ethical (or unethical) *Rezeptionästhetik* (see Jauss, 1982).

There remains the question, however, of the later reception of Plato's critique of poetry as falsehood, interpreted outside of the theory of Forms—the accusation that poetry is lies, and therefore immoral. Boccaccio replies to this accusation by saying that "I had supposed that a lie was a certain very close counterfeit of the truth which served to destroy the true and substitute the false" (Osgood, 1956: 63). Poetry is not falsehood by virtue of its dissimilarity to the truth, as "in most instances it bears not only no close resemblance to the literal truth, but no resemblance at all" (ibid.). Moreover, poetry differentiates from a lie by virtue of its *telos*, as "it is not a poet's purpose to deceive anybody with his inventions" (ibid.). Sidney responds to the charges of poetic falsehood in a similar manner in his *Defence*:

> Now, for the poet, he nothing affirms, and therefore never lieth. For, as I take it, to lie is to affirm to be true that which is false. [...] The poet never maketh any circles about your imagination, to conjure you to believe for true what he writes. [...] And therefore, though he recount things not true, yet because he telleth them not for true, he lieth not [...] What child is there, that coming to a play, and seeing *Thebes* written in great letters upon an old door, doth believe that it is Thebes? (2002: 235)

Again, Sidney differentiates from Boccaccio in his inclusion of drama; Boccaccio would not have considered tragedy and comedy in the first instance as being dramatic forms, but as narrative poetry, and would have inherited the Dantean prescription for the two forms as it appears in the Epistle to Can Grande (see Alighieri, 1920: 200-1; Hollander, 1994). Sidney also makes a key point concerning what Coleridge would term the "suspension of disbelief" (1983: 312). According to Sidney's perspective, there is truth—or at least a moral stimulus—to be found in drama whilst maintaining one's disbelief, which perhaps puts him at odds with Shakespeare's exhortation to "[p]iece out our imperfections with your thoughts" (23) in the Prologue to *Henry V* (Greenblatt *et al.*, 1997: 1455).

This moral stimulus within drama, specifically within comic drama, and the distinction between "scurrility" and "the right use of comedy", is echoed in Ben Jonson's Epistle to *Volpone* (1605):

> The too-much licence of *Poetasters*, in this time, hath much deformed their mistress [...] that now, especially in *dramatic*, or (as they term it) *stage poetry*, nothing but ribaldry, profanation, blasphemy, all licence of offence to God, and man, is practised. [...] the principal end of poesie [is] to inform men, in the best reason of living [...] it being the office of a comic-Poet to imitate justice, and instruct to life, as well as purity of language, or stir up gentle affections. (Jonson, 1968: 9)

Jonson, like Sidney before him, bemoans the current state of English drama, and like his predecessors he is defending his craft. Yet whereas Petrarch, Boccaccio and Sidney were responding to critiques of poetry per se, Jonson is responding to attacks on the theatre by Puritans, who saw it as a den of vice. Ironically, the sleights upon the stage that we read in Boccaccio are not a million miles away from the charges laid against it by Puritans such as Anthony Munday, who described the theatre as "the chapel of Satan" and claimed that there was "no want of young ruffians, nor want of harlots utterly past all shame, who press to the fore-front of the scaffolds to show their impudency and to be as an object to all men's eyes" (Chambers, 1923: IV: 211). Jonson's defence of the theatre draws upon the same language as that used by the poetic apologists, arguing that the *telos* of drama is the instillation of moral virtue within the audience. Jonsonian satire, aiming as it does "to reduce [restore] the ancient forms" (Jonson, 1968: 8), certainly corresponds to Sidney's argument that comedy represents "the common errors of our life [...] in the most ridiculous and scornful sort", and thereby prevents the audience from lapsing into vice.

There is an obvious question that needs to be asked here—why should it be the case that tragedy causes the audience to imitate virtuous actions, whereas comedy causes the audience to avoid vicious actions? Is it not possible for the vicious actions to be attractive, and therefore imitable? To answer this we must return the question of disposition—what Jonson would call a person's humour—and *Rezeptionästhetik*. Boccaccio posits that a perverse mind will pervert what is pure, whilst Sidney argues that "the force truth hath set in nature" causes the member of the comic audience to shun vicious behaviour (not to mention that the wicked are always punished at the end of the play, as in *Volpone*). Jonson in turn argues for "the impossibility of any man's being a good Poet, without first being a good man" (1968: 6), so that the good poet will imbue his works with a moral persuasion. However, Sidney's somewhat ambiguous "force" suggests an essential or natural virtue, which does not correspond with Aristotle's account of virtue in book II of the *Ethics*. According to Aristotle, moral goodness "is the result of habit", and "none of the moral virtues is engendered in us by nature, since nothing that is what it is by nature can be made to behave differently by habituation". By extension, "our virtues are expressions of our choice, or at any rate imply choice" (Aristotle, 1976: 91, 99). How then do we account for Boccaccio's conception of the perverse mind, or Sidney's conception of the natural force of truth, or the potential for poetry to have a positive moral effect on someone who is immoral? It is worth recalling Boccaccio's claim that certain kinds of comic drama "prompted lascivious men to crime, [and] unsettled those who were established in virtue". Such a statement is predicated upon typology, but not necessarily essentialism. Rather it is a matter of disposition. Aristotle argued that there were three forms of modification found in the soul: feelings, faculties, and dispositions:

> By feelings I mean desire, anger, fear, daring, envy, joy, friendliness, hatred, longing, jealousy, pity, and in general all conditions that are attended by pleasure or pain. By faculties I mean those susceptibilities in virtue of which we are said to be capable of the feelings in question, e.g. capable of anger or sorrow or pity. By dispositions I mean conditions in

virtue of which we are well or ill disposed in respect of the feelings concerned. (Aristotle, 1976: 98)

Sidney's ethical playgoer and Boccaccio's perverse reader are thus moral or immoral through disposition, which is reinforced by choice and habit. The effect, and hence the meaning, of each text is thereby made morally multiform in accordance with ethical hermeneutics. We see an example of this multiple ethical hermeneutics in Shakespeare's *Titus Andronicus*, a play which includes two re-readings of an exemplary classical text (Ovid's *Metamorphoses*) and re-readings of classical modes of moral conduct. It also blurs the line between the moral lesson taught by literature, and that taught by history. As such, it is worth first recapitulating humanist distinctions between literature and history.

Sidney, as we have seen, adheres to the Aristotelian position that poetry's universality is superior to history's particularity in terms of the moral lesson it teaches. And whilst it must be borne in mind that ethical codes are specific to the societies in which they inhere, it is also worth recalling that there are "continuities as well as breaks in the history of moral concepts" (MacIntyre, 1966: 2). Boccaccio had conceded that "the heroic poets seem to be writing history [...] Yet by their art they portray varieties of human nature and conversation, incidentally teaching the reader" (Osgood, 1956: 48-9). Boccaccio also notes that poets and historians differ in terms of their process, as historians "begin at some convenient beginning and describe events in the unbroken order of their occurrence to the end", whereas poets begin *in medias res* (as Horace prescribed), "or sometimes even near the end" (Osgood, 1956: 67-8). Petrarch, however, asserts equivalence between poetry and history in terms of process, *telos* and effect. In the prologue to *De viris illustribus* (*Concerning Illustrious Men*), he says that he has followed "the law of history" as prescribed by Cicero:

> I have joined together many things which were found dispersed in many histories, by one author or by several, and I have made them a whole. [...] For, unless I am mistaken, this is the profitable goal for the historian: to point up to the readers those things that are to be followed and those to be avoided, with plenty of distinguished examples on either side. (Kohl, 1974: 141)[9]

In one of his letters to Boccaccio (*Familiares*, XXIII. 19), Petrarch outlines the process of writing poetry in similar terms, whereby unity comes of plurality:

> We must thus see to it that if there is something similar, there is also a
> great deal that is dissimilar, and that the similar be elusive and unable to be
> extricated except in silent meditation, for the resemblance is to be felt
> rather than expressed [...] we must write as the bees make honey, not
> gathering flowers but turning them into honeycombs, thereby blending
> them into a oneness that is unlike them all, and better. (Petrarch, 1985:
> 301-2)[10]

The "oneness" of the new work of poetry is produced in accordance with
the principle that guides Petrarch's moral historicism—and which may be
linked to what C. S. Lewis termed the medieval Principle of Plenitude
(1964; repr. 2005: 44). This interdisciplinarity is unsurprising given that in
his *Letter to Posterity* (*Seniles* XVIII. 1) Petrarch describes himself as
having been "especially inclined to moral philosophy and poetry" and
"charmed by the historians, though I was no less offended by their
disagreements" (Petrarch, 1992: 673-74). Sidney, writing two centuries
later, was also offended, and does not subscribe to Petrarch's implicit
connection between poetry and history precisely on the grounds that the
former teaches a more moral lesson than the latter, which might even be
used to disseminate immorality:

> Now, that to which is commonly attributed to the praise of history [...]
> therein a man should see virtue exalted and vice punished—truly that
> commendation is particular to poetry, and far off from history. For indeed
> poetry ever sets virtue so out in her best colours [...] But the history, being
> captived to the truth of a foolish world, is many times a terror from well-
> doing, and an encouragement to unbridled wickedness. (2002: 225)

Sidney's divergence from Petrarchan moral historicism might be seen as
corresponding with his slight upon those poets who insist on reheating
"poor Petrarch's long-deceased woes" in his great sonnet sequence,
Astrophil and Stella (Sidney, 2002: 158 [*AS* 15. 7]). What is interesting,
however, is his view of history as "an encouragement to unbridled
wickedness", as Shakespeare would appear to endorse this argument in
Titus Andronicus (1592).[11] However, Shakespeare goes further than this
by creating a correspondence between history and poetry—as Petrarch
had—and by suggesting that *both* might serve as incitements to moral
degeneracy, depending upon the disposition and habit of the reader.
Shakespeare thus combines Aristotelian ethical hermeneutics (disposition,
choice, habit) with humanist ethical hermeneutics (the classical past as
moral tiller), and in doing so questions a culture—that of the period
formerly known as the English Renaissance—which looked to both the

literature and history of antiquity as a means of confirming the human condition.[12]

Whilst the character of Titus Andronicus is not an historical figure in the way that Julius Caesar or Antony and Cleopatra are, he is informed by a plurality of figures from Roman history—Shakespeare would appear to be following Petrarch's Senecan honeybee method. Indeed, Katharine Eisaman Maus cites a number of Roman patriarchs who might have informed Titus, such as Gaius Mucius Scaevola, Titus Manlius Torquatus, Marcus Portius Cato, and Appius Claudius (Greenblatt *et al.*, 1997: 372; see also Law, 1943; West, 1982). These figures, embodiments of Stoic virtue (in the sense of a specifically masculine moral ethos, stemming as it does from *vir*, man), combined, inform Shakepeare's honour-bound Titus, who kills his daughter Lavinia following her rape and mutilation at the hands of the Goths Chiron and Demetrius in order to preserve her honour. Titus's unswerving adherence to Roman codes of honour, codes which might be seen to have disintegrated by the period in which the play is set (late fourth century AD), lead him to acts such as the killing of both his son (Mutius) and daughter, acts which blur the division between the honourable Romans and the barbaric Goths. Tellingly, Titus is himself a reader of Roman history:

TITUS	My lord the Emperor, resolve me this:
	Was it well done of rash Virginius
	To slay his daughter with his own right hand
	Because she was enforced, stained, and deflowered?
SATURNINUS	It was, Andronicus.
TITUS	Your reason, mighty lord?
SATURNINUS	Because the girl should not survive her shame,
	And by her presence still renew his sorrows.
TITUS	A reason mighty, strong, effectual;
	A pattern, precedent, and lively warrant
	For me, most wretched, to perform the like.
	Die, die, Lavinia, and thy shame with thee,
	And with thy shame thy father's sorrow die.
	He kills her.

(5.3.35-46)

Titus's reading of the story of the Roman centurion who killed his daughter to preserve her (or rather his) honour, which Shakespeare took from Livy, provides him with a "pattern, precedent, and mighty warrant" for killing his own daughter. What is to us a barbaric act of "unbridled wickedness", yet one which is ostensibly legitimized by Lavinia's earlier plea to Tamora, Queen of the Goths, that she be killed rather than be defiled by Tamora's sons (2.3.168-78), and by Titus's profession that he "can interpret all her martyred signs" (3.2.36), is in Titus's eyes a moral action—whether it was thus for Shakespeare's audience remains to be seen. It is an action shaped by reading the tale of Virginius's daughter and reinforced by Titus's disposition, choice, and habit.

It was a similar act of reading reinforced by disposition, choice and habit which led to Lavinia's rape and mutilation. Chiron and Demetrius re-enact Tereus's rape of Philomel as it is recounted in Ovid's *Metamorphoses*. In this tale, Philomel is molested and has her tongue cut out by her sister Procne's husband. As she can no longer speak, and is held prisoner by Tereus, she weaves a tapestry relating what has happened to her, which reaches her sister. Upon being freed, Philomel, together with Procne, take revenge upon Tereus by butchering his and Procne's son, Itys, and feeding him to his father after he has been baked in a pie. Chiron and Demetrius evidently have read Ovid's tale, for they chop Lavinia's hands off in addition to cutting her tongue out, so that she cannot repeat Philomel's revenge:

DEMETRIUS So, now go tell, an if thy tongue can speak,
          Who 'twas that cut thy tongue and ravished thee.
CHIRON   Write down thy mind, bewray thy meaning so,
          An if thy stumps will let thee play the scribe.
DEMETRIUS See how with signs and tokens she can scrawl.
          [...]
CHIRON   An 'twere my cause I should go hang myself.

                                              (2.4.1-9)

Chiron and Demetrius have read the literature of antiquity and have found in it the "encouragement to unbridled wickedness" which Sidney ascribed to history. In the play the reading of history (Virginius) would appear to remedy the reading of literature (Ovid), although this is somewhat too facile—as we know, it is dependent upon the reader and his or her moral disposition. Just as Ovid's tale of Philomel and Tereus gave Chiron and Demetrius the idea for their hideous plan, so does it give Titus the means of revenge. It is only when young Lucius is reading Ovid's tales, much to the consternation of the mute Lavinia, that Titus realizes what has happened to his daughter: "Lavinia, wert thou thus surprised, sweet girl, / Ravished and wronged as Philomela was, / Forced in the ruthless, vast, and gloomy woods?" (4.1.51-53). Titus thus learns revenge from Ovid, killing and baking both Chiron and Demetrius, and feeding them to their mother, "For worse than Philomel you used my daughter, / And worse than Progne I will be revenged" (5.2.193-94). As Jonathan Bate argues,

Shakespeare "implicitly offers a critique of the very humanism he is embodying" (1993: 107).

In *Titus Andronicus* we appear to reach the point at which humanism turns on itself. Shakespeare's play is dependent upon a culture which venerates the classical past, and yet depicts that past as immoral, concupiscent and bloodthirsty. It might be argued that the Goths in the play (Chiron, Demetrius, Tamora) are supposed to be represented thus, but Titus himself, in his reading of Livy, exemplifies an ethical hermeneutics and a moral code founded upon a sense of honour which manifests itself as butchery. As Bate argues, "[w]hat kind of education by example is it, he [Shakespeare] seems to ask, that leads you to murder your daughter?" (1993: 107). This "education by example" might be brought into correspondence, however, with the earlier humanist view of history as teaching "those things that are to be followed and those to be avoided". Shakespeare's play, whilst it is not a history, corresponds to Petrarch's moral historicism. It also corresponds to Petrarch's Senecan model of literary production, and in doing so perhaps creates a link between humanist models of history and literature. Nevertheless, the overall impression that the play leaves is that history, and the literature of antiquity, teach lessons in "unbridled wickedness". This does not negate Boccaccio's Aristotelian emphasis upon the disposition of the reader informing the meaning of the text, however. Chiron and Demetrius possess an "innate foulness of mind" which cannot but lead to immoral interpretation. Titus is not thus, but might be guilty of moral misprision, to use one of Shakespeare's own words.[13]

What becomes apparent when examining the progress of humanist literary ethics is its blend of continuity and divergence. A constant factor in humanist defences of poetry is the view that poetry has the potential to make us morally better, if we are of the right disposition, and impelled by the natural force of truth. What is inconstant is the nature of this poetry— for example, Boccaccio would not agree with Sidney and Jonson that the comic poet has a moral vocation. Nevertheless, Boccaccio's admission that "[n]o word, however pure, was ever wholesomely construed by a mind that was corrupt" entails that impure words can, potentially, be construed morally. Indeed, according to Boccaccio poetry can "subdue the criminal". In tracing this pattern of continuity punctuated by divergence, humanist literary ethics can be seen to correspond with the progress of ethics as a whole, in that ethical codes differ between societies and epochs, whilst certain moral principles are maintained. For the humanist, poetry has the power to inspire moral virtue, and by extension illustrates the moral codes of the period in which it is produced. As Hamlet says, "the purpose of playing [...] is to hold as 'twere the mirror up to nature, to show virtue her own feature, scorn her image, and the very age and time his form and pressure" (Greenblatt *et al.*, 1997: 1708 [*Hamlet*, 3.2.18-22]).

Notes

[1] This passage, as Anna Maria Chiavacci Leonardi argues, poses "a difficult question—and indeed it is one which is still discussed today—because it is linked to an apparent incongruity in [Dante's] text" (Alighieri, 1991: 352). During (Aligheri, 1996: 182) provides a brief account of the critical debate as to the alleged Aristotelian referent.

[2] I have used Thomson's translation of the *Ethics* rather than that of Ross and Urmson as the former translates *diathesis* (διαθεσις) as "disposition" (1976: 98), correspondent with Dante's "disposizion", whereas the latter prefer "state" (1984a: 1746). I have however consulted Barnes' edition throughout.

[3] See *Convivio*, II. 14 and IV. 8 (Dante, 1908; Dante, 1988). On Dante and Aquinas see Wicksteed (2002).

[4] Roberto Weiss (1969) claims that Dante's outlook was humanist, but his argument involves redefining humanism to "fit" Dante, as it were. On the continuing influence of Aristotle's *Ethics* in the early modern period see Schmitt (1984: 87-112) and also the chapter by Unhae Langis in the present volume.

[5] Montrose's new historicist dictum refers to "the historicity of texts and the textuality of history" (1989: 20).

[6] Although Petrarch himself was not immune to Christian allegoresis—see for example the letter to his brother Gherardo (*Familiares* X. 4), which accompanied his first eclogue.

[7] The seven liberal arts consisted of the *trivium* (grammar, rhetoric, logic) and the *quadrivium* (music, astronomy, arithmetic and geometry).

[8] Petrarch frequently seeks to defend Aristotle against Aristotelians. In his *Invective contra medicum* (*Invectives against a Physician*), for example, Petrarch routs a physician with philosophical pretensions who has attacked poetry:

> Go wretch; read and re-read that passage in Book Three of Aristotle's *Rhetoric* [...] Don't cull a single word here or there in ignorance, pretending to have read Aristotle. Examine the whole passage. If you can understand it, you will find that this man of ardent genius desired to embrace all disciplines. In his fashion he amply discusses the eloquence proper to oratory and to poetry. (Petrarch, 2005: 95)

Similarly, in *De sui ipsius et multorum ignorantia* (*On His Own Ignorance and That of Many Others* [1371]), a treatise written in response to an attack on Petrarch's knowledge by four professed Aristotelians, Petrarch refers to Aristotle as

> a sweet and pleasant writer to whom they [Aristotelians] have given a scaly hide. They deviate and depart so far from their leader that they think eloquence an impediment and a disgrace to philosophy. But in fact Aristotle considered it a great ornament and strove to unite eloquence and

philosophy, incited, we are told, by the glory of the orator Isocrates. (Petrarch 2005: 233; see also 313)

[9] The "law of history" to which Petrarch is referring may be found in *De oratore*, II. 62: "Everybody knows that the first law of history is not daring to say anything false; that the second is daring to say everything that is true" (2001: 139). Boccaccio echoes Petrarch's moral historicism in his *De casibus virorum illustrium* (ca. 1373-1374): "For what is better than to use all one's resources in order that the errant might be called back to the better, virtuous life, in order that the sleep of death might be shaken from the indolent, in order to repress vices and extol virtue?" (1983: 3).

[10] See Seneca's Epistle LXXXIV, "On Gathering Ideas" (1918-25: II: 276-85). Seneca draws the image from Virgil (*Aen.*, I. 432-23), but see also Horace, *Carm.*, IV. 2. 27-32: "ego apis Matina / moro modoque / grata carpentis thyma per laborem / plurimum circa nemus uvidique / Tiburis ripas operosa parvus / carmina fingo" ("I, in manner and method like a Matine bee that with incessant toil sips the lovely thyme around the woods and riverbanks of well-watered Tibur, fashion in a small way my painstaking songs" [2004: 222-23]). Greene's discussion of the passage from *Familiares* XXIII. 19 in *Light in Troy* (1982: 95-100) is superlative.

[11] Whether Shakespeare read the *Defence* remains to be seen. In his review of Alwin Thaler's *Shakespeare and Sir Philip Sidney: The Influence of the Defence of Poesy* (1947), Geoffrey Bullough argued that it "is unlikely that Shakespeare did *not* read *The Defence*, but alas, Professor Thaler has not quite proved that he did" (Bullough, 1949: 560).

[12] I would agree with Robin Headlam Wells' argument that the early modern mind believed in a human condition, rather than the New Historicist imposition— informed by Foucault—of an anti-essentialist, ideologically constructed persona upon the early modern period. As Headlam Wells points out, "[t]he belief that Shakespeare and his contemporaries were radical anti-essentialists is not supported by historical evidence" (2005: 4). See also Mousley (2007).

[13] In sonnet 87 (line 11) the poet-speaker refers to "thy great gift upon misprision growing" (Greenblatt *et al.*, 1996: 1952). Misprision as wilful, creative misreading, is central to Bloom's anxiety of influence (1997: 19-45).

References

Alighieri, Dante. 1908. *The Convivio*. Trans. Philip H. Wicksteed. 2nd edn. London: Dent.

—. 1920. *Dantis Alagherii Epistolae: The Letters of Dante*. Ed. and trans. Paget Toynbee. Oxford: Clarendon Press.

—. 1988. *Convivio*. Ed. Cesare Vasoli and Domenico De Robertis. *Opere minori*, Tome I/2. Milan: Ricciardi.

—. 1991. *Commedia. Volume 1: Inferno*. Ed. Anna Maria Chiavacci Leonardi. Milan: Mondadori.

—. 1996. *The Divine Comedy of Dante Alighieri: Inferno*. Ed. and trans. Robert M. Durling. Oxford: OUP.

Aristotle. 1976. *Ethics*. Trans. J. A. K. Thomson. Rev. Hugh Tredennick. London: Penguin.

—. 1984a. *Nichomachean Ethics*. Trans. W. D. Ross and J. O. Urmson. *The Complete Works of Aristotle: The Revised Oxford Translation*. Ed. Jonathan Barnes. 2 vols. Princeton, NJ: Princeton University Press, 1984. 2: 1729-1867.

—. 1984b. *Poetics*. Trans. I. Bywater. *The Complete Works of Aristotle: The Revised Oxford Translation*. Ed. Jonathan Barnes. 2 vols. Princeton, NJ: Princeton University Press, 1984. 2: 2316-40.

Auerbach, Erich. 1984. *Scenes from the Drama of European Literature*. Trans. Ralph Manheim and others, Theory of History and Literature, 9. Manchester: Manchester UP.

Barthes, Roland. 1977. Image-Music-Text. Trans. Stephen Heath. London: Fontana.

Bate, Jonathan. 1993. *Shakespeare and Ovid*. Oxford: OUP.

Bloom, Harold. 1997. *The Anxiety of Influence: A Theory of Poetry*. 2nd edn. Oxford and New York: OUP.

Boccaccio, Giovanni. 1983. *De casibus virorum illustrium* . Eds. P. G. Ricci and Vittore Zaccaria. *Tutte le Opere di Giovanni Boccaccio*, IX. Gen. Ed. Vittore Branca. Milan: Mondadori.

—. 1985. *Decameron*. Ed. Vittore Branca. Milan: Mondadori.

—. 1995. *The Decameron*. Trans. G. H. McWilliam. 2nd edn. London: Penguin.

Bullough, Geoffrey. 1949. "Review of *Shakespeare and Sir Philip Sidney: The Influence of the Defence of Poesy* by Alwin Thaler", *Modern Language Review*, 44: 559-60.

Chambers, E. K. 1923. *The Elizabethan Stage*. 4 vols. Oxford: Clarendon Press.

Cicero. 2001. *On the Ideal Orator*. Trans. James M. May and Jakob Wisse. Oxford: OUP.

Coleridge, Samuel Taylor. 1983. *Biographia Literaria: Biographical Sketches of My Literary Life and Opinions*. Ed. James Engell and W. Jackson Bate. Princeton, NJ: Princeton UP.

Cornford, F. M. 1941. *The Republic of Plato*. London: OUP.

Greenblatt, Stephen, Walter Cohen, Jean E. Howard, Katharine Eisaman Maus (eds). 1997. *The Norton Shakespeare: Based on the Oxford Edition*. New York and London: Norton.

Greene, Thomas M. *The Light in Troy: Imitation and Discovery in Renaissance Poetry*. New Haven, CT: Yale UP.

Headlam Wells, Robin. 2005. *Shakespeare's Humanism*. Cambridge: CUP.

Hollander, Robert. 1994. *Dante's Epistle to Cangrande*. Ann Arbor, MI: University of Michigan Press.

Horace. 1926. *Satires, Epistles, Ars Poetica*. Trans. H. Rushton Fairclough. Cambridge, MA: Harvard University Press.

—. 2004. *Odes and Epodes*. Ed. and trans. Niall Rudd. Cambridge, MA: Harvard University Press.

Iser, Wolfgang. 1974. *The Implied Reader: Patterns of Communication in Prose Fiction from Bunyan to Beckett*. Baltimore, MA:

Jauss, Hans Robert. 1982. *Toward an Aesthetic of Reception*. Trans. Timothy Bahti. Brighton: Harvester.

Jonson, Ben. 1968. *Volpone*. Ed. Philip Brockbank. London: Black.

Law, Robert Adger. 1943. "The Roman Background of *Titus Andronicus*", *Studies in Philology*, 40: 145-53.

Lewis, C. S. 1964; repr. 2005. *The Discarded Image: An Introduction to Medieval and Renaissance Literature*. Cambridge: CUP.

MacIntyre, Alasdair. 1967. *A Short History of Ethics: A History of Moral Philosophy from the Homeric Age to the Twentieth Century*. London: Routledge and Kegan Paul.

Minnis, A. J. 1988. *Medieval Theory of Authorship: Scholastic Literary Attitudes of the Later Middle Ages*. 2nd edn. Philadelphia, PA: University of Pennsylvania Press.

Montrose, Louis. 1989. "Professing the Renaissance: The Poetics and Politics of Culture", in H. Aram Veeser (ed.), *The New Historicism*. New York and London: Routledge. 15-36.

Mousley, Andy. 2007. *Re-Humanising Shakespeare: Literary Humanism, Wisdom and Modernity*. Edinburgh: Edinburgh University Press.

Osgood, Charles G. 1956. *Boccaccio on Poetry: Being the Preface and the Fourteenth and Fifteenth Books of Boccaccio's Genealogia Deorum Gentilium*. Indianapolis, IN: Bobbs-Merrill.

Petrarch, F. 1976. *Petrarch's Lyric Poems: The Rime sparse and Other Lyrics*. Ed. Robert M. Durling. Cambridge, MA: Harvard UP.

—. 1982. *Letters on Familiar Matters: Rerum familiarium libri IX-XVI*. Trans. Aldo S. Bernardo. Baltimore, MA: Johns Hopkins University Press.

—. 1985. *Letters on Familiar Matters: Rerum familiarium libri XVII-XXIV*. Trans. Aldo S. Bernardo. Baltimore, MA: Johns Hopkins University Press.

—. 1992. *Rerum senilium libri: Letters of Old Age*. Trans. Aldo S. Bernardo, Saul Levin and Reta A. Bernardo. 2 vols. Baltimore, MA: Johns Hopkins University Press.

—. 2003. *Invectives*. Ed. and trans. David Marsh. Cambridge, MA: Harvard UP.

—. 2005. *Canzoniere: Rerum vulgarium fragmenta*. Ed. Rosanna Bettarini. Turin: Einaudi.

Schmitt, Charles B. 1984. *The Aristotelian Tradition and Renaissance Universities*. London. Variorum Reprints.

Seneca. 1918-1925. *Ad Lucilium Epistulae Morales*. Trans. Richard M. Gummere. 3 vols. London: Heinemann.

Sidney, Sir Philip. 2002. *The Major Works*. Ed. Katherine Duncan-Jones. Oxford: OUP.

Thaler, Alwin. 1947. *Shakespeare and Sir Philip Sidney: The Influence of the Defence of Poesy*. Cambridge, MA: Harvard University Press.

Thompson, N. S. 1996. *Chaucer, Boccaccio, and the Debate of Love: A Comparative Study of The Decameron and The Canterbury Tales*. Oxford: OUP.

Trinkaus, Charles. 1970; repr. 1995. *In Our Image and Likeness: Humanity and Divinity in Italian Humanist Thought*. Chicago, IL: University of Chicago Press; Notre Dame, IN: University of Notre Dame Press.

—. 1979. *The Poet as Philosopher: Petrarch and the Formation of Renaissance Consciousness*. New Haven, CT: Yale UP.

Weiss, Roberto. 1969. "Dante e l'umanesimo del suo tempo", *Letture Classensi*, 2: 11-27.

West, Grace Starry. 1982. "Going by the Book: Classical Allusions in Shakespeare's *Titus Andronicus*", *Studies in Philology*, 79: 62-77.

Wicksteed, P. H. 2002. *Dante and Aquinas: Being the Substance of the Jowett Lectures of 1911*. Honolulu, HI: University Press of the Pacific.

VIRTUE, JUSTICE AND MORAL ACTION IN SHAKESPEARE'S *HAMLET*

UNHAE LANGIS

The range of *Hamlet*'s language, styles, and forms makes it "a theatrical matrix and gathering place", not only, as James Calderwood observes, "for the plays that [...] follow it" (1978: 103) but also, I would add, for the works that precede it. As one of the features that make it a pre-eminent piece of tragic art, *Hamlet* presents an impressive assemblage of intellectual ideas, ethical systems, social mores, and literary conventions of the Renaissance, as evolved from the classical period through the medieval era. The eponymous hero is Hamlet, Prince of Denmark, "courtier, scholar, soldier" (3.1.150), who might have been Castiglione's ideal, adept with the sword, the word, and the lady, but lacks political ability, purpose, and strategy—qualities of governance requisite of a prince. Viewed as "Th'expectancy and rose of the fair state" (3.1.151), Hamlet, to some degree, betrays his nation Denmark when the ghost of his father commands him to avenge his murder. Apprised of this foul play, Hamlet, in his grievous state, is all the more inclined to idealise his father as the warrior king, whom he must emulate and avenge by manly martial action. A heroic ethos still operative in Denmark expects him to avenge a violation of family honour with impassioned dispatch.

At the same time, however, Hamlet, a student of (Christian) humanism, strives for moderation, the rational guidance of passions towards virtuous ends. Sir Philip Sidney, Shakespeare's contemporary, asserted in his *Apology for Poetry* (1595) that "the ending end of all earthly learning" is virtue, in his words, "as high a perfection as our degenerate souls, made worse by their clayey lodging, can be capable of" (2001: 71, 70). By all accounts of English Renaissance literature and culture, virtue figured as an important social ideal of intellectual, moral, and civic excellence. Conduct books from Castiglione's *The Book of the Courtier* (English translation 1588) to Henry Peacham's *The Complete Gentleman* (1622) to Richard Brathwait's *The English Gentleman* (1630) taught one how to be the virtuous man in the humanist aspiration to intellectual, moral, and physical excellence. Edmund Spenser's *The Faerie Queene* (1596), presenting virtues as a fusion of classical and Christian ethics, is grounded on the importance of virtue in the education of a gentleman. The aim of his epic poem, as revealed in his letter to Sir Walter Ralegh, is "to fashion a gentleman or noble person in virtuous and gentle discipline" (Spenser, 1993: 1). In short, virtue was the hub of the Renaissance discourse of ethical action grounded on ontological reflection.

Aristotle's *Nicomachean Ethics* was the standard text in moral philosophy at the universities, with more than sixty editions published before 1600 (Menut, 1943: 317), emerging from the Reformation struggles as "a keystone of both Catholic and Protestant education" (Schmitt, 1979, 1984: 94), and the golden mean, a cultural staple of the Renaissance.[1] Whether Shakespeare read Aristotle's *Nicomachean Ethics* is less important for my argument than the fact, as abundantly evidenced by his works, that Shakespeare, working within a rich humanist milieu, was familiar enough with his ethics to make *Hamlet* (and other plays) nuanced and complex dramatisations of the Aristotelian concept of virtuous action. *Hamlet*'s central focus on virtue and its status as the paradigmatic tragedy of moral action beg a neo-Aristotelian examination.

According to Aristotle, wisdom is of two parts, philosophical and practical: philosophical wisdom is virtue, the knowledge of what makes a good life, and practical wisdom, the ability to achieve that end. Together, they achieve flourishing at both the personal and civic level: "virtue makes us aim at the right mark, and practical wisdom makes us to take the right means" (VI.12.1144a6-9). In this manner, Aristotle brings a lofty Platonic pursuit of the noble and beautiful down to earth with a pragmatic emphasis on action in day-to-day civil and political life. Specifically, practical wisdom through moderation is the ability "to deliberate well about what is good and expedient for himself" (VI.5.1140a27) in human affairs, choosing the right response of affect and action in a particular situation regarding "the end, the manner, and the time" (VI.9.1142b27). In reference to the play, Hamlet, inheriting the task of avenging his father and redressing a corrupt state, is, first off, a victim of circumstances and of conflicting cultural imperatives. Nonetheless, the tragedy of Hamlet is not merely the result of an unfortunate accident but one to which the hero contributes, thus prompting a moral examination of his actions. Hamlet's inconsistent and ineffective execution of his task stems from an error of philosophical wisdom, or virtue: the pursuit of personal revenge rather than the more legitimate end of civil justice. Unclear about how to proceed towards justice in the wake of a regicide, Hamlet seeks "by indirections

[to] find directions out" (2.1.65) through the murky waters of clashing cultural dictates.

Hamlet's way is especially unclear because even if the pursuit of civil justice is the right path, it is one that cannot be dispatched with the quickness that vengeance requires to appease outrage. The conception of his task as public justice would have "spurred" stronger passion but ultimately would have been "dulled" (4.4.9.22-23) by his respect for the juridical process, which cannot investigate a regicide simply upon the evidence proffered by a supernatural witness / victim. "Let Hercules himself do what he may, / The cat will mew, and dog will have his day" (5.1.276-77), even if this reasoned justice, as opposed to vengeance, may take more time. A delay in "proceed[ing] by process" (*Coriolanus* 3.1.315) would, moreover, garner more sympathy than Hamlet's erratic efforts to execute private vengeance, which lack heart and purpose to see it through. Dramatising Hamlet's all too human errors in his efforts to fulfil his moral task, the play underscores the difficulty of taking just action "in a world where destiny is molded by forces beyond man's control or comprehension" (Ornstein, 1964: 508).

Hamlet's ultimate arrival at composure supports a theme of moral growth. Caught between an older code of honour governing a heroic society and newer imperatives of the early modern state enjoining obedience to the state and to personal conscience, Hamlet is a dual-sided "green" hero, who outgrows the role of an accomplished yet politically subordinate courtier but never quite attains the mark of the capable prince fit to govern Denmark. Alluding to a medieval poem, Hamlet mediates between a young Gawain figure, an "adventurous knight" (2.2.309) whose virtue is tested, and the Green Knight, an older trickster figure whose tests involve beheading, or the death's head—and the moral and sexual corruption imaged in mortal decay. As attested by the longstanding controversy over his age—early twenties as his university studies might imply or thirty as the text indicates in 5.1, Hamlet, I argue, is purposely presented as both youthful—as suggested by his attachment to his mother, sexual squeamishness, and adolescent vying with Laertes—and older—as evidenced by his frequent philosophising in his signature soliloquies, which mark him as one of the most intensely subjective characters ever created and the play, a compelling reflection on mortality and morality. By the same token, Hamlet is both mentor and student in this drama of moral growth as he metes out instruction, which he himself has trouble following, attesting not only to personal shortcoming but, more importantly, the enormous challenges of the ethical enterprise in a world of uncertainties and perplexing possibilities.

Much scholarly ink has been spilled on the examination of Hamlet's delay / neglect of duty with critics, on the one side, defending his moral sensibilities and philosophical approach as proper checks on unthinking, bloody vengeance and, on the other side, baffled and frustrated by his inconsistent—sometime inert, sometime impulsive—actions: "Hence the long tradition of regarding Hamlet as irresolute, paralyzed in will, unhealthy, morbid, neurotic, a dreamer who appears a very disturbing figure in the context of Western ideologies that value men of decision and action who are ready to do their duty" (Foakes, 2002: 88). Hamlet himself does not understand the reasons for his inertia: "I do not know / Why yet I live to say 'This thing's to do'. / Sith I have cause, and will, and strength, and means, / To do't" (4.4.9.35 Quarto 2). As his own puzzlement suggests, Hamlet's dilemma and the reasons for his non-performance are too complex to summon the single-minded passion and purpose that bloody revenge requires. Contrary to Hamlet's belief that all the elements for executing his duty are present, a more detailed historicist and Aristotelian examination of these—cause, will, strength, and means— reveals that his dilemma is vastly more complicated than his understanding of it.

I

The very fact that Hamlet avoids naming that which he must do— "This thing"—betrays his ambivalence towards the "cause." Hamlet's psychomachia between honour and conscience poignantly dramatises the contemporary moral controversy regarding revenge, as also lexically supported by a prolixity of meanings for "cause" across the moral spectrum. As a morally neutral word, it means both "motive" (OED 3a) and the "object of action" (4). "Cause", with a positive valence, denotes the "proper ground for action" (3b), but, with a negative spin, can mean "charge, accusation, blame" (9) as well as "disease, sickness" (12). Two other meanings extend the term into juridical and political spheres: "an action, process, suit" (8) and "That side of a question or controversy which is espoused, advocated, and upheld by a person or party" (11). Starting with the morally neutral sense, Hamlet, in learning about his father's murder, certainly has "cause," or "motive," to seek justice, which could be regarded as the "object of action." His father's command to "Revenge his most foul and most unnatural murder" (1.5.25) is situated within early modern culture, officially denouncing vengeance as an unchristian act of violence and a profane arrogation of divine retribution. As Peter Mercer observes, the "frequency and vehemence of condemnations of personal revenge by the clergy and moralists of the sixteenth century make it clear that it was unequivocally abhorred, and treated under the law—at least in theory—as severely as murder. The weight of denunciation [however suggests] that it was an all-too-frequent recourse in everyday life" (4). Sir William Segar in *The Booke of Honour and Armes* (1590), indeed, defends vengeance from a realist perspective:

> The cause of all Quarrel is Injury and reproach, but the matter of content, is Justice and Honour [...]. True it is, that the Christian law wills men to be of so perfect patience, as not only to endure injurious words, but also quietly to suffer every force and violence. Notwithstanding, for so much as none (or very few men) have attained such perfection, the laws of all Nations, for avoiding further inconveniences, and the manifestation of truth, have (among other trials) permitted, that such questions as could not be civilly proved by confession, witness, or other circumstances, should receive judgement by fight and Combat, supposing that GOD [...] would give victory to him that justly adventured his life, for truth, Honour, and Justice. (sigs. A2-A2v)

Segar wittily elides the causational meaning of "cause" (OED 3a) with its ideational meaning (11) to justify vengeance. His endorsement of self-help justice extends to an eye-for-an-eye blood revenge (Kinney, 2002: 17).[2]

The divine right of rulers, insofar as Hamlet is the crown-hopeful prince, muddies the moral issue of revenge even further. As R. A. Foakes observes, a "ruler, however bad, may be God's 'minister' in punishing the evil subjects do, according to St. Paul, as 'a revenger to execute wrath upon him that doeth evil' (Romans 13.4), and the people must accept this, 'for conscience sake'" (2002: 96). In this manner, Pauline doctrine could endorse Hamlet's undesired claim to God's "scourge and minister" (3.4.159), to the pursuit of revenge. Hamlet is technically not the ruler of Denmark, however—it is, rather, the vicious Claudius who has murdered his brother-king and usurped his throne. Yet against even vicious rulers, *The Trew Law of Free Monarchies* (1598), endorsed by James I, forbids rebellion: "the wickednesse [...] of the King can never make them that are ordained to be judged by him, to become his judges" (Lemon, 2002: 38). The clash between the doctrine of non-resistance and the concept of self-help justice exhibits itself most significantly in *Hamlet*'s issue of legitimate rule in the wake of a regicide: a rogue monarch's attempt to maintain power using any means available vs. the rightful heir's wish to restore civic justice without becoming a bloody revenger. "In neglecting his revenge," Hamlet, Foakes explains, "is not 'stifled by remembrance' (Kerrigan 186) so much as by his inheritance of conflicting classical and Christian values. The heroic code he associates with his father urges him to action, while the Christian code that is given lip-service in Claudius's Denmark condemns revenge and inhibits him from murder most foul" (2002: 96; Terry, 1999: 1082). Revenge, as mode of tragic action, is, moreover, largely a dramatic performance, which relies on rhetoric and emotion that incites motion. Hence, in addition to an ethical issue of revenge contributing to his inertia, Hamlet, Peter Mercer argues, fails to "find an authentic voice of woe" (191) and just anger that will stir him to retributive action. Accordingly, Hamlet upbraids himself for feeling less regarding his father's cause than an actor vis-à-vis fictious epic characters: "I, / A dull and muddy-mettled rascal, peak / John-a dreams, unpregnant of my cause" (2.2.543-45). While Gail Kern Paster argues an "interactivity of self and world" (2004: 49) in seeing his nature in terms of earthy mud, I read his "muddy-mettledness" as an indication of his ethical, emotional, and humoural conflict between anger and grief, choler and melancholy, which reason will guide towards balance. Though the player's speech "acting out the ancient passion of Aeneas" is "the authentic language of tragedy" (189), it is art—not easily translatable to real-life situations with no moral directive perhaps than the urgency to act humanly rather than bestially.

As a humanist, Hamlet strives for virtue, the rational guidance of passions towards good ends. But in his dilemma presenting a conflict between honour and conscience, he finds it difficult to carry out his father's commandment to revenge his foul murder *and* ("howsomever thou pursuest this act") to "Taint not thy mind" (1.5.84-85)—an enigma and test of virtuous self-control like the Delphic oracles. A successful execution of retributive action requires the self-possession on Hamlet's part to lead the commandment rather than let it lead him astray. In other words, Aristotelian moderation. Without obeying merely one or the other element, Hamlet must find a just mean that addresses both without canceling each other. The virtuous mean is not simply a middle state but the just response of affect and action in a particular situation.

This moderation is a "mean relative to us" (II.6.1106b37), particularised to take into consideration differences in individual abilities and limitations. By no stretch, however, does it entail moral relativism, granting each person sovereign will, for the mean is "determined by a rational principle, and by that principle by which the man of practical wisdom would determine it" (II.6.1107a1-2). Skilled "in discovering what is best in each situation," the virtuous person's judgement, "regarded as authoritative by other members of the community," serves as a standard and measure of good action and thereby "settles disputes" (Kraut, 2005: sec. 5.2).

Revenge, the carrying out of murder in the name of personal justice, epitomises the conflict between arbitrary will and the rule of law. As much as an avenger's inability to seek justice in a legal system controlled by corrupt authorities gains our sympathies, the notion of private justice entails an opposing danger—the potential onslaught of lawlessness in society. The university-educated Hamlet has too much respect for the rule of reason not to be wary of vengeance fuelled by passion. In Hamlet's dilemma, the mean is the integration of passion and reason, anger and virtue towards the end of justice, not bloody vengeance re-enacting the initial outrage. Hamlet's irresolution, paralysis of will, and erratic action— inability to kill Claudius at prayer, accidental murder of Polonius, and complicity in the deaths of Ophelia and Laertes, pursuant to their father's death—suffer from an ambivalence regarding the virtuous end, which must guide his actions: "This thing's to do" (4.4.9.34 Quarto 2).[3] Although Hamlet makes a few references elsewhere to his role as avenger (2.2.559, 3.1.125, 3.3.79), his vagueness here suggests moral ambivalence and reluctance that cramps vengeful action. Despite his self-recrimination of "thinking too precisely" (4.4.31), all his philosophising does little to cast the "cause" in a form that he can justifiably advance.

The Ghost of his father is partly to blame in presenting the problem as a cause of private honour. He appeals to Hamlet as father to son, claiming him for revenge. Revealing to Hamlet that a human rather than a natural serpent, Claudius, poisoned him, King Hamlet explains, "the whole ear of Denmark / Is by a forgèd process of my death / Rankly abused" (1.5.36-38). The use of metonymy indicates royal conscience, that he is the head of Denmark. The "Ghost's order that Claudius be killed seems partly a posthumous attempt to discharge a royal obligation, to show mercy, if not to a brother, to the moral welfare of those 'many many bodies' whose safety was annexed to that of the old king" (Tiffany, 2005: 119). Surely, this is unwarranted extrapolation, for no explicit words in the text indicate that King Hamlet considers his death as a regicide, baneful to the Danish people. Instead, he is more concerned about his tainted manhood—he wants the death of the man, his own brother, who cuckolded him. In addition, he wants "the royal bed of Denmark" to cease being "A couch for luxury and damnèd incest" (1.5.82-83)—because its continuance, by re-enacting the crime over and over, would redouble his shame. Guildenstern and Rosencrantz's expression of royal deference and concern over safety of the sovereign, "upon whose weal depends and rests / The lives of many" (3.3.14-15), indirectly highlights the reciprocal duties to the public that sovereigns in this play—the two Hamlets and Claudius— consistently seem to neglect in a figurative "cease of majesty" (3.3.15;

Tkacz, 1992: 22). As Catherine Brown Tkacz rightly observes, no member of Denmark's royal family, throughout the play, "ever speaks of his duty to the state. This omission is symptomatic of their abdication of that responsibility. Shakespeare leaves it to Polonius to link 'majesty' and 'duty'" (2.2.88) and Laertes, in advising Ophelia regarding Hamlet, "alone speaks clearly of that responsibility" (1992: 22):

> His greatness weighed, his will is not his own,
> For he himself is subject to his birth.
> He may not, as unvalued persons do,
> Carve for himself, for on his choice depends
> The safety and health of this whole state,
> And therefore must his choice be circumscribed
> Unto the voice and yielding of that body
> Whereof he is the head. (1.3.17-24)

If the "To be or not to be" question is inflected, in the case of Hamlet, towards "what majesty should be" and do, the prince should look beyond vengeance for personal honour and choose to act for the public good of Denmark (Tkacz, 1992: 23, see also Lee-Riff, 1981: 108).

Instead, Hamlet continues to conceive his obligation as revenge, without the requisite passion inciting him towards its fulfilment. Tellingly, Hamlet never brings up the notion of (public) justice as a counterpoint to revenge; in the single usage of the word in the play, "justice" is mentioned by Claudius in a cynical sense, equating it to mere power: "In the corrupted currents of this world / Offence's gilded hand may shove by justice" (3.3.58). Claudius's statement frankly acknowledges the rottenness in Denmark and highlights *a fortiori* the need for real justice through virtuous leadership. In his famous "To be or not to be" speech, Hamlet complains disingenuously that "conscience does make cowards of us all, / [...] the native hue of resolution / [...] sicklied o'er with the pale cast of thought" (3.1.85-87). But Hamlet's rational self knows that revenge, to use Harold Skulsky's words, "is an indulgence of the fallen will" (1970: 84), defying civil and moral laws that a society collectively prohibits. As Hector in *Troilus and Cressida* warns, "pleasure and revenge have ears more deaf than adders to the voice / Of any true decision" (2.2. 170-72; Skulsky, 1970: 81). Hamlet is at an impasse and cannot find a way to direct passion towards a just end. Since revenge is the action of arbitrary will (i.e., personal vendetta), he must reconceptualize the redressing of personal violation through vengeance into a redressing of regicide in the name of public justice. In this way, may his cause of revenge with its negative valences of "charge, accusation, blame" (OED 9) and "disease, sickness" (12) turn into a "proper ground for action" (3b) for the welfare of the entire Danish state. As Tiffany argues, Hamlet "must set things right in Denmark through violence, yet must avoid "coupl[ing] hell" by engaging in private vengeance [...]. At every turn Hamlet's response to the Ghost's call for revenge demonstrates the felt obligations" (2005: 123) of a prince who "may not [...] / Carve for himself" (1.3.19-20): who must not assassinate Claudius, but execute him for the good of the nation.[4]

One might raise the objection here that Hamlet cannot take the cause against regicide public because he lacks allies. Despite the fact that Hamlet is surrounded by danger with Claudius's men constantly spying on him, he is not without recourse. While the nobility, in electing Claudius to kingship seems generally to endorse him, Hamlet reportedly is popular with the people. Through the instance of Laertes rallied by the people in 4.5, the play seems to suggest that the commoners exercise a powerful voice in proclaiming a new ruler. Historical evidence also indicates that

> vengeance against the monarch's enemies was appropriate in a Christian realm. Helen Gardner relates Hamlet's mission to that described in the 1584 Bond of Association, in which Lord Burghley and thousands of English citizens signed a claim that they would "prosecute to the death" any pretender to England's throne. The signers swore "to take the uttermost revenge on them [...] by any possible means [...] for their utter overthrow and extirpation." (Tiffany, 2005: 119)

This pursuit of public justice would be endorsed by two meanings of "cause": "an action, process, suit" (8) and "That side of a question or controversy which is espoused, advocated, and upheld by a person or party" (11). Malcolm and Donalbain, sons of the murdered King Duncan in *Macbeth*, successfully gathered up an opposition force of Scotsmen and English allies. If Hamlet is desperately low on military support, he could even consider enlisting the aid of Fortinbras—in exchange for a return of Norwegian territories—to depose Claudius and try him for regicide. At any rate, Hamlet himself does not doubt his strength and means to oppose Claudius.

Despite the promises of public recourse against a rogue monarch, a civic remedy is not ready at hand—typical of revenge tragedies—because Hamlet lacks legal grounds to prove Claudius's murder of King Hamlet. While Hamlet and Horatio's viewing of Claudius's expression of guilt during The Mousetrap would satisfy the two-witness rule in order to lay a charge (or to satisfy the requirements for private vengeance according to Mosaic law) (Moore, 1997), the evidence of the regicide is based on inadmissible hearsay—what's more, from a ghost, which could be construed as an evil spirit—insubstantial proof to build a case against Claudius. If Hamlet and Horatio had witnessed the king's murder with their own eyes, they would have cause to organise a party to arrest Claudius and place him on trial. Hamlet would stir to action—passion and reason integrated in a cause of civil justice. But, alas, he has far less to go than another nephew, Brutus, in *The Rape of Lucrece*, who overthrew his uncle Tarquin and established the Roman republic, after the latter's rape of Lucrece, a virtuous noblewoman, and her ensuing suicide incited a wholesale revolt against the monarchy. In the absence of ocular proof or strong circumstantial evidence, Hamlet can only remain the reluctant scourge, balking at the "cursed spite of his task" (Ornstein, 1964: 507). Hamlet is admittedly a victim of adverse circumstances, but what is troubling in his situation is the complete neglect of public justice in his deliberations. A virtuous person in his shoes, having gone through these deliberations, would have reached the conclusion that he cannot proceed with retributive action until and unless stronger evidence of Claudius's crimes emerges, and, on the strength of this knowledge, would not yield thereafter to vehement acts of violence.

Because practical wisdom depends on "aim[ing] at the right mark" (VI.12.1144a6), justified inaction, which Hamlet cannot seem to locate within the misleading dualism of vengeance (action, good; inaction, bad), the "darkly striving prince" (Skulsky, 1970: 87) wavers at best between hesitation and impetuous reaction, his inability to execute revenge "corrected" by yet worse blunders. His state of moral irresolution reveals its dangers as Hamlet, "passion's slave" (3.2.65)—like most of us— succumbs to impulses of violence. As Foakes rightly notes, the central issue in the play, "is not the matter of revenge, but rather the control or release of instinctual drives to violence" (2002: 97). After "The Mousetrap" successfully exposes Claudius's agitation, convincing the prince of his uncle's guilt, Hamlet is primed for revenge, but he is summoned first to his mother:

> 'Tis now the very witching time of night,
> When churchyards yawn, and hell itself breathes out
> Contagion to this world: now could I drink hot blood,
> And do such bitter business as the day
> Would quake to look on. Soft! now to my mother [...].
> I will speak daggers to her, but use none.
> My tongue and soul in this be hypocrites [...]. (3.2.358-62, 366-67)

The temporal criss-crossing of goals—killing Claudius and chastising Gertrude—reveals how the course of revenge, like that of another strong passion, love, never does run smooth, revealing irony upon irony. One might think, like the Ghost who reappears to get his son back on course, that Hamlet's meeting with his mother would break the momentum toward bloody vengeance. Just when Hamlet is trying to control his anger to "speak[ing] daggers" to Gertrude short of physical violence, he happens upon Claudius kneeling in prayer, an icon of vulnerability subconsciously prompting an up close encounter with conscience, testing as never before his will to kill a man in bloody vengeance. Critics have puzzled over Hamlet's refusal to cut Claudius down at this ripe occasion. As Hamlet explains it, the niceties of *lex talonis* prevent him from "taking him [apparently] in the purging of his soul" (3.4.85) while Claudius "cut off" his father "even in the blossoms of my sin, / Unhouseled, dis-appointed, unaneled" (1.5.76-77).

Yet immediately thereafter in his mother's room, Hamlet berates his mother, who, upon hearing, "You go not till I set you up a glass / Where you may see the inmost part of you" (3.4.19-20), takes his dagger-sharp words literally and cries for help. This vignette is melodrama straight out of revenge tragedy: Hamlet's vehement castigation causing Gertrude's overreacting fright causing Polonius's imprudent yelp for help. As precise as he is in calculating how he will execute the act of vengeance at the sight of Claudius praying, Hamlet, in this scene of melodrama and violence, carelessly stabs into the arras. Critics have often remarked the inconsistency between Hamlet's refraining from killing Claudius at prayer and his subsequent act of violence. It is, as Gertrude calls it, "a rash and bloody deed" (26), vaguely hoping that its victim is Claudius, but more like a stab in the dark, a release of unthinking, pent-up fury: as Ornstein observes, "he must lash out even if the victim be only the foolish Polonius" (1964: 507). This quick sequence of non-action and impulsive reaction seems so inconsistent that one is tempted to think that metadramatically, the satire of revenge tragedy got the better of Shakespeare to present this rather absurd scene of melodrama and violence. It is through this lens of satire that readers sympathetic to Hamlet are encouraged to view his imprudent actions that reverberate into tragic deaths of innocents.

At the same time, however, this play of passions serves as an important commentary on "the basic problem of human violence" and the limits of moral action (Foakes, 2002: 98). Hamlet's impulsive stabbing exposes as mere excuse his inability to kill Claudius when the opportunity presented itself. Contrary to his overt explanations, which we cannot often trust, it seems more phenomenologically plausible that despite his boast of bloodthirstiness, he found himself morally and psychologically unprepared to do the deed at this sudden visceral confronting of his task. The moment past, Hamlet is possibly stricken by his weakness of will. To compensate for this failure, he impulsively thrusts his sword at the slightest whiff of his enemy. For a reluctant revenger, stabbing into the dark literally is perhaps the easiest way to carry out his bloody task, which from the outset has been problematically a command to "stab in the dark", to kill in the face of nagging rational and moral uncertainty. Hence, Hamlet's plaint: "O cursèd spite / That ever I was born to set it right!" (1.5.189-90).

Aristotelian ethics explains in explicit detail what we would see as Hamlet's complete botching of revenge. If virtue is the just response of affect and action "at the right times, with reference to the right objects, towards the right people, with right motive, and in the right way" (II.6.1106b20-22), then Hamlet has aimed, maimed, and killed the wrong person, at the wrong time, with the wrong motive, and in a blind, woefully wrong way. With this murder, however, Hamlet has symbolically if not successfully executed the act of revenge, as suggested by his reply to Gertrude, christening his "fallen will": "A bloody deed—almost as bad, good-mother, / As kill a king and marry with his brother" (3.4.27-28). To the morally sensitive Hamlet, the tainting of his soul is a far graver sacrifice than revenge's exaction of blood.

II

What is, moreover, disturbing about this impulsive release of violence is that it falls so shortly after Hamlet's instruction to others on ethical conduct. In act 3, Hamlet tells the players to exercise "mediocritie" (Wright, 1603, 1971: 179), or laudable moderation, linking ethics to the aesthetics of acting since both are grounded in truth: "Suit the action to the word, the word to the action, with this special observance, that you o'erstep not the modesty of nature. For the purpose of playing ... is ... to show virtue her own feature, scorn her own image" (3.2.16-21). According to this advice with Stoic resonances of decorum—acting in accordance with nature—to play a character naturally, or authentically, one must harmonise word with action, mind with body, emotion with motion. Discourse, or language, is the core of *ethos*—character—and fuels corporeal action. Like action in real life, which must ground itself in a "cause"—causal and ethical—an actor must discover a character's *modus operandi*—the particular psychic and physical features that ground the character, make him tick, and integrate his words with his actions. After discovering the unifying essence of a character, the player must then enact the character faithfully through an integration of bodily and vocal expression. To bring credible unity to the character, the actor, on a metadramatic level, must be "to double business bound" (3.3.41), rendering invisible the gap between his own subjectivity and the fictitious one he embodies. The skilful actor, according to early modern thought, achieves this consummate illusion through "mediocritie," the discipline of moderation by which he marshalled passions through his body—"larynx, limbs, torso, and head together—thereby transforming invisible impulse into spectacle and unspoken feeling into eloquence" (Roach, 1985: 32-33). Physiologically, the player adroitly "discover[s] a *via media* between the Scylla of [animating] spirit and the Charybdis of [affective] humours," between purposeful passion and aimless disorder, "not by freeing his actions, but by confining them in direction, purpose, and shape. He has to keep his flammable inner mixtures stable even in the heat of passion" (Roach, 1985: 52).[5] As Hamlet advises the players, "in the very torrent, tempest, and as I may say the whirlwind of your passion, you must acquire and beget a temperance that may give it smoothness" (3.2.5-7). Hamlet patronisingly instructs the players, at least one of whom, the First Player, is expert at his art, yet in his own real-life dilemma, he cannot remain calm and constant like the Aristotelian virtuous man or the Stoic sage. At "the mercy of opposing currents like a strait of the sea" (IX.6.1167b7) buffeted by his "sea of troubles" (3.1.61), Hamlet, in his mother's room, is caught by "the whirlwind of [his] passion," unable to "beget a temperance that may give it smoothness." Hamlet's inability to follow his own "instructions, which, being taught, return / To plague th'inventor" (*Macbeth*, 1.7.9-10),[6] calls attention not only to his moral deficiencies but also to the sheer complexity of enacting virtuous moderation, which, in some instances, entails a clear passage from desire to passion and action but, in others, requires the dissembling of desire, behind outward passion and action, for example, through an "antic disposition."

Hamlet, in a torrent of chastising passion in 3.4, also instructs Gertrude on how to abate her carnal passion:

Assume a virtue if you have it not [...].
Refrain tonight,
And that shall lend a kind of easiness
To the next abstinence; the next more easy;
For use almost can change the stamp of nature. (3.4.151.1, 5-8 Quarto 2)

Here, Hamlet reiterates Aristotle's ethical theory of how moral virtues are acquired through "custom" (3.4.151.2), or habituation: "some men become temperate and good-tempered, others self-indulgent and irascible, by behaving in one way or the other in the appropriate circumstances.

Thus, in one word, states of character arise out of like activities"
(II.1.1103b18-21). Despite his instruction of Gertrude and the players from
a morally superior position, Hamlet himself is evidently in moral training,
not having acquired a fully developed virtue through experience. Serving
as a foil, Horatio, "Whose blood and judgement are so well commingled /
That they are not a pipe for Fortune's finger / To sound what stop she
please" (3.2.62-64), displays Stoic virtues. By contrast, Hamlet, in his
mother's room, exhibits none of Horatio's Stoic calm. The prince's
chastisement of his mother is a combination of pent-up fury over her
overhasty marriage and displaced anger over his own recent failure at
vengeance. This castigation, in turn, stokes vengeful action, resulting in
the botched killing of Polonius. The episode is saturated with "hot blood,"
wholly void of "judgement" whereas in viewing Claudius at prayer,
Hamlet exhibits too much judgement and not enough blood.

"Unpregnant of [his] cause" (2.2.545), Hamlet had previously invoked
Pyrrhus in 2.2 as an example of purposeful action and the First Player's
ability to mourn over Hecuba, a fictitious character, as a foil to his own
lack of "gall" (2.2.554) to whet vengeance. David Kastan argues that
"Hamlet is angry that he, unlike the player, is incapable of acting
expressively, rather than angry that, unlike Pyrrhus, he is incapable of
acting effectively; the problem he admits is not that he can *do* nothing but
that he can *say* 'nothing'" (Kastan, 1987: 116). I contend, however, that
the two inabilities are expressions of the same: his feeling of feminine
powerlessness against "The slings and arrows of outrageous fortune"
(3.1.60). Hence, Hamlet moves flippantly from admiring Pyrrhus to
lauding a player's empathy with Hecuba to his own histrionic playing the
avenger and ultimately to his self-mockery:

> this is most brave,
> That I, the son of the dear father murdered,
> Prompted to my revenge by heaven and hell,
> Must, like a whore, unpack my heart with words
> And fall a-cursing like a very drab [...]. (2.2.560-65)

But these expressions, vented in an air of fiction than reality, only
disingenuously extol single-minded action and passion; rather than
suggesting serious choices of action, they bemoan Hamlet's powerlessness
of his predicament. Lacking substantive words that can denounce and
prosecute Claudius publicly, he is left "like a whore, [to] unpack [his]
heart with" futile curses or to conceal his real sentiments behind a varying
level of "antic disposition."

Hamlet's position of political powerlessness could also partially answer for what has disturbed some critics—his callous attitude towards the deaths of Polonius, Rosencrantz, and Guildenstern. Without exonerating Hamlet's rash act of stabbing into the arras, Hamlet's complicity in violence can be seen as unavoidable within the genre of revenge tragedy: having inherited the personal and political complications ensuing from a regicide, Hamlet, from his relatively powerless position, must *react* with dispassion to oppose Claudius's brutal actions of realpolitik effectively. As a subversion of the sovereign's duty to protect his subjects, in *Hamlet*, people in the service of Claudius and Gertrude become political pawns and innocent victims of the corrupt state. In the case of Hamlet, his own difficulties in opposing Claudius make it all the more understandable how he comes to adopt the ruthless methods of realpolitik. As Francis Bacon once averred as a universal truth about the temporal world, "an honest man can do no good upon those that are wicked to reclaim them," without recourse to the same tactics used by the wicked (Kahn, 1994: 117).

It is through the tainting of his soul, his participation in death (taking the lives of Polonius, Ophelia, Rosencrantz, and Guildenstern), combined with a first-hand encounter at sea with the strange workings of Fortuna bringing about his happy escape from death, that Hamlet comes to accept life's terms with Stoic Christian calm: that destiny is partly shaped by forces beyond man's control or comprehension. In so doing, he no longer reproaches himself in "false compare" (Sonnet 130: 14) with Fortinbras, a model of misguided passion, who, in risking the lives of thousands "Even for an eggshell," displays, according to Hamlet's criteria for action, strong "will" and "strength" but "means" unconscionably disproportionate with its unworthy "cause" (4.4.9.35, 43). Perhaps that is why Hamlet, now appeased about his avenger's duty, jumps into Ophelia's grave after Laertes, publicly denouncing ostentatious shows of passion against his own "natural" grief "within which passeth show" (1.2.85) but now will express itself like the cat's mew and the dog's bark:

> What is he whose grief
> Bears such an emphasis, whose phrase of sorrow
> Conjures the wand'ring stars and makes them stand
> Like wonder-wounded hearers? This is I,
> Hamlet the Dane [...].
> I loved Ophelia. Forty thousand brothers
> Could not, with all their quantity of love,
> Make up my sum [...].
> Let Hercules himself do what he may,
> The cat will mew, and dog will have his day. (5.1.238-42, 254-56, 276-77)

Hamlet, here, seems to be instructing the funeral gathering on a private and public level. On a private level, the prince recognises Laertes's tragic loss of father and sister as one akin to his own: "by the image of my cause I see / The portraiture of his" (5.2.78-80). Having experienced the moral ordeal of the avenger's task before Laertes, Hamlet subconsciously seems to caution him about the dangers of overwrought passion, wholly insensitive to his own culpability in the deaths of Polonius and Ophelia. Indeed, if one compares the prince's capital offences against Laertes's allegedly excessive claim of brotherly love, Hamlet's question to Laertes, "What is the reason that you use me thus? / I loved you ever" (5.1.274-75), shows such outrageous insensitivity of the solipsistic mind that Laertes tractably refrains from being provoked by "madness" (5.1.269).

Hamlet is hardly in a position, moreover, to boast about the strength of his love, which apparently was not enough to protect Ophelia and keep her from harm's way. We may perhaps, however, condone his swaggering claim to Ophelia's love as an undesirable by-product of his condemnation of an endemic dishonesty and dissemblance at the court of Denmark. Significantly, Hamlet proclaims himself with this critique, raising private to the level of public matter. Despite the indiscretion of shaming Laertes after initially causing ruin to the house of Polonius, Hamlet, according to the Stoic ethos of public service, has commendably risen from the shadow of private matter to the sun of public affair, a binary which criticises "private life, effeminacy, selfishness, idleness and vice" in favor of "public life, manliness, virtue, hard work" (Vickers, 1990: 25).

Hamlet's public affront to Laertes develops into a duel, thinly disguised as a manly contest of swordsmanship. Regretting his graveside bluster as well as heeding Gertrude's maternal guidance "to use some gentle entertainment" (5.2.146.11-12 Quarto 2), Hamlet accepts the challenge as a way to render Laertes satisfaction for his double wrong of bringing death to Laertes's family and publicly insulting him—as borne out by his request for Laertes's pardon at the beginning of the match. Interestingly, his conciliatory behavior goes against the "gain-giving" of his heart (5.2.150, 153), an inner voice, or daemon, disclosing an augury of his destiny. As if to compensate for his solipsistic graveside declamation, Hamlet now swings to the other extreme of other-centeredness against his "foolish" intuition, which "would perhaps trouble a woman" (5.2.153-54). Although Hamlet goes against his own better sense, his concern for virtue in the martial society of Denmark would effectively prevent his withdrawal from the contest. Hence, in his famous speech marking Stoic Christian composure, Hamlet affirms his participation, notably using the royal pronoun: "We defy augury. There's a special providence in the fall of a sparrow. If it be now, 'tis not to come. If it be not to come, it will be now. If it be not now, yet it will come. The readiness is all" (5.2.157-60). After scenes of racking deliberation over whether to act, how to act, and when to act, Hamlet is ready for whatever will come, even and especially death. No longer does he fear death, as he states in 3.1, as an "undiscovered country from whose bourn / No traveler returns" (3.1.81-82). He is ready to face calmly whatever may come because he has come to terms with the external forces beyond our control and comprehension instead of "thinking too precisely on th'event" (4.4.9.31). By yielding to the way of things, Hamlet rises closer to Aristotle's conception of the virtuous man, approaching "the active state of the soul that constitutes moral virtue and forms character": "the condition in which all the powers of the soul are at work together, making it possible for action to engage the whole human being" (Sachs, 2006: sec. 2). If the "work of achieving character is a process of clearing away the obstacles that stand in the way of the full efficacy of the soul" (Sachs, 2006: sec. 2), Hamlet, in doing just that, has grown through the play and attained a state of character more constantly disposed to virtue. Finally commingling "blood and judgement" (3.2.62), violence and reason, Hamlet kills Claudius upon knowledge of his new treachery, his poison plot, enacting both bloody vengeance and civil justice. But this act arises from provocation: Hamlet remains to the end the humanist courtier who eschews savage violence. His mantra, "Readiness is all" (5.2.160), takes on a different meaning here: not Stoic Christian resignation but a promptness to seize the opportunity of just vengeance.

Hamlet had proof earlier than the sword match, however, to advance his cause of civil justice. With Claudius's execution order to the King of England as evidence, Hamlet questions:

> And with such coz'nage- is't not perfect conscience
> To quit him with this arm? And is't not to be damn'd
> To let this canker of our nature come
> In further evil? (5.2.68-71)

One would have liked to have seen Hamlet, upon this proof, gather up an opposition force to oust Claudius, like Malcolm against Macbeth. But it was not to be in this play: *Hamlet* is the study of a man for whom a preoccupation with personal virtue largely impeded the imperatives of civil leadership. Hamlet's mottled attempts at justice reveal the sheer difficulty of taking good action in the world. Despite his dying plea to "report me and my cause aright / To the unsatisfied" (5.2.281-82), Horatio objectively speaks of the recent tragic events as

carnal, bloody and unnatural acts;
Of accidental judgments, casual slaughters;
Of deaths put on by cunning and forc'd cause;
And, in this upshot, purposes mistook
Fall'n on th'inventors' heads. (5.2.326-29)

Such an account includes Hamlet's complicity in erroneous actions that led to the death of others and to his own as an "even-handed justice / Commends th'ingredients of our poisoned chalice / To our own lips" (*Macbeth* 1.7.10-12). The numerous poisonings throughout the play are symbolic of the figurative poison that infects and kills all—from the innocent to the culpable—who find themselves enmeshed in the cankerous realpolitik of Denmark.

A neo-Aristotelian approach to examining Hamlet's moral action does much to illuminate Shakespeare's complex exploration of a fundamental ethical conflict between arbitrary will and the rule of reason, which crests in the dilemma of revenge. In so doing, the foray also explores more broadly the yet ill understood processes and experiences that go into forming moral character. If nothing else, the close examination of Hamlet's inaction has revealed the enormity of the challenge of becoming a good person, an enterprise obstructed by the self-delusions and the instinctive drives to violence to which human beings are prone in their strivings towards personal and public good. Aristotle attests to the difficulty of the task when he considers the different theories regarding the acquisition of goodness: "some think that we are made good by nature, others by habituation, others by teaching" (X.9.1179b19). While a few are fortunately endowed with virtue, for others aspiring to virtue, an instinctive love for "what is noble and hat[e for] what is base" (X.9.1179b30) must be fostered early on as a base for moral development. Even with this firm foundation, Hamlet's own difficulties in moral judgement and self-governance while instructing others reveal the enormity of the ethical enterprise, complicated by multiple variables— external forces beyond our control, our skills of social interaction, and our self-knowledge and capacity for self-control. While habituation guided by moral instruction directs one towards goodness, the example of Hamlet, an aspirant to virtue intermittently exhibiting impulses of verbal and physical violence, reveals ultimately the eternal human struggle to control and direct our passions towards salutary ends, a challenge without an easy fix that must be confronted day by day with moral vigilance.

Notes

[1] See also Schmitt and Skinner, 1992: Vol. 3, 778; Elton, 1997: 337, n. 2, for a copious bibliography; Turner, 2006: 47–50, 62–63, 65 and 86–90, with additional bibliography, for the influence of the *Nicomachean Ethics* on Sidney's *Defense of Poesy*; Poisson, 1966: 210–11.

[2] See also Pollard 2005: 57, for an early modern medical account of revenge as a "powerful but dangerous strateg[y] for alleviating suffering," in particular, melancholy.

[3] See, in contrast, Paster's humoral account: "the evanescence of Hamlet's several transformations in the play comes from humoralism generally, a way of thinking about bodily behavior that ... finds it much easier to account for a subject's moment-to-moment fluctuations in mood and action than to account for emotional steadiness and a high degree of psychological self-sameness.... From this point of view, the volatility that characterizes Hamlet's behavior and moods until his return from the aborted trip to England is to be understood less as a striking feature of his disembodied personality and more as a humoral inevitability, given the myriad complexities of his predicament as Shakespeare represents them. Early modern behavioral though understood such complexity and used humoralism and the pneumatic character of life—at least in part—to explain them" (59-60). I will reserve for another essay a humoral/historical phenomenological approach engrafted onto an Aristotelian ethical interpretation of *Hamlet*.

[4] While we agree on this notion, I am not as persuaded as Tiffany that Hamlet's actions are those of "an agent of public morality" (123), carried out for the civil and political well-being of Denmark.

[5] According to the humoral theory from ancient times, the human body was thought to be filled with four basic substances, or humours—black bile, yellow bile, phlegm, and blood—which needed to be maintained in balance for moral and physical health. "A vital *pneuma*, imbibed from a universal *aether*," Roach explains, "supposedly permeated the blood as spirits, and, radiating outward from the heart and lungs, displayed inward feelings as outward motions" (1985: 27).

[6] I would like to thank my student Brandie Derr for bringing my attention to this quotation.

References

Aristotle. 1947. *Nicomachean Ethics*, in Richard McKeon (ed.), *Introduction to Aristotle*. New York: The Modern Library.

Calderwood, James L. 1978. "*Hamlet*: The Name of Action", *Modern Language Quarterly*, 39 (4): 331-62.

Elton, William R. 1997. "Aristotle's *Nicomachean Ethics* and Shakespeare's *Troilus and Cressida*", *Journal of the History of Ideas*, 58 (2): 331–37.

Everett, Barbara. 1995. '*Hamlet*: Growing', in David Scott Kastan (ed.), *Critical Essays on Shakespeare's Hamlet*. New York: G. K. Hall.

Foakes, R. A. 2002. "Hamlet's Neglect of Revenge", in Arthur Kinney (ed.), Hamlet: *New Critical Essays*. New York and London: Routledge. 85-100.

Halpern, Richard. 2008. "Eclipse of Action: *Hamlet* and the Political Economy of Playing", *Shakespeare Quarterly*, 59 (4): 450-82.

Kahn, Victoria. 1994. *Machiavellian Rhetoric: From the Counter-Reformation to Milton*. Princeton: Princeton University Press.

Kastan, David Scott. 1987. "'His semblable is his mirror': *Hamlet* and the Imitation of Revenge", *Shakespeare Studies*, 19: 111-24.

Kinney, Arthur F. (ed.) 2002. *Hamlet: New Critical Essays*. New York and London: Routledge.

Kraut, Richard. "Aristotle's *Ethics*" in Edward N. Zalta (ed.), *The Stanford Encyclopedia of Philosophy*. 10 June 2006. <http://plato.stanford.edu/archives/sum2005/entries/aristotle-ethics/>.

Lee-Riff, Nancy M. 1981. "What Fortinbras and Laertes Tell Us about Hamlet", *Hamlet Studies*, 3: 103-09.

Lemon, Rebecca. 2002. "Scaffolds of Treason in *Macbeth*", *Theatre Journal* 54 (1): 25-43.

Mack, Maynard. 1963. "The World of *Hamlet*", in Edward Hubler (ed.), *The Tragedy of Hamlet, Prince of Denmark*. New York. New American Library. 234-56. Originally printed in 1952. *The Yale Review*, 41: 502-23.

Menut, Albert D. 1943. "Castiglione and the *Nicomachean Ethics*", *PMLA*, 58 (2): 309-21.

Mercer, Peter. 1987. Hamlet *and the Acting of Revenge*. Iowa City: University of Iowa Press.

Moore, Peter R. 1997. "Hamlet and the two witness rule", *Notes and Queries*, 44 (4): 498-503.

Nardo, Anne K. 1983. "Hamlet, 'A Man to Double Business Bound'", *Shakespeare Quarterly*, 34 (2): 181-199.

Ornstein, Robert. 1964. "*Teaching Hamlet*", *College English*, 25 (7): 502-508.

Paster, Gail Kern. 2004. *Humoring The Body: Emotions and the Shakespearean Stage*. Chicago: University of Chicago Press.

Plato. 1997. *Phaedrus*, in John Cooper (ed.), *Plato: Complete Works*. Indianapolis: Hackett Publishing Company. 506-56.

—. 1997. *Republic*, in John Cooper (ed.), *Plato: Complete Works*. Indianapolis: Hackett Publishing Company. 971-1223.

Pollard, Tanya. 2005. "A Kind of Wild Medicine: Revenge as Remedy in Early Modern England", *Revista Canaria de Estudios Ingleses*, 50: 57-69.

Poisson, Rodney. 1966. "Coriolanus as Aristotle's Magnanimous Man", *Pacific Coast Studies in Shakespeare*: 210–24.

Roach, Joseph R. 1985. *The Player's Passion: Scenes in the Science of Acting*. Newark: University of Delaware Press.

Sachs, Joe. 2006. "Aristotle", *Internet Encyclopedia of Philosophy*. 20 July 2009 <http://www.iep.utm.edu/a/aris-eth.htm>.

Schmitt, Charles B. 1979, 1984. "Aristotle's Ethics in the Sixteenth Century: Some Preliminary Considerations", *The Aristotelian Tradition and Renaissance Universities*. London: Variorum Reprints. 87-112.

Schmitt, Charles B. and Quentin Skinner. 1992. *A History of Western Philosophy: Renaissance Philosophy*. Vol. 3. Oxford and New York: Oxford University Press.

Shakespeare, William. 1997. *Hamlet*. In Stephen Greenblatt, Walter Cohen, Jean E. Howard, and Katharine Eisaman Maus (eds), *The Norton Shakespeare*. New York: Norton.

Sidney, Philip. 2001. *Sir Philip Sidney's An Apology for Poetry and Astrophil and Stella. Text and Contexts*. Glen Allen, VA: College Publishing.

Skulsky, Harold. 1970. "Revenge, Honour, and Conscience in *Hamlet*", *PMLA*, 85 (1): 78-87.

Spenser, Edmund. 1993. *Edmund Spenser's Poetry. A Norton Critical Edition*. Eds. Hugh McClean and Anne Prescott. New York. Norton.

Terry, Reta A. 1999. "'Vows to the Blackest Devil': *Hamlet* and the Evolving Code of Honour in Early Modern England", *Renaissance Quarterly*, 52 (4): 1070-1086.

Tiffany, Grace. 2005. "Hamlet, Reconciliation, and the Just State", *Renascence: Essays on Values in Literature*, 58 (2): 111-33.

Tkacz, Catherine Brown. 1992. "The Wheel of Fortune, the Wheel of State, and Moral Choice in *Hamlet*", *South Atlantic Review*, 57 (4): 21-38.

Turner, Henry S. 2006. *The English Renaissance Stage: Geometry, Poetics, and the Practical Spatial Arts 1580–1630*. Oxford: Oxford University Press.

Vickers, Brian. 1990. "The Ambivalence of *Otium*", *Renaissance Studies: Journal of the Society for Renaissance Studies* 4 (1, 2): 1-37; 107-54.

Watson, Robert N. 1990, 2003. "Tragedy", in A. R. Braunmuller and Michael Hattaway (eds), *The Cambridge Companion to English*

Renaissance Drama. Cambridge: Cambridge University Press. 292-343.

Wright, Thomas. 1971. *The Passions of the Minde in Generall.* Ed. Thomas O. Sloane. Urbana: University of Illinois Press.

A MAN'S OFFICE, A WOMAN'S SHIELD: THE ETHICS OF THE BODY IN SHAKESPEARE

JIM CASEY

In his book-length study of *Shakespeare and Violence*, R. A. Foakes observes that "Violence has always been associated chiefly with masculinity" (2003: 10). This is an important point for him, and he describes violence, and a fascination with violence, as inherent traits of human beings, but "especially males", "especially among males", "especially men", "especially males", "usually a man", and "especially in males" (2003: 1-17). This gendering of violence is so common that it is not even a cliché; it is a truism.[1] Declarations concerning masculine domination are so common that it almost seems as if violence, oppression, hegemony, and patriarchy are all synonyms for *male*. Derek Cohen is typical in his assertion that "women are the obvious and natural victims of violence within patriarchal structures" and "Acts of violence belong to patriarchy as surely as fathers do" (1993: 92, 1). But are they? Do they?[2]

Teresa de Lauretis asserts that "the subject of violence is always, by definition, masculine", and the object of violence is always, by definition, feminine (1987: 43), but this cannot be true or we would not have hundreds, thousands, even millions of men killed or maimed in armed conflict.[3] As Pierre Bourdieu observes, "Male privilege is also a trap, and it has its negative side in the permanent tension and contention, sometimes verging on the absurd, imposed on every man by the duty to assert his manliness in all circumstances" (2001: 50). In the plays of Shakespeare, the impositions of male privilege force men to engage in dangerous enactments of manhood. Male identity becomes formed and informed by the sociocultural expectation of masculine violence; although characters may be classified initially as male by their physical attributes, their appellative and effective manhood depends on their ability to perform the offices of men. Alongside this masculine definition, the plays reveal an ethics of violence that is grounded in corporeal reality: male bodies represent appropriate sites for violence, but non-male bodies must be protected, not attacked. This chapter will explore the legitimization and limitation of masculine violence in Shakespeare's plays, paying particular attention to the intersections of gender, violence, and the body.

In *Macbeth*, when Macbeth enlists the aid of the two murderers, he asks them if they can forgive Banquo's supposed wrongs against them, and they simply reply, "We are men, my liege" (3.1.92), as if this answers the question. Macbeth retorts,

> Ay, in the catalogue ye go for men,
> As hounds and greyhounds, mongrels, spaniels, curs,
> Shoughs, water-rugs, and demi-wolves are clept
> All by the name of dogs. (3.1.93-6)[4]

This indicates that biological maleness may make a man eligible for inclusion in the catalog as a man, but there are gradations of manhood. Individual men in the plays may each possess the physical and biological attributes that define him "in the catalogue" as a man. When challenged, however, he can only "prove" his manhood by submitting his body to possible destruction. Repeatedly in Shakespeare, there is a clear connection between an individual's manhood and his voluntary entrance into the realm of masculine violence. Later in *Macbeth*, for example, when Old Siward learns that his son has been killed by a wound "on the front" (5.11.13), he does not lament the death of his son, as MacDuff does with the news of his children's murder, but rather expresses his pleasure that his son died, as Rosse says, "like a man" (5.11.9).

In *As You Like It*, Jaques depicts the fourth age of man as that of a soldier, seeking honour "[e]ven in the cannon's mouth" (2.7.148-52). Similarly, Ptolemaic theories of life argue that a large portion of every man's life is spent under the influence of Mars: in *Tetrabiblos*, Ptolemy asserts that a man spends fifteen years under Mars (1940: 445); Pedro Mexia, following Ptolemy, also assigns fifteen years to Mars, referring to the period as the *Aetas virilis* (M2^r); and in his *Historie of the World* (1617), Sir Walter Raleigh notes that man's martial stage comprises many years "in which we seeke honor and victorie, and in which our thoughts trauaile to ambitious ends" (D4^r).[5] These anthrochronologies suggest that all men, regardless of social station, must be educated in war and must progress through a martial stage of life.[6]

Thus, the only way the "unrough youths" of the rebel army in *Macbeth* can "Protest their first of manhood" (5.2.10-11) is with sword and shield. Similarly, in *Coriolanus*, Volumnia proudly explains to Virgilia how her own son became a man:

> To cruel war I sent [Martius], from whence he returned his brows

bound with oak. I tell thee, daughter, I sprang not more in joy
at first hearing he was a man-child, than now in first seeing he
had proved himself a man. (1.3.12-15)

Ultimately, however, even when a man faces danger and establishes his
manhood through repeated martial acts, his socioculturally inscribed
gender identity is, by its very nature, impermanent. Caius Martius
Coriolanus has "proved himself a man" in combat countless times, but
even his manhood is not incontrovertible. Despite demonstrating his
manliness again and again, despite receiving over twenty-five wounds,
despite vanquishing all his enemies, Martius cannot rest assured of his
masculinity. At the end of the play, when Tullus Aufidius and Caius
Martius return to Corioles after abandoning their invasion at the gates of
Rome, Aufidius accuses Martius of treason and cowardice, calling him a
"boy of tears" (5.6.103). Martius Coriolanus acquired his *agnomen* by
almost superhuman martial feats in the very city where he stands, fighting
alone within the city gates and, as he reminds Aufidius, defeating
countless Volscians, including the general himself. How, then, can
Aufidius so brazenly impugn his manhood? Perhaps more disturbing,
however, is the critical reaction of scholars regarding this moment. Almost
universally, critics read Martius's response to the appellation "boy" as a
signal of his castration or emasculation. For example, Bruce Smith claims
that the contrast between open and closed bodies prompts "Coriolanus to
imagine his stabbing death at the hands of the Volsces as an act of
emasculation" (2000: 16).[7] But Martius's actual words are "[c]ut me to
pieces, Volsces. Men and lads, / Stain all your edges on me" (5.6.112-13).
Martius is not imagining emasculation; rather he is inviting evisceration.
Nor does he fear a violent encounter. He says that he wishes he "had him
with six Aufidiuses, / Or more, his tribe, to use [his] lawful sword"
(5.6.127-8). The interpellation of this warrior as a "boy" demonstrates the
interminability of corporeal interpretation. Bodies are texts. They can be
read and re-read. And since his manhood is inscribed on his body, Martius
must continually demonstrate his manliness until he finally "proves" it
beyond question through his death. I am not suggesting that death is the
only marker of manhood in Shakespeare's plays—I would not even
suggest that it is the primary one—but it is the ultimate one, the final one.
By offering up his body for complete destruction, a character proves once
and for all that he is a man. Thus, the wages of manhood is death, and the
stage becomes a shambles.

Of course, early modern masculinity is a polysemous concept, not
constructed solely within the context of male violence but also connected
to honor, class, sexuality, humours, and various other matters.[8] Nevertheless,

manhood becomes "proven" only within the arena of ethically appropriate physical conflict. As Cohen notes, there are limits and rules to masculine violence:

> The violent act [...] has been naturalized by patriarchal social formations. Violence stands as one of the most flexible practices in the social structure and has been appropriated in most societies as the prerogative of the state. As a matter of social necessity the unsanctioned use of violence is constructed and understood as contrary to the public interest and is made illegal in order to protect both the potential victims of violence and the interests of those for whom it is a means of control, in particular those who dominate and direct state authority. (1993: 126)

Domestic disputes, personal vendettas, and private brawls are all inappropriate expressions of violence. Men are encouraged to involve themselves in violence and activity, but only if that violence is useful. Uncontrolled personal violence leads to chaos. For instance, in terms of masculinity, skill with a blade is manly, but indiscriminate use makes one effeminate, as seen in Joseph Swetnam's *The Schoole of the Noble and Worthy Science of Defence* (1617):

> hee which hath tried his manhoode, afterwards the world will iudge and say, that he is a man of his hands, and that he dare fight vpon a good occasion; but if he make a common occupation of fighting, hee will then bee accounted for a common quarreller, and his friends will refuse his company many times for doubt of his quarrelling, and yet hee shall neuer be accounted, more then a man againe. (I4^r)

Thus, the selfish, personal conflict of characters such as Pistol in *Henry 5* results in what Foakes describes as a "trivializing of violence, using it for robbery and pillage, or in petty quarrels and civil brawls"; this bears "the stigma attached to violence carried out for display or for corrupt purposes, in contrast to the violence of a war fought, as Henry claims, with the sanction of God" (2003: 100).

Jennifer Low (2003) suggests that duels and mock duels reveal the interconnectivity of manhood and social rank and Shulamith Shahar notes that "In the nobility, elderly women indeed outnumbered men because of the frequency of violent death among males" (Shahar, 2005: 79). But even non-aristocratic men could be drawn into deadly disputes, such as when Peter the apprentice kills Horner the armorer in *2 Henry 6*. Like the defendant in a high-born duel of honor, described in Saviolo's *Vincentio Saviolo His Practise* (1595), Peter is "both accused and constrained to fight" (BB2^v). Similarly, the pressures of manhood force the Capulet serving-men in *Romeo and Juliet* to both stand and stir against the house of Montague. According to Robert Appelbaum, the "insoluble double bind" of the "ambivalent prosthetics of masculinity" creates an internal conflict regarding male self-identity, so that "Sampson and Gregory, or, for that matter, Tybalt and Mercutio, are compelled to try to complete themselves in ways that can only result in their death" (1997: 252). Even Romeo succumbs to the expectations of bloodshed, despite Marianne Novy's claim that he overcomes his initial belief in "the manhood of violence" and, with Juliet, transcends the "aggressions and stereotypes of the outside in their secret world" (1984: 107-8). But these "civil brawls" (1.1.82) represent illicit manifestations of male violence, and the Prince declares that if any men engage in similar acts of unauthorized aggression, their "lives shall pay the forfeit of the peace" (1.1.90).

Alan Sinfield speaks of "legitimate violence" (1992: 95), licensed by the state and comprising activities such as war, training, and policing.[9] But violence is also licensed by the culture, particularly with regard to masculinity. Within the *habitus* of acceptable male violence, healthy, adult male bodies are ethically appropriate sites for violence. In contrast, female bodies, old bodies, and very young bodies are all read as inappropriate recipients of violence. Lavinia's death in *Titus Andronicus* is particularly immoral not only because she is innocent, but also because her body is not coded for destruction. In contrast, when Young Siward dies, or John Talbot, or Rosencrantz, or another male innocent, audiences accept (and even applaud) the death because the male body represents an appropriate location for the enactment of violence. R. S. White (1986), in his book-length study of "innocent victims", does mention the two male servants who die in *Lear*, but his chapter headings and full discussions include no adult males, only women and children: *Lavinia, Lucrece, Children, Ophelia, Desdemona, Cordelia*. This emphasizes the fact that women are conceived as both innocent and victims, whereas men are both guilty and victimizers. Thus, although men are encouraged to engage in masculine violence for the protection of women, children, and the state, although they sometimes die in this service, in general, they receive no recognition or appreciation for their own sacrifice. It is simply what their bodies are made to do.

Judith Butler claims that sex is not a "bodily given", but rather a "cultural norm which governs the materialization of bodies"; she advocates a rethinking of the materiality of the body "as the effect of power, as power's most productive effect" (1993: 2-3). In terms of Shakespearean male bodies, the governing norms of early modern culture insist on the bodily destruction of men, often in the service of the state. Of course, women also die in Shakespeare, but their deaths are more notable because they confound corporeal expectations. "The imminent death of twenty thousand men" (4.4.9.50) over an insignificant plot of land forms an accepted, almost quotidian backdrop in *Hamlet* because the soldiers are merely fulfilling their duties as men. In contrast, the accidental poisoning of Gertrude represents an unacceptable villainy enacted on an inappropriate feminine recipient. Early modern society, like Hamlet, would "speak daggers to her, but use none" (3.2.366). Similarly, the death of Ophelia is much more powerful dramatically than the deaths of Rosencrantz or Guildenstern, even though all three deaths occur offstage. No one, I expect, would leap into the graves of Hamlet's erstwhile friends—"They are not near my conscience" (5.2.59), the prince declares—and no one cries, "[l]ook to the King there, ho!" The women may be outnumbered in death ten thousand to one, but the play takes greater notice of them.

There is more going on here than a playwright's or a playgoer's personal necrOphelia. Culturally, historically, audiences are taught that women are not *made* to die, so entrance into the arena of masculine conflict is prohibited. For example, Jean Howard argues that in *Much Ado About Nothing*, when Beatrice and Benedick fall in love, they "reveal their successful interpellation into positions within a gendered social order" (1987: 178). Beatrice is portrayed as weakly feminine and Benedick demonstrates his manly nature and "rescues" her. But within the play as a whole, this interpellative gender positioning occurs particularly in relation to violence and death. When Benedick agrees to "[k]ill Claudio" (4.1.287) because "[i]t is a man's office" (4.1.265), he reveals his successful interpellation into a dangerous position within a gendered social order, conforming to the male role that society prescribes. Nor does Beatrice resist this limiting categorization. When Benedick exclaims, "[b]y my sword, Beatrice, thou lovest me" (4.1.272), she replies, "[d]o not swear and eat it" (4.1.273). He is making a surprised observation. She, on the other hand, is binding him to an oath of violence. When he accepts the office, he accepts the gender role that both she and society press upon him. Eager to be a man for her, he agrees to defend his honour, as well as Hero's, with the very weapon upon whose cross-shaped hilt he has just sworn.

Shakespeare's plays may appear to subvert the categories of gender, but their conclusions always re-establish stable gender identities. Smith suggests that "Shakespeare's comedies often invite the conclusion that masculinity is more like a suit of clothes that can be put on and taken off at will than a matter of biological destiny" (2000: 3). Looking at the situation of Beatrice in *Much Ado* or of Viola in *Twelfth Night*, however, reveals the limitations of Smith's "suit of clothes". Although Viola dresses and acts like a man for most of the play, eventually her (sartorial) performance must end. She cannot perform the offices of a man because she lacks the necessary equipment, as alluded to in her lines, "[a] little thing would make me tell them how much I lack of a man" (3.4.268-9). Similarly, Rosalind must abandon her "swashing" and "martial outside" (1.3.114) in *As You Like It*, and Portia must surrender her judge's robes in *The Merchant of Venice*. Like Viola, each of these women must relinquish her masculine disguise and reclaim her woman's weeds. These reversions are not merely returns to normativity, but returns to possibility. Just as it is not socially possible for the actors to remain kings or queens after the conclusion of the play, it is not physically possible for women to remain men. Viola cannot be Cesario because her body precludes her from doing so.

Discussing the dueling and cross-dressing of *Twelfth Night*, Smith argues that "[m]asculinity in all these instances is a matter of contingency, of circumstances, of performance" (2000: 4). Yet Viola's misadventures are not truly instances of masculinity, but rather moments of mistaken, misplaced, and misrepresented masculinity. This is part of what makes the scene funny. Were she truly made into a man (with a body coded for destruction), then the dueling scene could not be funny in the same way, because the audience would fear for Viola/Cesario's safety. There could be moments of macabre, ironic humor, such as when Mercutio is stabbed in *Romeo and Juliet*, but the threat of bodily destruction would frustrate not only the generic expectations of the comedy, but the generic expectations of the female body. In contrast, Shakespeare presents the dangerous exchange between Antonio and Sir Toby or the injuries suffered by Sir Toby and Sir Andrew in their confrontation with Sebastian as the logical consequences of masculinity. Because the audience knows that Viola is a woman, and because women's bodies are not read as acceptable sites for violence, Viola is in no real danger when she pseudo-duels Sir Andrew. Women are neither appropriate agents nor appropriate recipients of violent attack, so, despite the farcical mock-threat, Viola is never in any real danger of a bloody coxcomb. In contrast, we might compare the fates of other potential duelists in Shakespeare's plays: cross-dressed women may escape without incident, but Tybalt, Mercutio, Laertes, and Hamlet all fulfil the expectations of manhood.

In *King Lear*, when Lear encounters the eyeless Gloucester, he commiserates with the blinded man about the injustices of the world. In this scene, Lear utters the famously misogynistic speech in which he claims that "Down from the waist [women] are all Centaurs" (4.6.121). He has already cursed his daughters and has promised to visit the "terrors of the earth" upon them (2.4.277). Notice, however, that when he gives voice to his fantasy to stealthily approach and "kill, kill, kill, kill, kill, kill!" (4.6.181), he is not referring to his daughters, but rather to his sons-in-law. After all his rage and posturing, he cannot physically harm his wicked daughters. That this reticence to harm the female is grounded in her corporeal body is apparent in Albany's words to Goneril when he learns of her wicked deeds:

> Were't my fitness
> To let these hands obey my blood,
> They are apt enough to dislocate and tear
> Thy flesh and bones. Howe'er thou art a fiend,
> A woman's shape doth shield thee. (4.2.64-8)

Despite the fact that he identifies her as a devil, she *looks* like a woman so he cannot harm her. This prohibition also protects Regan during the scene of Gloucester's blinding. The servant who tries to intervene and is killed delivering Cornwall's death-blow tells her, "[i]f you did wear a beard upon your chin, / I'd shake it on this quarrel" (3.7.78-9). But she has no beard, no markers of manhood on her body; therefore, the servant cannot assail her.

There are times, of course, when women's bodies are attacked, but in these situations, the attackers are consistently represented as less rather than more manly.[10] The men who attack Macduff's family are simply "Murderers". These men lose honor and masculine fame because they violate ethical codes and attack the helpless. This gendered weakness is articulated in Lady Macduff's "womanly defence / To say [she has] done no harm" (4.2.78-9). To ask for pity simply based on an assumption of innocence is portrayed as effeminate. In contrast, the manly reaction is to act, to fight against the injustices of the world. Even Joan *la Pucelle* in *1 Henry 6*, who appears to wield a manly sword, succumbs to the fate of her biological body.[11] M. L. Stapleton (1994) argues that Joan is punished for her attempt to establish feminine identity in a martial, phallocentric world and depicts Joan as a woman engaged in the transgressive seizure of masculine power, but *la Pucelle* does not die a man's death on the battlefield. In fact, Young John Talbot will not even fight her, making her complain, "He left me proudly, as unworthy fight" (4.7.43). Even when she is condemned to death, Warwick urges her executioners to curtail the torture during her execution "because she is a maid" (5.6.55-8). Like Viola, her sojourn into maleness is temporary. Joan herself eschews all masculine agency and fully re-feminizes herself when she announces her (potentially fictitious) pregnancy. Many women escaped execution by pleading for the lives of their unborn children and Joan declares both her sex and her gender with the claim; not only does her pregnancy mark her as female, but her attempt to avoid torture and death also codes her as decidedly not-male. In the end, she is executed not because she is a woman, but because she is a witch, an "accursèd minister of hell" (5.6.93).

Normal women may avoid torture and death through protestations of innocence (although these womanly defences do little good against immoral murderers), but men must protest their manhood daily through seeking out torture and death. A woman may testify that she is "a right maid for [her] cowardice" (3.2.303), as Helena does in *A Midsummer Night's Dream*, and flee from conflict with no shame. If a man runs from battle, however, as Fastolf does in *1 Henry 6*, then the markers of manliness (in this case, the man's Garter) are torn from his "craven's" leg (4.1.15). In *Coriolanus*, Martius refers to such men as "souls of geese / That bear the shapes of men" (1.5.5-6). Like the demonic women mentioned above, these individuals have violated the gender expectations of their biological bodies and are condemned for it. Men, to be called men, must stir and stand. The only exception to this rule would be when the ostensibly male body has been transformed, through old age or excessive wounding, into a feminized body.[12]

As Elizabeth Foyster points out, Hippocratic humoral theory, still widely believed in Shakespeare's time, asserted that the biological sex of a person resulted from a combination of temperature and moisture: "Men had a propensity to be hot and dry; women cold and moist" (1999: 28-9). In his *De Temporum Ratione* (725) the Venerable Bede describes old age as cold and moist (Burrow, 1986: 12).[13] Therefore, old men were like women not only in their sociocultural exclusion but also in their physical/humoural constitution. In *King Lear*, when Lear confronts Goneril, he says,

> Life and death! I am ashamed
> That thou hast power to shake my manhood thus;
> That these hot tears, which break from me perforce,
> Should make thee worth them. (1.4.273-6)

Since the humoral element most connected to old age is water, old men are often depicted as particularly susceptible to tears. In Shakespeare, weeping consistently figures as feminine, countered only by masculine anger and eventual action. For example, in *Macbeth*, when Macduff learns of the murder of his family, he is overcome with emotion. Malcolm urges him to "Dispute it like a man" (4.3.221) and to turn his pain into useful anger:

"Be this the whetstone of your sword. Let grief / Convert to anger: blunt not the heart, enrage it" (4.3.230-1). Macduff admits that he "could play the woman with [his] eyes" (4.3.232), but he rejects such an unmanly option, choosing instead to take arms against a murdering usurper and by opposing, end him. Of course, old men are often denied this option in Shakespeare. Lear prays to the gods, "touch me with noble anger, / And let not women's weapons, water-drops, / Stain my man's cheeks!" (2.4.463-7), but the noble anger that might have sustained Lear when he was younger no longer works because he no longer has the power to exercise his will. Anger without implementation leads to frustration, even madness. "You think I'll weep", he tells his daughters, "No, I'll not weep" (2.4.277-8). Yet he does. What else can he do?

For the effeminized old man, the transformation of his body releases him from the bodily obligation of masculinity, as seen in *Much Ado About Nothing*. After the public denunciation of his daughter, Leonato confronts Claudio, challenging him to a "trial of a man" (5.1.66) and promising bodily harm. The young man does not take the old man's threat seriously, any more than he would take such a challenge from Beatrice. Unlike Benedick's challenge only minutes later, which could have serious consequences indeed, Leonato's provocation, like the old man himself, has no teeth. Even when played straight, the sound and fury of the two old men often leaves the audience "tittering" as in as is Douglas Seale's 1958 production (Cox, 1997: 209n). Most audience members, like Claudio, simply cannot take the old man's challenge seriously. They know that no harm can come from the encounter because, like Viola in her duel with Aguecheek, Leonato's body is not coded for destruction. Like women, old men are to be protected, not destroyed.

We see this sentiment at work when Leonato accuses Claudio of reaching for his sword. The young man responds, "[m]arry, beshrew my hand / If it should give your age such cause of fear. / In faith, my hand meant nothing to my sword" (5.1.55-7). Not only does this passage demonstrate the deference that the young owe their elders; it also displays the unsuitability of Leonato's old body as a site for violence. Were it not for the age of Hero's father, Claudio would not be able to withdraw so easily from the quarrel without injuring his own honour. As it is, accepting Leonato's challenge would be more dishonourable than ignoring it. When he realizes that the young man cannot face him without flouting social prohibitions, Hero's father tries to dissociate himself from age and veneration, saying,

Tush, tush, man, never fleer and jest at me.
I speak not like a dotard nor a fool,

As under privilege of age to brag
What I have done being young, or what would do
Were I not old. Know Claudio to thy head,
Thou hast so wronged mine innocent child and me
That I am forced to lay my reverence by,
And with grey hairs and bruise of many days
Do challenge thee to trial of a man. (5.1.58-66)

Clearly, these words attempt to displace age as an excuse for Claudio to disregard the old man's challenge, but they also work to (re)establish Leonato's manhood. Just two scenes earlier, when Beatrice urges Benedick to "[k]ill Claudio" because "[i]t is a man's office", she clearly delineates the boundaries of manhood. When Leonato tries to challenge Claudio, he attempts to prove that, despite his age, he is still a man and able to do his office. This declaration of masculinity is reiterated when Claudio won't fight him and Leonato asks indignantly, "[c]anst thou so doff me? Thou hast killed my child. / If thou kill'st me, boy, thou shalt kill a man" (5.1.78-9). By offering up his body for potential destruction, by engaging in an action in which he may kill or be killed, Leonato endeavors to assert his masculinity in an unequivocal manner. That the brothers see the dismissal of their challenge as an affront to their manhood may be seen in the fact that, in only six lines, they address Claudio as "boy" four times (5.1.79-84). The rhetorical *perseverantia* of "boy" attempts to re-categorize the bodies on stage, figuring the two brothers not as *old* men, but as *proven* men, in opposition to the *boys* they face. The taunting appellative underscores the discourse of manhood and demands a response in the same way that Aufidius's "boy" demands a response from Martius Coriolanus.

The problem, of course, is that Leonato's manhood is liminal at best. In fact, the play demonstrates that old age has emasculated him by grouping him, at different times, with both Beatrice and his brother Antonio. For example, when Leonato tells Claudio that, if the young man should kill him, he would kill a man, Antonio adds, "He shall kill two of us, and men indeed" (5.1.80). Antonio is introduced in the stage directions of the First Folio as "old man, brother to Leonato", and his braggadocio here is often characterized as "caricature dialogue" (Zitner, 1993: 38). On stage, Antonio's blustering usually comes across as either humorous or pathetic, depending on the action, but even if they induce pity, the old man's warlike overtures are always ridiculous. His body simply cannot meet the requirements of manly action. He is like Old Capulet in *Romeo and Juliet*, who can barely walk, yet calls for a sword, prompting his wife's "[a] crutch, a crutch—why call you for a sword?" (1.1.69). Clearly, in scenes such as these, the humour and the horror of the angry old man's predicament resides in his ineffectual nature, in his essential impotence. No matter how much he threatens, Leonato cannot take up the sword because his body excludes him from dangerous and violent action. In this, he is similar not only to Antonio and Old Capulet, but to Beatrice as well.

After Claudio's public disavowal of Hero, Beatrice cries out, "O God that I were a man! I would eat his heart in the market place" (4.1.303-4). Her indignation and anger are at least as great as Leonato's, but she has been precluded from the office of killing Claudio solely on the basis of her gender.[14] Moreover, she acknowledges that "[she] cannot be a man with wishing, therefore [she] will die a woman with grieving" (4.1.317-18). At the beginning of Act 5, Leonato laments his own grief at the public defamation of his daughter. Rather than die with grieving, however, he challenges Claudio to his "trial of a man". When Claudio denies him, the young man does so entirely as a result of Leonato's age. In this context, then, Leonato and Beatrice occupy analogous positions of powerlessness: Leonato's "[w]ere I not old" becomes dramatically equal to Beatrice's "O God that I were a man!"

The prohibition of violence against feminine and effeminized bodies generally obviates dire physical threat and makes violence against those bodies much more notable. For example, audiences watching *Titus Andronicus* witness the reported deaths of Titus's twenty-one soldier-sons, the ritualized killing of Alarbus, the slaying of Mutius, the murder of Bassianus, the maiming of Titus, the beheadings of Martius and Quintus, the hanging of the Clown, the cooking of Demetrius and Chiron, the dual stabbings of Titus and Saturninus, and the live burial of Aaron. Yet the critical discussion of bodies in the play focuses almost entirely on the female body of Lavinia. Male bodies, when mentioned, most often appear within other discussions, such as those regarding economic, class-based, or political power structures. Francis Barker, commenting on the "homology of the spectacularity of the scaffold of punishment with that of the theatricality of the [early modern] stage", asserts that the "theatricality of power" in plays such as *Titus Andronicus* helps to underwrite the signifying practices of the dominant culture (1993: 165). Thus, the senseless, seemingly random hanging of the Clown (4.4.39-48) solidifies the power of the ruling class and legitimizes an otherwise unreasonable royal authority. At the same time, the execution obfuscates the hanging of real non-aristocratic people: "To be sure occlusion does not entail a complete erasure of death by hanging; rather it puts death by hanging 'under erasure.' Not exactly hidden, it is more naturalised and exscribed at the same time" (Barker, 1993: 192-3). In a similar way, the hundreds of males who die or are wounded on and offstage in Shakespeare's plays help to put masculine death "under erasure" by both naturalizing and exscribing male injury and quietus.

Elisabeth Bronfen argues that "Because they are so familiar, so evident, we are culturally blind to the ubiquity of representations of feminine death. Though in a plethora of representations feminine death is perfectly visible we only see it with some difficulty" (1992: 3). But if we compare the number of male and female deaths, we find that cultural and artistic representations of masculine death are far more common. Three female bodies are dead at the end of *Titus Andronicus*, for example (Lavinia, Tamora, and the Nurse), but they are accompanied by thirty-one male bodies (or pieces of them) and the promise of one more (one Moor). Perhaps because they are so prevalent, so multitudinous, we are culturally blind to the ubiquity of representations of masculine death. These deaths are perfectly visible, but we only see them with some difficulty.

Pascale Aebischer, discussing "the relative restraint of Shakespeare's playtext" when it places Lavinia's rape offstage, asks the insightful question, "[i]f Titus can chop off his hand on-stage and Hieronimo, in Kyd's roughly contemporary play, *The Spanish Tragedy*, can bite off and spit out his own tongue, why is the playtext so reluctant to portray the process of Lavinia's mutilation?" (2004: 24). She observes that, in contrast to the performance text (the play on stage), the playtext (the play on page) removes Lavinia's rape from her body and re-places it into the words of her male relatives; her suffering is thus subsumed by their grief. On stage, however, Lavinia's textual erasure is necessarily reversed by her very real physical presence on stage. In her body, the "unspeakable" is spoken, the "unrepresentable" represented. Thus, bodies in performance open up the play in ways the playtext can only suggest. Aebischer notes that the stage direction for Lavinia's return after her rape and mutilation, "in its explicit display of the opened-up female body, borders on sadistic pornography" (2004: 29). The rape is both "ob-scene" and obscene.

These are excellent observations, but Aebischer does not answer her original question, nor does she explore the implications of that answer. Why is it that audiences are able to witness male bodies suffering horrific acts of cruelty but cannot bear to see a woman's body violated?[15] Looking at Lavinia's rape and mutilation, Aebischer quotes Lynda Nead's description of obscenity: "Art is being defined in terms of the containing of form within limits; obscenity, on the other hand, is defined in terms of excess, as form beyond limit, beyond the frame of representation" (1992: 20). Lavinia's rape is something the early moderns would have considered obscene. Consequently, it occurred ob-scene. Titus's mutilation, Hieronimo's self-mutilation, Mutius's death—none of these was considered obscene, so none was performed ob-scene. The answer to Aebischer's question, then, seems to imply that female mutilation exists beyond appropriate limits and is somehow more disturbing than male mutilation.

Appelbaum notes that the current "critical community's ideological moment" figures masculinity as perpetually "*at fault*", as something that "must be refused, denied, pathologized, subverted, or otherwise abjected" (1997: 256-7). But re-examining the otherwise normalized performance of male death in literature allows for a potentially positive reading of men, with male death understood within a conceptual paradigm similar to that of Celia Daileader's depiction of female death. Using the phraseology of Laurie Finke, who describes "'killing' a woman into art" (1984: 361), Daileader connects female sacrifices to the sacrifice of Christ:

> not only is Christ's passion a necessary precondition for the eroticization of a woman's death (or a man's)—but the erotic element itself perpetuates this theme in art. The word "martyr" is Latin for "witness": a witness of God; a death to be witnessed. Sacrifice requires an audience; thus, martyrdom is *redeemed* as a subject for art. After all, Christ is killed into art every day. (1998: 105-6)[16]

Daileader and Finke are speaking of the objectification of a woman's body, particularly her beauty, but "killing into art" also performs a memorializing function. A woman's beauty becomes timeless inside a painting.

For men, there is a similar dialectic of sacrifice and immortalization, although bravery and manhood, rather than beauty, are usually what becomes transformed into art. For example, in a passage in *Pierce Penilesse* (1592) that probably refers to *1 Henry 6*, Thomas Nashe, commenting on the revival of "our forefathers valiant acts" asks, "what can be a sharper reproofe to these degenerate effeminate dayes of ours" (F3[r])? He exclaims,

> How would it haue ioyed braue *Talbot* (the terror of the French) to thinke that after he had lyne two hundred yeares in his Tombe, hee should triumphe againe on the Stage, to haue his bones newe embalmed with the teares of ten thousand spectators at least, (at seuerall times) who in the Tragedian that represents his person, imagine they behold him fresh bleeding. (F3[r])

Nashe's laudatory lines behold Talbot not in any engagement where he defeats the French, but when he is "fresh bleeding". In this, men are also sacrificial, perhaps like Christ, but their deaths and the deaths of women are read differently. When men are sacrificed, it is glorious, but when women or children die, it is a tragic occurrence, a "crime". Thus, we have Hamlet's reaction to the death of Ophelia, or Fluellen's outrage at the killing of the boys and the luggage. In Shakespeare, men remain on stage to have hands chopped off and eyes gouged out because extreme violence against male bodies was not read as ob(-)scene for the early moderns, not considered "beyond the frame of representation".

Discussing death and the female body, Carol Chillington Rutter suggests that "[f]or us, as for Shakespeare, the experience of death is gendered, and death is a site where the work of gender gets (finally) done. If you want to know what any culture thinks of women, read its representations. Read the theatre. Read Cordelia. Read the body" (2001: 26). I agree with Rutter's statement here, although perhaps beyond what she means. The experience of death is gendered. For us, as for Shakespeare, useless male death is tragic: "Promising young athlete dies in a car crash". But virtually all female deaths are useless, and therefore tragic: "Aid agencies report as many as 47 non-combatants killed, including 3 women and 2 children". We can infer from reports such as this one that the deaths of three women and two children are more notable than the deaths of forty-two men. We never hear, for example, that "20 die, including 2 men". There is an interesting chiasmus here if we but look for it. Death may be a site where the work of gender gets done, but we should also note that, in the case of men, gender is a site where the work of death gets (finally) done. If you want to know what any culture thinks of men, read its representations. Read the theatre. Read Lear (AntonyMacbeth CoriolanusTitusTalbot). Read the body.

Notes

[1] According to conceptual artist Jenny Holzer's *Truisms* (1977-), for example, "fathers often use too much force" while "mothers shouldn't make too many sacrifices".

[2] Numerous feminists have challenged such assertions; see, for example, Rene Denfeld (1997), Alix Kirsta (1994), and Cathy Young (2000).

[3] At the Battle of the Somme in 1916, for example, British casualties were 420,000; French casualties were 195,000; and German casualties were 650,000 (Laffin, 1986: 399). These one million, two hundred and sixty-five thousand soldiers were all males.

[4] All quotations from *The Norton Shakespeare* (Greenblatt *et al.*, 2008).

[5] The Loeb Classical Library edition of the *Tetrabiblos* appears in a common volume set following the text of *Manetho*, edited by W.G. Waddell, and is usually

catalogued under that title. Mexia's *Silva de Varia Lección* was translated into English by Thomas Fortescue in 1571 as *The Foreste*.

[6] For more on the martial education of young men in early modern England, see my essay, "Honest Payneful Pastymes" (2010).

[7] Numerous scholars make similar claims; Janet Adelman, for example, argues that the language here "represents a kind of castration" (Adelman, 1976: 121n), and Coppélia Kahn appears to agree with Aufidius's assessment of Martius: "this god is but a boy, finally, a 'boy of tears'" (Kahn, 1981: 158).

[8] These myriad aspects of masculinity have been discussed extensively by a number of critics, including Smith (2000), Robin Headlam Wells (2000), and Kahn (1981).

[9] Although he never explicitly says so, Sinfield appears to be following Max Weber's influential definition of a state as an entity that has a monopoly on legitimate violence.

[10] There are exceptions to this rule, but in almost all of situations of admirable violence against female bodies, the women are figured as fiends, hell-kites, witches, and other demonic creatures, *not* as women.

[11] The editors of the Oxford *Textual Companion* have shown that significant portions of *1 Henry 6* were written in collaboration with Thomas Nashe and other unknown playwrights, including the portion quoted here (Taylor *et al*, 1997: 217), but dual and multiple authorship occurs often in the period and Shakespeare himself was a collaborative playwright, so I have treated the entire play as part of the Shakespeare canon, rather than parsing this play according to theories of attribution.

[12] Peter Rudnytsky argues that the "precious stones" (testicles) and "bleeding rings" (vaginas) mentioned during the blinding of Gloucester in *King Lear* (5.3.188-9) suggest symbolic "castration" (Rudnytsky, 1999: 292-3).

[13] Galen believed that men became drier as they aged, but "the elderly also had 'external moisture' and a secondary nature. Often viewed as 'bad,' these external moistures were produced by the elderly themselves, through their tears, phlegm and mucus, rendering their secondary natures cold and moist" (Botelho, 2005: 127).

[14] As Benedick says, "A most manly wit [...] will not hurt a woman" (5.2.13-14).

[15] Of course, there is no crime against a man that is precisely analogous to the sexualized violation of Lavinia's rape. For discussions of rape and sexual attack on female bodies in early modern England, see Bamford (2000), Daileader (1998), Spierenburg (1998), Little (2000), and Donaldson (1982).

[16] Finke herself appropriates this phrase from Sandra Gilbert and Susan Gubar's *Madwoman in the Attic* (Gilbert and Gubar, 1979: 14-17).

References

Adelman, J. 1976. "'Anger's My Meat': Feeding, Dependency, and Aggression in *Coriolanus*", in D. Bevington and J. L. Halio (eds),

Shakespeare: Pattern of Excelling Nature. Newark: University of Delaware Press, 108-24.

Aebischer, P. 2004. *Shakespeare's Violated Bodies: Stage and Screen Performance*. Cambridge: Cambridge University Press.

Appelbaum, R. 1997. "'Standing to the wall': The Pressures of Masculinity in *Romeo and Juliet*", *SQ*, 48 (3): 251-72.

Bamford, K. 2000. *Sexual Violence on the Jacobean Stage*. New York: St. Martin's Press.

Barker, F. 1993. *The Culture of Violence: Tragedy and History*. Chicago: University of Chicago Press.

Botelho, L. A. 2005. "The 17th Century", in P. Thane (ed.), *A History of Old Age*. Los Angeles: J. Paul Getty Museum. 113-74.

Bourdieu, P. 2001. *Masculine Domination*. Trans. R. Nice. Stanford: Stanford University Press.

Bronfen, E. 1992. *Over Her Dead Body: Death, Femininity and the Aesthetic*. Manchester: Manchester University Press.

Burrow, J. A. 1986. *The Ages of Man: A Study of Medieval Writing and Thought*. Oxford: Clarendon Press.

Butler, J. 1993. *Bodies That Matter: On the Discursive Limits of "Sex"*. New York: Routledge.

Casey, J. 2010. "Honest Payneful Pastymes: Pain, Play, and Pedagogy in Early Modern England", in K. M. Moncrief and K. R. McPherson (eds), *Performing Pedagogy in Early Modern England*. Burlington, VT: Ashgate. 108-28.

Cohen, D. 1993. *Shakespeare and the Culture of Violence*. London: Macmillan.

Cox, J. F. (ed.) 1997. *Much Ado About Nothing*. Shakespeare in Production. Cambridge: Cambridge University Press.

Daileader, C. R. 1998. *Eroticism on the Renaissance Stage: Transcendence, Desire, and the Limits of the Visible*. Cambridge Studies in Renaissance Literature and Culture Series. Cambridge: Cambridge University Press.

De Lauretis, T. 1987. *Technologies of Gender: Essays on Theory, Film, and Fiction*. Bloomington: Indiana University Press.

Denfeld, R. 1997. *Kill the Body, the Head Will Fall: A Closer Look at Women, Violence, and Aggression*. New York: Warner.

Donaldson, I. 1982. *The Rapes of Lucretia: A Myth and Its Transformations*. Oxford: Clarendon Press.

Finke, L. A. 1984. "Painting Women: Images of Femininity in Jacobean Tragedy", *Theatre Journal*, 36 (3): 357-70.

Foakes, R. A. 2003. *Shakespeare and Violence.* Cambridge: Cambridge University Press.

Foyster, E. A. 1999. *Manhood in Early Modern England: Honour, Sex and Marriage.* Women and Men in History Series. London: Longman.

Gilbert, S. and S. Gubar. 1979. *Madwoman in the Attic: The Woman Writer and the Nineteenth Century Literary Imagination.* New Haven: Yale University Press.

Greenblatt, S. *et al* (eds) 2008. *The Norton Shakespeare: Based on the Oxford Edition.* 2nd edn. New York: Norton.

Headlam Wells, R. 2000. *Shakespeare on Masculinity.* Cambridge: Cambridge University Press.

Howard, J. 1987. "Renaissance Antitheatricality and the Politics of Gender and Rank in *Much Ado About Nothing*", in J. E. Howard and M. F. O'Connor (eds), *Shakespeare Reproduced: The Text in History and Ideology.* New York: Methuen. 163-87.

Kahn, C. 1981. *Man's Estate: Masculine Identity in Shakespeare.* Berkeley: University of California Press.

Kirsta, A. 1994. *Deadlier Than the Male: Violence and Aggression in Women.* London: Harper Collins.

Laffin, J. 1986. *Brassey's Battles: 3,500 Years of Conflict, Campaigns, and Wars from A-Z.* London: Wheaton.

Little, A. L., Jr. 2000. *Shakespeare Jungle Fever: National-Imperial Re-Visions of Race, Rape, and Sacrifice.* Stanford: Stanford University Press.

Low, J. A. 2003. *Manhood and the Duel: Masculinity in Early Modern Drama and Culture.* Early Modern Cultural Studies, 1550-1700. New York: Palgrave.

Nead, L. 1992. *The Female Nude: Art, Obscenity, and Sexuality.* London: Routledge.

Novy, M. 1984. *Love's Argument: Gender Relations in Shakespeare.* Chapel Hill: University of North Carolina Press.

Ptolemy. 1940. *Tetrabiblos.* Trans. F. E. Robbins. [*Manetho.* Trans. W. G. Waddell]. Loeb Classical Library. Cambridge, MA.: Harvard University Press.

Rudnytsky, P. L. 1999. "'The Darke and Vicious Place': The Dread of the Vagina in *King Lear*", *Modern Philology*, 96 (3): 291-311.

Rutter, C. C. 2001. *Enter the Body: Women and Representation on Shakespeare's Stage.* London: Routledge.

Shahar, S. 2005. "The Middle Ages and Renaissance", in P. Thane (ed.), *A History of Old Age.* Los Angeles: J. Paul Getty Museum. 71-111.

Sinfield, A. 1992. *Faultlines: Cultural Materialism and the Politics of Dissident Reading.* Oxford: Clarendon Press.

Smith, B. 2000. *Shakespeare and Masculinity.* Oxford Shakespeare Topics. Oxford: Oxford University Press.

Spierenburg, P. 1998. "Masculinity, Violence, and Honor: An Introduction", in P. Spierenburg (ed.), *Men and Violence: Gender, Honor, and Rituals in Modern Europe and America.* [Columbus]: Ohio State University Press. 1-29.

Stapleton, M. L. 1994. "'Shine it like a comet of revenge': Seneca, John Studley, and Shakespeare's Joan la Pucelle", *Comparative Literature Studies*, 31 (3): 229-50.

Taylor, G. *et al.* 1997. *William Shakespeare: A Textual Companion.* New York: Norton.

White, R. S. 1986. *Innocent Victims: Poetic Injustice in Shakespearean Tragedy.* 1982. London: Athlone Press.

Young, C. 2000. "Taking It Personally". *Guardian Unlimited: The Guardian.* 8 Feb. 2000.
<http://www.guardian.co.uk/women/story/0,,237578,00.html>.

Zitner, S. P. (ed.) 1993. *Much Ado About Nothing.* Oxford Shakespeare. Oxford: Oxford University Press.

MILTON'S "CHASTE THINKING" IN PROLUSION VI

JIM DAEMS

How might we account for accusations of sexual transgression in the polemical battles that John Milton entered? Such accusations are remarkably prevalent in Milton's writings and in those of his opponents—also remarkable is the sheer range of transgressions: adultery, effeminacy, sodomy, promiscuity, rape, and uxoriousness, to cite but a few examples. My focus in this paper, however, will not be on the accusations themselves, whether they have any basis in reality, but rather on the instructional aspect of the broader context from within which the sexual conduct, real or imagined, of an author enters into the rhetorical arena. This broader context is humanism. As John Hale states, Milton's writings demonstrate "an interested, appreciative audience for insults, indeed, a humanist taste for such" (1998: 166). The "humanist taste" for insults, often explicitly sexual insults, prompts some very interesting questions, and reading their occurrence throughout Milton's prose works provides a means of interrogating a continuity in his thought—a politics of virtue. In what follows, I will discuss one particular trope which recurs frequently in humanist writings—the rape of Lucretia, a narrative which is implicated in a political logic that Stephanie Jed (1989) calls "chaste thinking" and analyses in relation to humanist and republican discourse. Specifically, I will examine Milton's sixth prolusion (1628). Though not published until 1674, I choose this work because it is Milton's earliest appropriation of the Lucretia narrative and thereby allows us to foreground the significance of "chaste thinking" in his literary career.

My argument, then, is relevant to the much debated topic of Milton's republicanism, though I am not so much interested here in ascribing a date for Milton's republican conversion. As Martin Dzelzainis' cogent summary of the debate demonstrates, there are competing definitions of the term which contribute to views of Milton's republicanism that "vary according to which of these definitions we adopt" (2001: 296). The current chapter is, undoubtedly, an example by focusing on the rape of Lucretia and Milton's politics of virtue. Be that as it may, Dzelzainis argues for an early date for Milton's republican conversion, a date prior to the execution of Charles I: "if the key to understanding Milton's republicanism is his commitment to a politics of virtue, then it is hard to see 1649 as a watershed. For an outline of this politics is already visible in the pamphlets he wrote in the mid-1640s" (2001: 300). But a politics of virtue is evident even earlier than the mid-1640s. It is evident, for example, in the sixth prolusion. In this work, Milton rather disturbingly constructs a politics of virtue by using the rape of Lucretia as a controlling metaphor to berate his fellow undergraduates. He takes on the role of Lucius Junius Brutus, the model humanist chaste thinker.

In *Chaste Thinking: the Rape of Lucretia and the Birth of Humanism*, Jed examines the fifteenth-century Florentine appropriation of the Roman republican tradition. Jed sees Florentine philological practices as commensurate with their political ideals, but also, importantly, as figuratively complicit with the rape of Lucretia. The humanist tradition constructs a logic—a cause and effect relationship—whereby Tarquin's rape of Lucretia is a historically transcendent prologue to republican freedom. "[T]he Florentines", Jed argues, "figured themselves as the legitimate conservators of the topoi of republican freedom, on the basis of their exclusive, chaste relations with the Roman texts" (1989: 37). The purity of the republican cause of liberty is dependent upon the chastity of that tradition's textual transmission. In this way, the Florentines represented themselves as the rightful heirs of the republican tradition—by purifying that tradition's textual transmission and making it into a direct line of descent to themselves, they purified their own historically specific struggle against the tyranny of the Visconti. While this humanist project involves the paradox of what Jed calls "chaste thinking"—the use of rhetorical devices to cover their own contact with the Roman texts through editorial means aimed at producing a text in it original, pristine state, thereby asserting the tradition's transcendence—one thing is certain within the logic of this tradition: Lucretia *had* to be raped for tyranny to be overcome.

This clearly foregrounds the relationship between the effacement of the historical specificity of ideological competition and the existence of textual homosocial bonds in humanism. These work in tandem in the service of desired political aims. The struggle over, and possession of, Lucretia, becomes a politicised one which aids in the construction of a republican masculinity based on a politics of virtue which is metaphorically linked to a transcendent concept of chastity—the restraint of passions and sexual purity. Through "chaste thinking", Lucretia's rape is read by succeeding generations of humanists in much the same way that Brutus is represented as having "read" the original situation that led to the establishment of republican liberty. Indeed, by focussing on Brutus as the avenger of this crime and the liberator of the people from tyranny and slavery, humanists draw our attention away from the sexual violence committed on Lucretia's body. This is accomplished in a fascinating way. Jed argues that,

> Any emotional involvement we might feel in what happened to Lucretia is quickly displaced by our admiration of Brutus for liberating Rome[...]. Livy tells us that when Brutus found the Romans grieving over the fate of Lucretia, he "castigated" them for their tears and emotions and urged them to take up arms instead of weeping. This figure of Brutus as a *castigator lacrimarum* functions not only as a cue to the Romans to subordinate their emotions to the cause of liberty, but also as a cue to the readers to consider the rape of Lucretia "objectively"—that is, as a necessary prologue to Brutus' act of liberation. (1989: 10-11)

Brutus castigates himself, at first, to hide his true character under the tyranny of the Tarquins. Following the rape of Lucretia, he turns his self-castigation on the Roman populace, creating an emotional detachment that Jed associates here with "objectivity." Brutus as castigator, the "chaste thinking" humanist philologists, and Lucretia (who, in Livy's account, argues that she should be punished to the full extent of the law even though, while her body has been polluted, her mind remains chaste) all assert a primacy of mind over body—the rational restraint of passions of the sort that the tyrannical Tarquins have given themselves up to.

Indeed, Lucretia's decision to commit suicide reproduces the central political point of the story which is resolved only after the rebellion, involving Brutus's sons, later in the text. Livy clearly establishes the significance of law to republicanism when he writes that the rebellion

> began with a group of young aristocrats who had found life under the monarchy very agreeable; accustomed to associate with the younger members of the royal family, they had been able to give freer rein to their appetites and to live the dissolute and irresponsible life of the court. (1974: 108)

The dissolute life of the court will become a familiar element of Milton's work. But here, it is important to recognise how Lucretia's decision, because of its foreshadowing of more strictly political concerns, tends also to move attention away from herself to the man who will avenge the crime committed against her and found the republic. Lucretia, like Brutus when he condemns his sons, believes in an impersonal law, one not subject to the vagaries of one man's will, the monarch's. As Jed points out, humanists still follow this rhetorical shift of focus, and it is a major caveat of her book—one which, at times, has been ignored. For example, Debora Shuger writes, "Jed's tendentious philology simply erases the fact that, from antiquity through the Renaissance, 'chaste thinking' regularly concerned issues of male purity, of the (violent) constraints placed on male sexuality, of the need to control male bodies" (1998: 530). That "need to control male bodies" is precisely the rhetorical move produced by chaste thinking (modelled on Brutus's self-castigation), a move which prompts Shuger's shift of focus away from the violated Lucretia, whom she effaces, to "the (violent) constraints placed on male sexuality". The chaste thinking humanist remains, however, a desiring masculine subject inscribing a discourse complicit with violence, specifically, with the rape of Lucretia.

The body (physical or textual) is a site of potential violation; hence, Shuger's confusion of cause and effect in regards to the logic of chaste thinking. Brutus's castigation and Lucretia's suicide confirm that the chaste body in fact invites violation—it motivates both Tarquin's rape and subsequent appropriations of the narrative. As Jed points out, it is precisely from Lucretia's

> refusal to live with this contradiction of 'chastity of a corrupt body' [...that] a new freedom is born which reproduces, in Florence and the Roman texts supporting Florentine identity, this same contradiction—the claim to restore a pure and integral descent from Republican Rome as proof of a political mission. (1989: 46)

Jed's analysis of fifteenth-century Florentine humanism—of chaste thinking—is relevant to Milton's relationship with texts, both classical and biblical, and how he represents the distinction between liberty and tyranny as one of rational restraint (law) over passions (licence). In order to explore Milton's place in this tradition, I want to begin with Milton's earliest, and perhaps most fascinating appropriation of the Lucretia narrative: Prolusion VI. Milton and his polemical opponents, I want to suggest, are trapped within the humanist rhetorical logic of chaste thinking, developed in response to a foundational sexual transgression and its textual transmission.

In Prolusion VI, Milton almost immediately alludes to Brutus and draws an analogy to his own situation:

> If that famous second father of Rome and great avenger of a king's lust, Junius Brutus, could bear to hold down a mind almost equal to the immortal gods and a wonderful inborn genius under a pretence of idiocy,

there is no reason why I should hesitate to put on a sophomoric show.
(1957: 613)

Milton's comment highlights Brutus's self-castigation, the burden of holding
"down a mind almost equal to the immortal gods" while he feigned folly.
Apparently, however, Milton does not seem as mentally burdened by his
own "sophomoric show" (as is clear from his sarcasm throughout the
prolusion). But, in the oration that follows, Milton enacts Brutus's role as
castigator. In addition, the "second" founding is a repurification of a body
politic which has fallen into corruption and is in need of this castigation in
order to revive its liberties—a situation commensurate, in a more
humorous way, with the context sketched out in Milton's text. And,
importantly, Milton follows this allusion with a significant republican
allusion—"our Republic of Letters" (1957: 616). Together, the allusion to
Brutus and the allusion to a "Republic of Letters" serve to conflate
Lucretia and the textual transmission of her story.

In the *Discourses*, Machiavelli draws an important political lesson
from Brutus's dissimulation of character. Brutus feigned folly in order to
"live in greater security and preserve his patrimony" (1950: 403). But,
significantly, he asserts that there is more than just self-interest in Brutus's
actions. Machiavelli provides a more politically pragmatic reason:

yet if we well consider his conduct we are led to believe that he had
another reason, which was that by thus avoiding observation [... Brutus]
would have a better chance of destroying the kings, and of liberating his
country, whenever an opportunity should offer. (1950: 403)

Machiavelli's comments foreground the causal logic of the narrative that
Jed points to. By stressing that there is more than self-interest in Brutus's
actions, Machiavelli removes those actions from a historically specific
time up to a transcendent, universal icon of the struggle for republican
liberty. Too weak to wage open war on the Tarquins, Brutus cunningly
awaits his opportunity to liberate Rome under the guise of folly, and,
indeed, his patience is, horrifically, rewarded when Tarquin rapes Lucretia.

Milton, while castigating his audience for their passions, ostensibly
claims to hide his true character for other purposes:

it is to give you pleasure that I have put off and for the moment laid aside
my usual habit, and if anything I may say is loose or licentious, put it down
to the suggestion, not of my real mind and character, but of the needs of
the moment and the genius of the place. (1957: 617)

Milton's feigned foolishness lowers him in order to mock his fellow undergraduates whom he sees as having turned away from diligent, scholarly pursuits in "our Republic of Letters" to debauchery. Like Brutus, however, Milton becomes a castigator of passions which, if allowed free reign, can lead only to tyranny—the distinction made in the above quotation between "mind" and "pleasure." Milton is made the "Dictator" who must attempt to save the "commonwealth of fools" from the brink of disaster (1957: 617). The ironies here, as Joseph Wittreich argues, work in Milton's favour: "open abuse brings out antagonism toward the orator whereas irony creates sympathy for him" (1973: 7). Through irony, Milton is able to recreate Brutus's emotional detachment, the "objectivity" of chaste thinking.

But, by associating himself with Brutus, Milton's transformation as castigator or dictator is problematically linked to Lucretia's body. Brutus removes the knife from Lucretia's body and, in Shakespeare's version of the story, buries "in Lucrece's wound his folly's show" (1997: 1810). In a sense, Milton is replacing the knife into Lucretia's wound in order to take on Brutus's folly. Milton's rhetorical action curiously re-enacts an originary moment, a transitional political moment poised between liberty and tyranny. History is compressed into Lucretia's self-inflicted wound, and, as Jed argues,

> the knife by which Lucretia cuts off every trace of Tarquin's violation (i.e., by suicide) also serves as a cue to the reader to cut off the meaning of Lucretia's rape from the historical materials in which it is transmitted [...]. [T]he word *chastity* comes from the root "to cut," and it refers, in particular, to a quality of being "cut off" from contact or contamination. In Livy's text, Brutus receives the torch of chastity from Lucretia by virtue of this cutting. (1989: 12)

Like Brutus, Milton also "receives the torch of chastity from Lucretia". In the Prolusion, Milton's cutting marks off the boundary between liberty and tyranny (rational self-control, a form of self-castigation, and passions); but it also cuts off the humanist textual tradition, so essential to the continuance of the "Republic of Letters," from potential contamination. More specifically, in the context of Milton's oration, his cut marks off those given into their passions and those of the "Republic of Letters."

Not only does Milton represent himself as the avenger of tyranny and transgression by comparing himself to Brutus; he also, figuratively, embodies the very site of that political struggle—the female body, and, significantly, a chaste female body. Milton represents himself before his audience as the "Lady". It is important also to note the criticisms Milton is levelling at his fellow students by, ironically, acknowledging this nickname. In regards to humanist editing practices, the gender and grammar confusion that Milton calls attention to symbolise the potential contamination of a textual tradition and point to the moral and political urgency of castigation. Milton's comments link both his virtuous behaviour and his fellow students' poor Latin grammar for his nickname—he alludes to classical tales of sexual transformation and a lack of respect to Priscian, asking, "Do these grammaticasters attribute the marks of the masculine to the feminine gender?" (1957: 620). This rhetorical move clearly links the body and the text, a sexual and textual politics, in a way that demonstrates how chaste thinking prompted a code for "representing a relation between reader and text, full of all the ambiguities and contradictions characterizing human relations" (Jed, 1989: 27). Milton constantly moves effortlessly between texts and his audience's promiscuity, rotten teeth, bad breath, bloating, and flatulence in order to highlight the bodily purity of the "Lady". Milton, then, like Brutus,

> finds in Lucretia's chastity the female version of his self-castigation [...]. It is Brutus' identification with the self-castigating dimension of this act [suicide] which gives him the courage to give up his disguise as a fool. He now sees the inimical feelings and emotions—previously located only within himself—in the expression of Sextus Tarquinius' lust. (Jed, 1989: 15)

Or, more specifically in Milton's case, in the expression of his fellow undergraduates' passions.

There is one more comparison between Milton and Brutus in the prolusion that I want to discuss before considering chaste thinking in some of Milton's later prose works. The notion of paternity in the prolusion, and Milton's ironic warning to his "sons" not to "degenerate" (1957: 621), is suggestive of Brutus's final act of castigation—the execution of his rebellious sons. As "Father", all eyes are on Milton, as "all eyes were on the father's face" when Brutus watched his sons "stripped, flogged, and beheaded" for conspiring against the new Republic (Livy, 1974: 110). Milton takes on the role of a man who unflinchingly passed judgement on his sons. Also, whereas Brutus has the Roman people take an oath against monarchy, Milton sets up a prologue to an oath, which is not administered: "let no one who wants to keep me for his father develop a fondness for Father Liber" (1957: 621). The point again distinguishes between restraint and passion, to a commitment to a politics of virtue. By not administering the oath, Milton ironically calls attention to the fact that his sons will not be able to keep such an oath. Like Brutus's sons and the young aristocratic rebels, they prefer "a dissolute and irresponsible life" (Livy, 1974: 108).

We meet with the rhetorical strategies of chaste thinking throughout Milton's prose, particularly in the recurrence of rape stories which function as narratives of liberation in very different political circumstances. In his writings, Milton continually put himself on the line for the individual, political, and religious liberties of the people: "The people of England know that I am not sorry to be either the defender of their rights or the hunter of their beasts" (1953-1982: 4: 746). Milton textually entwines his body with the body politic, and this is a manifestation of his chaste thinking—self-identification with castigation, bodily and rational purity, and the maintenance of a desired, integral textual tradition. Milton's attacks on his opponents' sexual behaviour, like theirs on his sexual character, are clearly motivated by the association of the integrity of the book and the body: "If I prove him who has so vehemently defended the royal cause to be corrupt and villainous", writes Milton, "I know sufficiently well that I have with no light argument impugned the royal cause itself" (1953-1982: 4: 736-7).

Within this rhetorical configuration, both books, when invested with a corporeal dimension, as they so notably are in *Areopagitica*, and bodies remain the potential targets of violent sexual assault (at least metaphorically). If the body can be violated, so, of course, can the book that marks out its margins. Chaste thinking aims at defending the chaste integrity of the body and the book against potential contamination. In Milton's work, there are two particularly interesting examples of his defence of the book as body—the state licenser in *Areopagitica* and his attack on Vlacq's pirated editions of the *Second Defence*. In *Areopagitica*, Milton complains that licensing forces the author to "appear in Print like a punie with his guardian, and his censors hand on the back of his title to be his bayl and surety, that he is no idiot, or seducer" (1953-1982: 2: 532). It is in comments such as this that Dzelzainis locates the development of Milton's republican politics of virtue. For Milton, however, the censor's hand, his touch, contaminates the integrity of the book and disgraces the author as well as the "dignity of Learning" (1953-1982: 2: 532). The pre-publication censor is situated at the lascivious level of Milton's earlier undergraduate audience, jeopardising the "Republic of Letters." As Jed states, "the humanists' practice of restoring the Roman texts to a state of *integritas*, or severance from contact, was invented in defence against the contaminating effects of touching" (1989: 30). Printing his "chaste" mind, Milton challenges the Licenser's potential accusation that his book may enter the world a "seducer" by questioning the character of the Licenser as the more significant source of potential contamination to the body of "Truth", a figure that demonstrates many of the concerns evident in relation to the Lucretia narrative.

The fear of contamination by another's hand recurs later in Milton's writings. In *Pro Se Defensio*, Milton complains of Vlacq's editions of the *Second Defence* which are bound with *The Public Faith of Alexander More*. He asserts that Vlacq's pirated edition mutilates his text and opens it to potential contamination, "sometimes with whole words omitted, and not without either the destruction or the distortion of the whole structure and sense" (Milton, 1953-1982: 4: 718). These textual gaps are important in terms of the book as body—its chastity and integrity. Whereas Milton had upheld the cause of the English people against tyranny in the pristine *Second Defence*, he must defend the integrity of those ideas in terms of its corrupted textual transmission by Vlacq. But Milton continues, "[t]hus I find those whom I thought to have been banished and removed farthest from me to be most closely joined with me, against my will, even under the same covers" (1953-1982: 4: 719). This coercive, contaminating contact compromises not only the book as the embodiment of English liberty; it also suggests a physical aspect that attacks Milton's own body— a potential sodomitical implication in that Milton finds himself under the covers with the licentious More through Vlacq's procurement.

These two brief examples specifically highlight how the corporeal dimension of texts can be compromised and contaminated. While there are no explicit references to Lucretia in these examples, the logic of chaste thinking is evident. The maintenance of Lucretia's purity and the textual transmission of that narrative as a prologue to republican liberty can also be demonstrated as underlying Milton's other significant, and repeated use of a rape narrative—the concubine of Judges. Appropriately, in regards to the attempt of the Florentine humanists to claim an *exclusive* and chaste relation to the republican tradition through Lucretia, Milton appropriates the *exclusion* literature of the Old Testament in which "the idea of holiness was given an external, physical expression in the wholeness of the body seen as a perfect container" (Douglas, 1966: 53). Milton argues for the sexual purity of the concubine, countering the charge that she "playd the whoor" (1953-1982: 2: 335). In this way, the concubine, like Lucretia, becomes an example of Milton's chaste thinking.

Milton uses the Judges narrative in *The Doctrine and Discipline of Divorce*. The similarity between the concubine's and Lucretia's rapes are striking. The Levite, following the gang rape of his concubine (whom he actually forces out the door to face the unbridled lust of the rapists), finds her the next morning on the doorstep. It is unclear whether she has even survived the repeated assaults of the night before. The Levite loads her on a donkey, "And when he was come into his house, he took a knife, and laid hold on his concubine, and divided her, *together* with her bones, into twelve pieces, and sent her into all the coasts of Israel" (1611: Judges 19: 29). A knife and cutting: a cutting so violent that the compiler of Judges felt it necessary to stress the fact that the cut went through the bones. In Judges, this cutting reaffirms the integrity of the body politic—scattering the twelve parts of the concubine throughout Israel, the tribes are united as "one man" (a term that occurs twice in Judges 19).

In *The Doctrine and Discipline of Divorce*, Milton wrestles with the definition of fornication, clearing the concubine of the charge of adultery and whoredom: "Fornication then," Milton argues, "in this place of the *Judges*, is understood for stubborn disobedience against the husband, and not for adultery" (1953-1982: 2: 336). Milton makes the same point in the *Christian Doctrine* when discussing Christ's response to the Pharisees in regards to divorce. While Milton's distinction is essential to his argument for the legitimacy of divorce on the grounds of incompatibility, he argues that the commentators of Judges, and the other scriptures that he enlists to support his argument, have misread, corrupted, and violated the biblical texts. Significantly, however, we should recall that, in contrast to Brutus's and Lucretia's moments of castigation, which insist on the letter of the law, Milton castigates his opponents here for not reading in terms of the spirit of the law, of not reading with Christian charity. But, in so doing, he appeals to a rape narrative. Milton connects the interpretive, textual violation by commentators that read the concubine's actions as adultery (in the physical sense) to her bodily violation by the men of Gibeah—both are "sons of Belial." This again puts Milton, rhetorically, in a similar position to that of Brutus: he takes on the role of castigator and figuratively possesses the concubine's chastity and the Levite's knife, a role implanted in humanism and chaste thinking and used here in order to counter the textual violation of scriptures relevant to divorce by misinterpreting Pharisees.

We might, then, be willing to agree with Stanley Fish's statement that Milton's own reading of scripture is a violation of the text: "In the *Doctrine and Discipline of Divorce*", writes Fish, "the scripture is the object not only of direct scrutiny, but of an interpretation so strenuous that even the word 'manipulation' is too mild to describe it" (1990: 54). Yet, this is, in fact, the very paradox of chaste thinking—that chaste touching is a violation; that chastity, indeed, invites such violation. Milton's defence of the concubine's sexual purity and his castigation of previous interpretations of her conduct reproduces the logic of the Lucretia narrative in his divorce tract—the concubine's rape and dismemberment becomes the prologue to "domestic or personal liberties" and, in terms of scriptural interpretation, "ecclesiastical liberties". She, too, had to be raped.

Having cleared the concubine from charges of sexual transgression in order to use her story as a narrative of ecclesiastical and domestic or personal liberties, Milton would return to Judges as a narrative of political liberation. In *Eikonoklastes* and the *First Defence*, Milton alludes to the concubine in the context of the Irish Rebellion. In *Eikonoklastes*, Milton discusses the fury of the Irish rebels and royalist complicity with the rebellion. In countering the Dinah rape story from Genesis in chapter 12 of *Eikon Basilike* (wherein the fury of the Irish rebels is, understandably, blamed on the measures taken by Parliament), Milton substitutes the rape of the concubine:

> Did not all Israel doe as much against the Benjamits for one Rape committed by a few, and defended by the whole Tribe? and did they not the same to Jabesh Gilead for not assisting them in that revenge? I speak not this that such measures should be meted out rigorously to all the Irish, or as remembering the Parlement ever so Decreed, but to shew that this his Homily hath more of craft and affectation to it, then of sound Doctrin. (1953-1982: 3: 481-2)

The contrast of "craft and affectation" and "sound Doctrin" serves to rationalise violence through Judges and paves the way for liberation.

Milton picks up the torch of chastity from the concubine in the face of what is seen as a bunch of anti-Christian, barbaric Irish rebels. The cut he makes here is especially violent. But, then, so is the repeated re-exposure of Lucretia and the concubine to the social forces of disorder: unruly undergraduates, Pharisees, Irish rebels, or the Tarquin / Stuarts. The violence involved here, however, is more than merely textual—it is a disturbing manifestation of the humanist imagination. While the context I have discussed goes some way in explaining accusations of sexual transgression in the writings of Milton and his opponents, we must resist the logic of these appropriations of rape narratives or else, as Jed states, we are in danger of reproducing humanistic chaste thinking and its "nostalgia for past freedoms [which] is dependent upon the representation of rape" (1989: 14).

This is clearly evident in Milton's undergraduate address in 1628. Published in 1674, however, Prolusion VI once again nostalgically re-exposes Lucretia to possible violation, suggesting that Milton still believes in the need to castigate his audience in the service of the defeated "Good Old Cause," in the language of republicanism—indeed, to reactivate a politics of virtue by, as he has throughout his literary career, figuratively re-enacting a rape. As Wittreich states, "[w]ith their publication, the academic audience becomes fictive and the reader becomes the new audience. Paradoxically, by assaulting a fictive audience that represents the most oppressive forces in English society, Milton is able to elicit the goodwill of his new audience (prospective readers)" (Wittreich, 1973: 7). Milton's prolusions serve as a fascinating set of bookends for his literary career, and Prolusion VI becomes one example of the "fundamental continuities in Milton's thought"—a commitment to a politics of virtue (Dzelzainis, 2001: 308). My argument, however, does not necessarily reveal a republican, undergraduate Milton lurking behind a guise of folly in 1628, patiently awaiting the events of the 1640s in order to drop the mask and wage open war with *The Tenure of Kings and Magistrates* and the tracts following the execution of Charles I. But what I have demonstrated is the need to be aware of that fundamental originary sexual violence that underlies Milton's, and his contemporaries, political thought.

References

Douglas, M. 1966. *Purity and Danger: an Analysis of Concepts of Pollution and Taboo*. London: Routledge & Kegan Paul.

Dzelzainis, M. 2001. "Republicanism", in T. N. Corns (ed.), *A Companion to Milton*. Oxford: Blackwell.

Fish, S. 1990. "Wanting a Supplement: the Question of Interpretation in Milton's Early Prose", in D. Loewenstein and J. Grantham Turner (eds), *Politics, Poetics, and Hermeneutics in Milton's Prose*. Cambridge: Cambridge University Press.

Hale, J. K. 1998. "Milton and the Rationale of Insulting", in S. B. Dobranski and J. P. Rumrich (eds), *Milton and Heresy*. Cambridge: Cambridge University Press.

Jed, S. 1989. *Chaste Thinking: the Rape of Lucretia and the Birth of Humanism*. Bloomington and Indianapolis: Indiana University Press.

Livy. 1974. *Early History of Rome*. Trans. Aubrey de Selincourt. Harmondsworth: Penguin.

Machiavelli, N. 1950. *The Prince and the Discourses*. Trans. Luigi Ricci and Christian E. Detmold. New York: Random House.

Milton, J. 1957. *The Complete Poems and Major Prose*. Ed. M. Y. Hughes. New York: Macmillan.

—. 1953-1982. *The Complete Prose Works of John Milton*. Ed. D. M. Wolfe *et al.* 8 vols. New Haven: Yale University Press.

Shakespeare, W. 1997. *The Norton Shakespeare*. Ed. S. Greenblatt *et al.* New York: Norton.

Shuger, D. 1998. "Castigating Livy: the Rape of Lucretia and *The Old Arcadia*", *Renaissance Quarterly*, 51: 526-48.

Wittreich, J. A., Jr. 1973. "Another 'Jest' in Milton's 'Sportive Exercises'", *Milton Quarterly*, 7: 5-8.

WRITING WOMEN'S LIVES
AND THE "ROAD TO DIVORCE":
MARY WOLLSTONECRAFT, FEMINISM
AND LAW, 1700-1800

LI-HUI TSAI

While constructing a history of sexuality and marriage, Lawrence Stone (1995: 15) argues that eighteenth-century feminist writers, prominently Mary Wollstonecraft, fail to achieve a significant effect on emancipating women from sexual oppression through a political reform of nuptial culture and law. This chapter offers some evidence against Stone's argument about Wollstonecraft and feminism. The construction of the history of sexuality and marriage in this chapter is complementary to the works of other cultural and legal historians. Ursula Vogel investigates how lawsuits of divorce become indistinguishable from legal cases of extra-marital, illicit sex so that in "nineteenth-century England 'divorce [means] adultery'" (1992: 160). David Turner (2002: 2) suggests that while known by its legal term as *criminal conversation* in court, adultery in eighteenth-century England is traditionally associated with sexual slander in print culture. Li-Hui Tsai (2010) shows that the print culture of sexual slander is later related to an ongoing debate on adultery and bigamy as legitimate grounds for women to obtain a divorce, and how this sheds light on the complex relationship between visual culture and the writings of Mary Robinson, a Romantic-era woman writer known as a follower of the teachings of Wollstonecraft's feminism.

This chapter argues that a rewriting of literary and cultural history related to Wollstonecraft's life and works would also rewrite the traditional historical narrative of feminism, through a better understanding of Wollstonecraft's sexuality and her attitude towards marriage as a legal, social and political institution, and what constitutes the legacy of feminism for her precursors and successors. The chapter advances the thesis that the debate on sensibility in the 1790s does not decline, but rather revives and merges into a wider debate on sexuality, morality and marriage, and that the debate reaches its peak in the posthumous reception of Wollstonecraft. This would contribute to our understanding of the cultural debate on sensibility, including the discourse on "Jacobin Morality", as exemplified by the poem "New Morality" in *The Anti-Jacobin Review* (July, 1798) and the poem *The Unsexed Females*, where Richard Polwhele attacks Wollstonecraft and her fellow women writers for their moral "corruptions" and "evil" teachings. This chapter discusses what it means for eighteenth-century readers to read and interpret her sexual and married life and the life writings by and about Wollstonecraft. It examines the debate on her posthumous reception among the readers and reviewers of her husband William Godwin's biography of Wollstonecraft as occasioned by their understanding of the moral of her life story and the differences between Godwin's version and her own version. It explores these writings and their relations to the traditions of feminist and legal treatises published between 1700 and 1800, to suggest the extent to which eighteenth-century discourses on sexuality and matrimony constitute the origin of modern feminism.

This chapter also considers the life and works of Wollstonecraft as intimately related to the broader argument of this volume (can literature instruct readers to be better or worse people, virtuous or licentious?). It examines the complex relationship between literature and ethics in a wide historical, literary and legal context; exploring how women's life stories, especially those about their sexual and married lives, function as a method for a philosophical ethics among eighteenth-century and Romantic-era writers, critics and reviewers, and how Wollstonecraft's life stories reveal a moral and legal debate on sexuality and marriage, an important historical debate that has been largely overlooked in current scholarship. In many ways, this chapter about Wollstonecraft and her contemporary writers explore the intersection of women's lives and the reception of women's writings among their critics, detractors and sympathetic readers, and are thus relevant to the themes of instruction, judgment and justice underpinning this volume.

This chapter consists of three sections. Section I explores the relation between the cultural meaning of female sexuality, embodied in the form of wifely adultery, and the polemic for and against divorce in eighteenth-century legal treatises. It then explores the relation between the reform of the divorce laws in revolutionary France and Wollstonecraft's discourse on matrimony in *A Vindication of the Rights of Woman* (1792). It goes on to look at the history of her union with her ex-lover Gilbert Imlay in Paris as her practice of "revolutionary marriage", and how this throws lights on our readings of Wollstonecraft's other writings. Section II examines the posthumous reception of Wollstonecraft from September 1797 to December 1798, in the periods between her death and a year after the publications of Godwin's *Memoirs*, in relation to the life writings about Wollstonecraft in various genres, including obituaries and book reviews. It offers a new reading of the debate among Godwin's reviewers in eighteenth-century periodicals. This reveals an ethical and legal debate on matrimony and divorce between her opponents and supporters, under the influence of Wollstonecraft's own writings. Section III explores the relation between Wollstonecraft's posthumous reception and the publication of legal treatises on the subjects of marriage and divorce from January 1799 to December 1800. This chapter concludes with a close analysis of legal treatises on the subjects of morality, marriage and divorce published in this period to suggest that Wollstonecraft's feminism and her writings have a small, but significant impact upon the theory and practice of marital unions and separations in eighteenth-century nuptial culture and law.

Feminism, Wollstonecraft and Eighteenth-Century Legal Treatises on Adultery and Divorce

Cultural connotations of wifely adultery gradually come to signify a moral attitude towards female sexuality and then a way of divorce in the eighteenth century and beyond. Among these connotations is the biblical interpretation of "adulteress". In eighteenth-century society, while adultery is perceived as a moral failing and offence, the meaning of adultery is implicitly gendered: this gendered meaning takes its root from a biblical reference to the sin of committing adultery. It is said that "whoever shall put away his wife, saving for the cause of fornication, cause[s] her to commit adultery: and whoever shall marry her that is divorced commit[s] adultery" (King James Bible, Matthew 5: 32). This biblical reference concentrates on the sin of becoming an adulteress rather than an adulterer. The offence is not the act of sexual intercourse outside marital relations, because its biblical meaning does not apply to the guilty husband. The way in which the biblical meaning of adultery is construed suggests an intention of preventing an adulteress from obtaining her rights to divorce: it is said that "if a woman shall put away her husband, and be married to another, she commit[s] adultery" (Mark 10: 10-2). This cultural connotation of wifely adultery becomes one of the important moral issues in the debates on the rights of an adulteress to marry her lover between writers of legal treatises and Wollstonecraft in *Maria, or the Wrongs of Woman*.

Overlooked in critical studies is the writing of legal treatises on divorce as a legitimate subject in the long eighteenth century. The early works in this genre invariably suggest that divorces should be granted for the benefits of discontented husbands rather than those of miserable wives. One of the exceptions is *Social Bliss Considered: in Marriage and Divorce* (1745), where Peter Annet contends that lawful divorces and the legal rights to remarry should be granted for the benefits of women, especially those who are unhappily married and wrongly labelled as "adulteress". This legal treatise depicts unhappy marriages as "slavery", arguing that "this prohibition of divorce, this preachment of slavery [...] is not [a Christian] doctrine" (1745: 33).

The most important contribution that Peter Annet makes to the legal and moral discourse on matrimony is that his treatise questions the biblical interpretation of adulteress ("she [who] puts away her husband (so called), and marries again, commits adultery" (1745: 33). Annet points out that "*Jesus* [is] no enemy to the *Adulteress*", as Jesus "[pleads] her cause", asking the accusers that "[whoever] is without sin", may "cast a stone at her" (1745: 24). Thus, Annet argues on behalf of the so-called adulteress, pleading the public "not to condemn those [who] are guilty of this *innocent adultery* (if it must be called adultery), of putting away a tormentor" (1745: 24).

This contribution is important also because Annet, unlike other legal writers in this period, makes an ethical equation between adulteress and divorcee. An empathetic picture is portrayed to suggest the ways in which the adulteress could be considered as a "wrongly divorced" woman:

> suppose that the woman is cruelly used, or wrongly divorced, and accept the refuge and protection of an honest man, who would marry her, love her, and use her tenderly, how does she commit adultery, or he that marries her? (1745: 33)

Here, Annet presents a persuasive argument, suggesting a plausible reason of why divorce should be granted to an adulteress. This reinforces the idea that an adulterous woman can be equated with a divorced woman ("she [who] is divorced in soul, is not united to her husband mentally, and should be divorced bodily" [1745: 30]). Ultimately, *Social Bliss Considered: in Marriage and Divorce* advocates the ethical equation between an "adulteress" and a divorcee by evoking great sympathy for the condemned "adulteress", who is forbidden by laws and religion to obtain a lawful divorce in this period.

Although there was no actual reform of the divorce laws in England until the Divorce Act of 1857, the latter half of the eighteenth century saw the making of the legal history of divorce taking place during the French Revolution. Divorce became a legal issue and was heatedly debated among the French press from 1780 to 1792 (Phillips, 1991: 60; 28-46). A petition was made and a draft of marital laws was passed on 10 August 1792. This draft was significant, as it introduced the idea of "divorce by mutual consent, on the ground of incompatibility", "ill-treatment" and "desertion for at least two years" (Phillips, 1991: 60). The draft became the "law of 20th September": this enabled "marriage partners to seek divorce on the equal conditions of wife and husband" (Traer, 1980; paraphrased by Vogel: 151). This was known as the model of the revolutionary marriage discussed in this chapter.

The discourse on sensibility and matrimony in *A Vindication of the Rights of Woman* has been misunderstood: Wollstonecraft does not oppose matrimony, but argues that unhappy marriages should be considered as "slavery", an argument that is apparently influenced by *Social Bliss Considered: in Marriage and Divorce*. She argues that the cultivation of sensibility asks a woman to learn the "art of pleasing" her husband, but does not promise a happy marriage: "When the husband ceases to be a lover—and the time will inevitably come, her desire of pleasing will then grow languid, or become a spring of bitterness" (1792: 52). Here, by considering the dilemma of a neglected or deserted wife, Wollstonecraft shows sympathy towards female sufferings in marital relations.

Overlooked in critical studies is also Wollstonecraft's self-representation as a "legislator" in her discourse on matrimony in *A Vindication of the Rights of Woman*. Her treatise includes a letter entitled "Dedication […] to Talleyrand Perigord, [the] bishop of Autun", in which she states that "I address you as a legislator" with a view to promote "equitable laws": if "more equitable laws are forming our citizens, marriage may become more sacred" (1792: viii; xi). Her letter to the bishop warns that "if women are not permitted legitimate rights, they will render both men and themselves both vicious, to illicit privileges" (1792: xi). This is an allusion to adultery or bigamy ("illicit privileges"), echoing her earlier assertion that "faithless husbands will make faithless wives" (1792: x). Following her letter to the bishop, her treatise suggests that "adultery" should be considered as "a natural divorcement" (1792: 154). It also suggests that bigamy or "polygamy", as she calls it, should be considered as tolerable because it binds a man "legally obliged" to a mother and her child (1792: 154). As a whole, *A Vindication of the Rights of Woman* reveals Wollstonecraft's desire to contribute to the legalization of marriage and divorce in eighteenth-century England.

Thus, it is significant that after publishing *A Vindication of the Rights of Woman*, Wollstonecraft chooses to arrive in Paris in December 1792, in the aftermath of the heated debates on the reform of marital laws to include women's equal rights to divorce. Her travel to Paris signifies, amongst other things, her desire to witness the freedom of women's equal marital rights in revolutionary France. Before her departure, she writes a letter to her friend William Roscoe, a Liverpool lawyer: "I am still a spinster on the wing [...]. At Paris, indeed, I might take a husband of the time being, and get divorced when my truant heart longed again to nestle with old friends" (quoted in Tomalin, 2008: 156). This is suggestive when we read "the first contemporary account" of her relationship to Imlay, written by her friend Joel Barlow in a letter of 19th April 1793 to his wife Ruth Barlow: "Between you and me [...] I believe that she has got a sweet heart—and that she will finish by going with him to A[merica] a wife" [...]. He is of Kentucky & a very sensible man" (quoted in Verhoeven, 2008: 177). It is clear that the marriage plan between Wollstonecraft and Imlay is anticipated by an observant friend in April 1793.

Godwin's *Memoirs* disclosed her marriage plan with Imlay, a plan that involved Imlay's marital registration and their cohabitation in Paris in around August 1793. Although Godwin argued that Imlay's registration was merely to offer her political protection, it was also possible that she married Imlay for domestic affections. Imlay apparently drafted his novel *The Emigrants* when they were in love, as his novel was published in London in July 1793. Both Imlay and Wollstonecraft were attracted to the new revolutionary ideas about marriage and divorce that they understood to operate in Paris in 1793. Imlay's novel advocated free love and liberal divorce; Wollstonecraft perhaps believed that she found a good husband, a congenial spirit, who would not bind her by the traditional "ties of matrimony, which it [was] not possible to dissolve".[1] They lived as a family in Paris and Le Havre. When Imlay went on a business trip to London in around June 1794 and disappointed her by lengthening his stay in London and perhaps by his infidelity, her letters to Imlay, dating from December 1794, began to show her contemplation of the solutions to her unhappy marriage. During this period, Wollstonecraft was perhaps acutely aware that separation or "desertion", which lasted for six months or longer, was a legitimate ground for divorce in revolutionary France.[2]

Wollstonecraft attempts to contribute to the reform on marriage and divorce laws by formulating a political and moral discourse on sensibility, domesticity and matrimony in *A Vindication of the Rights of Woman* and *Maria, or the Wrongs of Woman*. We may also get a glimpse of this discourse in her letters published in *Posthumous Works*. In a private letter sent to Imlay from Paris on 10th February 1795, Wollstonecraft discusses the subject on "the desertion of women" through a deliberate allusion to Imlay's writing of the novel *The Emigrants*: "Reading what you have written relative to the desertion of women, I have often wondered how theory and practice could be so different, till I recollected that the sentiments of passion, and the resolves of reason, are very distinct" (*Posthumous Works*, Letter xxxvi). This is also an allusion to Imlay's own discourse on the moral positions of transatlantic marriage and divorce, and the pun is on his dissipation and moral corruptions: he deserted her because he had a liaison with an actress in London (hence "theory and practice"). In this way, her letter sketches a philosophical and ethical discourse on women's struggles in marital relations. This discourse on moral philosophy allows her to explore the fine line between "the sentiments of passion" and "the resolves of reason", and to formulate a wider theoretical and political discourse on morality, sexuality and matrimony.

Wollstonecraft's discourse on women's struggles in marital relations, sketchy as it might be at this stage, also emerges in her suicide note, written in letter form and sent to Imlay during one of her failed attempts to commit suicide, later also published in *Posthumous Works*. It is important to note that her suicide attempts occur just before and after her Scandinavian travel. In this journey lasting from July to October 1795, she is travelling on his behalf as his lawful wife. Upon her return to London, when she again discovers Imlay's infidelity, she writes her suicide note in despair. This is a note that depicts her suffering as a neglected, deserted wife by declaring: "let my wrongs sleep with me" (*Posthumous Works*: Letter lxlx). For Wollstonecraft, her "wrongs" represent her endurance of marital injustice. She survives and manages to have a private separation from Imlay in March 1796.

It is likely that between this period and her subsequent marriage to Godwin in March 1797, she decides to dramatize the marital injustice, which she experienced during her unhappy union with Imlay, in *Maria, or the Wrongs of Woman*. In a letter to her friend George Dyson, Wollstonecraft expresses her distress that Dyson fails to understand the significance of the novel, which advocates liberal divorce for "a woman of sensibility":

> I am vexed and surprised at your not thinking the situation of [my heroine] Maria sufficiently important [till I recollect] that you are a man - For my part I cannot suppose a woman of sensibility with an improving mind to be bound, to such a man as I have described, for life—obligated to renounce all the humanizing affections. (quoted in Todd, 1991: 41)

Dyson perhaps thinks it inappropriate for Wollstonecraft to model herself as the heroine Maria, or merely takes it as a novel written, under the influence of her wounded heart, as a satire on Imlay as the model of the tyrant husband. For Wollstonecraft, her novel clearly depicts the difficulty of Maria as a married woman, who is "bound, to such a man as [she has] described, for life", and the injustice of prohibiting her to seek domestic affections elsewhere by marrying her lover (she is "obligated to *renounce all humanizing affections*", italics added).

Wollstonecraft is perhaps acutely aware that the readers of her novel, such as Dyson, would inevitably associate the tyrant husband with Imlay. For Wollstonecraft, it is thus necessary to draw a line between herself and her heroine Maria, so as to make the distinction between the private and the public. In the "Author's Preface" to *Maria, or the Wrongs of Woman*, in a tone that is reminiscent of her letter to Dyson, Wollstonecraft asserts that "my sketches are not [... just] the strong delineation of a wounded heart" (1798: 59). To some extent, this is also reminiscent of her suicide note. Unlike her suicide note, however, this "Author's Preface" considers the "wrongs of women", or rather women's endurance of marital injustice, in a wider political and social context, as she argues that "'The Wrongs of Woman' [are only] deemed necessary by their oppressor" (1798: 59). Thus, despite the rich autobiographical elements in this novel, her novel makes a fine distinction between the private and public (as also suggested by its title "*Maria*" and the subtitle "*the Wrongs of Woman*").

Judged by its subtitle ("*the Wrongs of Woman*"), the novel is apparently intended as part of her feminist works, as it echoes the title of *A Vindication of the Rights of Woman* (women's wrongs as the impediment to women's rights). In her treatise, Wollstonecraft already warns that the wife, "who patiently endures injustice, and silently bears insults, will soon become unjust, or unable to *discern right from wrong*!" (1792: 184).

The novel repeatedly exploits the trope of slavery in marriage to depict Maria as an eighteenth-century married woman in her struggles to leave and divorce her tyrant husband. Maria is imprisoned in her marital home when she is about to leave her husband after she discovers his plan to "sell" her into prostitution. The marriage plot also exploits the archetype of a tyrant husband. Maria's husband considers himself as a master and exercises whatever power he has over his wife as a slave. Like a run-away slave, Maria escapes from her marital home and moves from one to another obscure lodging to avoid the traps of her husband, who always tracks her down. The trope of slavery is most apparent in the plot, where Maria is again imprisoned by her husband in a madhouse.

The novel advocates liberal divorce and the rights to remarry: this is suggested by the interweaving marriage plot. Maria falls in love with her fellow prisoner Henry Danford. She later declares Henry to be her new husband when they escape from the madhouse and openly cohabit in London. Notably, the novel gives Maria the rights to defend herself in the trial of her adultery, but not the rights to divorce. As a whole, the novel dramatizes the difficulty of women in obtaining lawful marital separations in eighteenth-century England.

"Jacobin Morality" and the Posthumous Reception of Wollstonecraft: Godwin's Reviewers and the Legal Debate on Matrimony

Scholars have assumed that given the severe attack on Godwin's *Memoirs*, Wollstonecraft's contemporary writers, even her fellow feminist writers, largely remain silent or feel powerless to defend her posthumous reputation. This underestimates the number of her supporters, including those who defend her character and conduct by paying tribute to her "talents and genius" as "original thinker" and expressing sympathy for her unhappy union with Imlay. Modern scholarship has been heavily influenced by Godwin's reading of Wollstonecraft as an abandoned lover, a reading that deliberately misrepresents her relationship with Imlay as nothing more than a romance. Godwin's reading is also influential in critical studies on Wollstonecraft's posthumous reception. Scholars have also assumed that Godwin is attacked by his reviewers because he discloses her attempted suicides and their pre-marital sexual relationship. I suggest that the reviewers attack Godwin largely because his biography argues against the legitimacy of Wollstonecraft's earlier, marital union with Imlay. Godwin argues that Imlay's registration of Wollstonecraft as his wife in the American Embassy is merely to offer her political protection, and that a ceremony does not take place to solemnize their union and so it does not constitute a legal marriage. This provokes a legal and moral debate on what constitutes marriage, adultery and divorce among Godwin's reviewers. As suggested below, this debate reveals the number of Wollstonecraft's supporters, and the significance of her own writings, including *Maria, or the Wrongs of Woman* and her private letters sent to Imlay, both published by Godwin in *Posthumous Works*.

In *A Vindication of the Rights of Woman*, Wollstonecraft makes political and moral appeals for women to be liberated from domestic sorrows in unhappy marriages: her appeals are apparently understood by her supporters and even her opponents. Following Wollstonecraft's unexpected death on 10th September 1797, *The Gentleman's Magazine* promptly publishes in October an obituary that pays tribute to her reputation as the writer of *A Vindication of the Rights of Woman*:

> [Wollstonecraft was] a woman of uncommon talents and considerable knowledge, and well-known throughout Europe by her literary works [...] particularly by [*A Vindication of the*] *Rights of Woman* [...] This tribute we readily pay to her character, however adverse we may be to the system she supported in politics and morals, both by her writing and practice. (quoted in Holmes, 1987: 15)

In this obituary, it is clear that despite the stance of the periodical against her political and moral views, *The Gentleman's Magazine* does not fail to see Wollstonecraft's theoretical treatise as consistent with her "writing and practice" in general ("her politics and morals, [as exemplified] both by her writing and practice"). Her friend and feminist writer Mary Hays pays tribute to her "unconquerable spirit" by publishing an obituary that depicts her as "a victim to the 'vices and prejudices of mankind'" (quoted in Holmes, 1987: 15). The phrase "unconquerable spirit" can be read, among other things, as an allusion to Wollstonecraft's triumph over the partial marital laws to liberate the female self from the burden of traditional matrimonial ties.

Godwin's biography of Wollstonecraft is published in January 1798; as the first to offer in February a review of Godwin's *Memoirs* among eighteenth-century periodicals, *The Monthly Visitor* defends Wollstonecraft's posthumous reputation by insisting on her legal and moral rights to a marital separation from Imlay. Although reviews in eighteenth-century periodicals are often written and published anonymously, this review unusually reveals its authorship by giving out the signature of John Evans, who is also a travel writer. Evans appeals for the reader's sympathy and a greater understanding of her unhappy union with Imlay, arguing that Imlay is "leagued to her by desire—not love: he [is] destined to her by honour—not affection! This is the truth, and we must pity her" (1798: 241). This merit of this review is that it throws light on our understanding of what it means for eighteenth-century readers to read her private, sexual and married life as a story of her struggles against social and marital injustice in laws and customs: "she [inveighs] bitterly against a code of regulations which she [deems] derogatory to her sex [...] the grand lines of her character have been confounded by persons of narrow comprehension, or by prejudice" (1798: 242).

In another review of Godwin's *Memoirs* published in March in *The Monthly Visitor*, Evans argues that what is problematic is Godwin's narrative style: "we object to the style of these 'MEMOIRS' [that narrate his] 'cohabitation' with Mrs. Wollstonecraft [...] beyond all moral consideration" (1798: 311). In April, *The Critical Review* expresses the same sentiments that "with disgust we have read [Godwin's] *Memoirs*" because "we are convinced that they are not calculated to do honour to her memory, although this may have been the sincere intention of the writer and editor" (1798: 414). The reviewer condemns this posthumous biography of Wollstonecraft also because Godwin, as it appears to the reviewer, only cares about his own defence against the charge of adultery:

> A period of only six months intervenes in this case; but, says, [Godwin], although "it was only six months since she had resolutely banished every thought of Mr. Imlay (the former lover), it was at least eighteen [months] though he [Imlay] ought to have been banished [...], had it not been her scrupulous pertinacity in determining to leave no measure untried to regain him". (1798: 416-7)

This review recalls Godwin's *Memoirs*, where he states that Imlay "ought to have been banished" (Holmes' edition, 1987: 259). Godwin's writing is deliberately used here as a satire on Godwin's justification of his sexual intimacy with Wollstonecraft, which, according to his biography, does not begin until "six months" after her final separation from Imlay. For the reviewer, Godwin's biography fails to treat Wollstonecraft with justice because his writing downplays the legitimacy of her earlier marital union (the phrase "the former lover" is satirically added by the reviewer) and her eighteen-month struggle to regain Imlay's affection.

This suggests that some of Godwin's opponents are not necessarily Wollstonecraft's opponents or detractors and we may count, for example, *The Critical Review*, *The Monthly Magazine* and *The Monthly Review* among Wollstonecraft's sympathetic, but passive supporters. Although these periodicals attack Godwin's *Memoirs* for his writing style, this does not necessarily suggest that they criticize Wollstonecraft and her writing. *The Monthly Review* expresses resentment against Godwin by pointing out the indelicacy of his own argument: "he relates with complacency" that "she [cohabits] with Mr. Imlay as his wife, without being married" (1798: 322). *The New Annual Register* also criticizes Godwin, stating that his "extraordinary method of doing honour to her memory" cannot but excite "living emotions of disgust and concern". Here it is important to note that *The New Annual Register* does not criticize Wollstonecraft and her writing: this reviewer supports her literary reputation by asserting that she is "a woman of *undoubted* talents and genius" (1798: 271, italics added).

Perhaps because of her struggles in her unhappy union with Imlay, *The Critical Review* does not criticize Wollstonecraft: instead, the reviewer reminds the readers of her status as a literary genius and "original" thinker: "[those who] censured Mrs. Godwin with attention and candour [would concede] that she was [...] possessed of great genius [and] original habit of thinking" (1798: 414). *The Monthly Magazine* contends that "it is not for us to vindicate Mary Godwin from the charge of multiplied immorality, which is brought against her by the candid as well as the censorious; by the sagacious as well as the superficial observer" (1798: 148). Nevertheless, *The Monthly Magazine* defends Wollstonecraft by commenting that "her character, in our estimation, is *far from being entitled unqualified praise*" (1798: 148).

By contrast, we may count *The European Magazine* and *The Anti-Jacobin Review* as Wollstonecraft's opponents or detractors, because of their severe attacks on her morality. These periodicals insist that she violates her chastity and the indissolubility of marriage during her union with Imlay. *The European Magazine* calls Wollstonecraft "a philosophical wanton, breaking down the bars intended to restrain licentiousness" (1798: 246-51). Here it is important to note that the "bars" or the barrier is likely an allusion to the indissolubility of marital union. The reviewers argue that one cannot "obliterate all state of decorum" and as Wollstonecraft has already done so by means of her "new philosophy", it is best for her friends Mrs. Siddons and Mrs. Inchbald to avoid further acquaintance with her after her marital union with Godwin and they "will be acquitted in the court of propriety". Here, what *The European Magazine* describes as her "new philosophy" is tainted by what they suppose about her morality or adultery. In July, *The Anti-Jacobin Review* argues that "she [becomes] the concubine of Mr. Imlay" because the "state to which [Godwin] attributes" to "the mind of her whom he afterwards [makes] his wife" is nothing but "concubinage" (1798: 94-102). This is a harsh satire on Wollstonecraft's sexuality, but also on Godwin's morality, based on his own argument that tampers with the legitimacy of her earlier marital union with Imlay.

Among her opponents, the legal and moral debate on matrimony is articulated clearly in a review of Godwin's *Memoirs* published in September in *The British Critic*. This review gives a brief summary of Wollstonecraft's argument concerning the breakdown of her marriage with Imlay as narrated in Godwin's *Memoirs*: that Imlay has "chosen another companion, and she [is] at liberty to follow his example" (1798: 228-37). This is a satire on Wollstonecraft's justification of her adultery with Godwin on the ground of Imlay's own liaisons with his mistress. This is immediately followed by a mockery of her "wedded love" to Godwin, where the reviewer depicts their union as "adulterous lust" through a literary allusion to Milton's poem: "Hail, wedded love! mysterious laws [...] By thee ADULTEROUS LUST [is] driven from men" (1798: 233). The purpose of this satire is to assert the legitimacy and indissolubility of her earlier marital union:

> She had even obtained from the American Ambassador at Paris, a *certificate* that she was his wife; her respected friends in England might think that, in a country like France, where all ancient forms are abolished, such a certificate was sufficient to constitute a legal marriage; and if so, how would they avoid deserting their acquaintance, who, during the life of Imlay, had married Mr. Godwin. (1798: 232)

Here, the reviewer asserts that her marriage certificate, issued by the American Embassy, is likely to be considered by English society as "sufficient to constitute a legal marriage". Accepting her nuptials with Imlay in Paris as a form of revolutionary marriage, *The British Critic* insists on the indissolubility of marital relation, in which, according to the English canonical laws, a separated wife is not free to remarry, as long as her husband is still alive.

This argument about the indissolubility of marital union is anticipated by Wollstonecraft's supporters among the early reviewers of Godwin's *Memoirs*: Wollstonecraft's supporters argue on her behalf, appealing to the public's sympathy and a tolerant view of her "divorce". Adopting a different narrative strategy than Godwin's *Memoirs*, *The Analytical Review* publishes a review of Godwin's biography in March to assert the legitimacy of her earlier marital union: "the ceremony of marriage performed or neglected, altered not the morality of the thing" or "the *legal* tie" of it; "[this] marriage ought to be an indissoluble union" (1798: 239, italics added). This narrative strategy is used to evoke the public's sympathy for her unhappy union with Imlay: "[yet] we daily [see that] thousand married, whose union is as unhappy as this lady with Mr. Imlay" (1798: 239). While anticipating that "her notions and practice respecting marriage will meet violent objection", the reviewer appeals for the public's sympathy to consider her marital separation as acceptable: "we think [...] that Milton [is] right and that *divorces should be allowed* in many cases, where they cannot in this country be obtained" (1798: 239, italics added). While on the subject of divorce, the reviewer alludes to Wollstonecraft's writing of *A Vindication of the Rights of Woman*:

> We have only to observe, that Mrs. G was an original thinker [..., who,] had long reflected on this subject [... when she] entered upon this connection

with Mr. Imlay, *in France*, and at a *moment when the discussion of the subject of marriage agitated the national councils, and when a new system of thinking on that point almost universally obtained*. That, therefore, may appeal to us in our circumstance indelicate, which *there* would not have appeared to be so. (1798: 239)

The reviewer argues that given her nuptials with Imlay in Paris, their union is a model of revolutionary marriage and is thus beyond the territory of English laws. This argument is eloquent because a marital union is apparently dissoluble in revolutionary France, where under the divorce laws of 1792, it would be possible for her to obtain a divorce on the ground of adultery. Apart from its eloquent argument about eighteenth-century nuptial culture, *The Analytical Review* adds to our understanding of the significance of Wollstonecraft's writing in *A Vindication of the Rights of Woman* as a theoretical discourse on matrimony and divorce (she is "an original thinker", who "[has] long reflected upon this subject").

Among Godwin's sympathetic reviewers, Wollstonecraft's own writings, particularly those published by Godwin in *Posthumous Works*, are frequently used as living proof of female sufferings because of the indissolubility of marital union. In the same volume where the review of Godwin's *Memoirs* is published, *The Analytical Review* also publishes a review of *Posthumous Works*. The review suggests that Godwin's biography of Wollstonecraft should be read along with her letters privately addressed to Imlay: "we think every one who reads these Memoirs ought, in justice to Mrs. G., to read her letters; and we wish, indeed, that they had not been separately printed" (1798: 240-45). This suggests the significance of Wollstonecraft's letters in *Posthumous Works*: *The Analytical Review* apparently considers her own account as a powerful discourse on the difficulty of an eighteenth-century woman to obtain a lawful divorce.

The significance of Wollstonecraft's own writings, such as her letters in *Posthumous Works*, is also asserted by early reviewers. *The Aberdeen Magazine* for instance, comments that this body of her letter-writing "[partakes] fully the lively sensibility and instructive sagacity of Mrs. G." and shall "remain a splendid and deserving monument of general worth and female renown" (1798: 365-68; 417-20). This is also suggested by *The Hibernian Magazine*:

Let no one speak of Mrs. G. who had not *seen her* letters; they form the true account of her life and character. They show, that *whatever* were Mrs. G.'s opinion respecting marriage, her love was pure, ardent, individual and exclusive. (1798: 289-296)

The Hibernian Magazine thus places her autobiographical account in her letters published in *Posthumous Works* as superior to the biographical account of Wollstonecraft in Godwin's *Memoirs* ("*whatever* were Mrs. G's opinion respecting marriage" as narrated by Godwin).

This echoes the view of *The Analytical Review*, which offers lengthy extracts of her letters addressed to Imlay in *Posthumous Works*, to demonstrate the impact of her own writing (1798: 243-45). The extracts of her letters include her suicide note that strongly depicts her poignant sufferings from domestic sorrows: "I shall appear before you, the victim of your deviation from rectitude" (1798: 245). As discussed earlier, this suicide note can be read as an allusion to her endurance of marital injustice (let you have "*your deviation*" and "let *my wrongs* sleep with me", italics added).

Perhaps because of this reference to her "wrongs", this reviewer pays tribute to *A Vindication of the Rights of Woman* by relating the merits of this work to *Maria, or the Wrongs of Woman*:

> Mary Wollstonecraft Godwin, farewell! Thou hast asserted the rights, and received an uncommon portion of the wrongs of woman [...] Thy name is pursued by the censures of the licentious and malignant. But better time approach, - and thy vindication is secure. Thy name shall be mentioned with those, who have been distinguished for virtue and talents; and under this persuasion, we are contented that, for a time thou should'st suffer the reproach of married and unmarried prostitutes. (1798: 245)

This reviewer perceptively illustrates the significance of the marital injustice, which is endured by Wollstonecraft and then depicted by her as "the wrongs of woman" in her novel *Maria, or the Wrongs of Woman*.

Conclusion

Apart from the literary and political circles, the posthumous influence of Wollstonecraft on the moral and legal discourses on marriage, adultery and divorce eventually extends to the publication of legal treatises. This is most apparent in a legal treatise anonymously published under the title of *Thoughts on Marriage, and Criminal Conversation [... as in] the Example of the Late Mrs Wollstonecraft Godwin* (1799). The book title deliberately includes a reference to Wollstonecraft: this title is apparently used here to illustrate the argument of the writer that her union with Godwin can be considered as an example of what constitutes a fine distinction between marriage and adultery (known in court by its legal term as *criminal conversation*). Whatever this writer thinks about her "adultery" with

Godwin, it is significant that the legal treatise opens its discussion on matrimony by paying tribute to her literary fame and political influence as the writer of *A Vindication of the Rights of Woman*: "[among] the competitors for fame" "is the celebrated author of [*A Vindication of The*] *Rights of Woman*", "herself a woman" "remarkable" "for her singular and new-spun theory, to which she daringly [entrusts] her conducts" (1799: 4-5).

While singling out Wollstonecraft's theoretical discourse on matrimony in *A Vindication of the Rights of Woman*, this legal writer makes an allusion to her practice of revolutionary marriage as disclosed in her letters in *Posthumous Works*. This allusion to Wollstonecraft's empirical discourse on matrimony again reappears at the end of the same passage:

> [her] remembrance, as it reveals the winning softness of her manners, will not fail to shed the tears which mercy loves and sanctions; while the severer genius of CIVIL ORDER enjoins, that the last, posthumous record of her name, be accompanied by an enquiry into [...] her doctrines, and the possible influence of her life and example. (1799: 5)

This passage explicitly discusses Wollstonecraft's "influence" with a particular reference to her letters in *Posthumous Works*, where she formulates a sentimental and ethical discourse on matrimony (her reader would "shed the tears which mercy loves and sanctions").

By contrast, this legal writer also discusses the influence of Godwin's discourse on matrimony in his biography of Wollstonecraft. Godwin famously argues that she chooses "deliberately to form with Mr. Imlay [...] a connection unsanctioned by the laws" (1799: 9-10). This writer remains skeptical of Godwin's argument about her unmarried state, especially when she submits to Imlay's request to travel in Scandinavia on his behalf:

> When the violence of [her suicide] was subsided, Mrs. Imlay, as she then called herself, submitted to undertake for her *master* (for what other name shall we give to the man, who continued to a dominion over her without love?) a task of drudgery, which she herself most practically abhorred; namely, the arrangement of some commercial affairs in Norway. (1799: 13-4)

Here, the trope of slavery in marriage is used as a satire on the husband's rights. This writer points out the contradiction between Godwin's discourse on matrimony and her own discourse on the same subject in her writings: "This heart-rending affliction" is "endured by Mrs. Wollstonecraft in an unmarried state"; "Yet in her writings, notwithstanding, she transfers all this mighty sum of unappalled misery to a supposed sufferer under the bonds of *matrimony*" (1799: 19). Here, this writer shows great sympathy for her unhappy marital union (her endurance of her "heart-rending affliction"; her "might sum of unappalled misery"). There is an allusion to *Maria, or the Wrongs of Woman*, where she dramatizes female sufferings in marital unions because the legal restrictions of eighteen-century marital laws insist upon the indissolubility of marriage ("the bonds of *matrimony*"). This helps to illustrate the subtle relation between Wollstonecraft's writing and eighteenth-century legal discourse on divorce: this legal treatise considers Wollstonecraft writings, in *Posthumous Works* and *Maria, or the Wrongs of Woman*, as a vindication of her personal conduct in her battle for a liberal divorce.

Though it is difficult to prove that eighteenth-century feminist writers, including Wollstonecraft, have direct influence on the legalization of divorce in this period, their opponents apparently blame Wollstonecraft for the rapid increase of divorce among the so-called adulteresses in the late 1790s. This view is suggested in a legal treatise entitled *Thoughts on the Propriety of Preventing Marriages Founded on Adultery*, anonymously published in 1800. This legal tract opens by observing that "Adultery [has] become more common in this country than it used to be [... in] our courts of laws" (1800: 3). Here, this writer offers a topical discussion of "the increase of this evil" of adultery (1800: 3). For the increase in divorce rates, this legal treatise offers some statistics of divorce cases that occur between 1796 and 1799:

> since [George III's] accession to the throne exhibits the titles of no fewer than ninety-nine Divorces-bills [sic], of which *the last four years furnish the large proportion of twenty-nine, and the year, which has just elapsed, ten*; a greater number than is to be found in the annals of any of those which have preceded it. (1800: 9, italics added)

It is perhaps curious that the chronicle of rapidly growing divorce cases offered in this legal treatise coincides with the chronicle of Wollstonecraft's writing and practice of matrimony (*A Short Residence* in 1796; her marriage to Godwin in 1797): as suggested earlier, her writing in this period shows great sympathy for deserted wives and the so-called adulteresses.

Perhaps to counter feminist supporters who advocate liberal divorce for unhappy wives, the writer of *Thoughts on the Propriety of Preventing Marriages Founded on Adultery* takes sides with the "injured" husbands: "I mean not to blame the interference of parliament, to free an injured husband from the bonds which yoke him to dishonor" (1800: 5). For this reason, this legal writer condemns the increase in divorce cases of adulteresses as a "vice":

> this vice [, which] has made rapid strides against us, is the frequency of intermarriage between the adulteress and the person with whom the offence has been committed; and *her restoration*, in consequence of that event, to society; not indeed to all its advantages, nor with unclouded fame, but *to so much of the regard which is due to virtue.*
>
> From this statement it appears how greatly the class of women divorced for Adultery has of late been augmented.—It is notorious, that of these many have married the Adulterer; some [...] perhaps, in a few instances, from their own share of personal merit, have, in a great measure, regained the countenance of the world. (1800: 9-10, italics added)

As suggested here by this lengthy, repetitive complaint and by the title of the legal treatise, the writer of *Thoughts on the Propriety of Preventing Marriages Founded on Adultery* condemns the impropriety of adulteresses and their subsequent marriages to their lovers.

Despite the complaint of this legal writer, the publication of *Thoughts on the Propriety of Preventing Marriages Founded on Adultery* reveals a shift in the moral view of the public towards adultery and divorce in the late 1790s: as this tract suggests, the moral of Wollstonecraft's story is that an adulteress is no longer condemned to suffer for the rest of her life: if she has some "share of personal merit", it is possible to restore her public reputation. If she wishes to marry her lover, it is also possible to legalize their union. According to this legal treatise, it is clear that in some of the cases, "the act of Adultery has been committed for the express purpose of *dissolving one marriage in order to contract another*" (1800: 15, italics added). For this legal writer, it is unsettling that many adulteresses are public women, "distinguished" by their own "accomplishments" ("whether led astray [by] their own vanity, or the arts of the seducer", these women are "not in general among the least distinguished of their sex for elegance and accomplishments" (1800: 4-5). For modern readers, what this legal treatise shows is the anxiety about female power, or rather, the anxiety about the feminist discourses on women's liberation to interfere with the legal theory and practice of marriage and divorce: "[we have] much reason to apprehend that a few instances of persons, who have succeeded in [divorce and remarriage], without forfeiting their situation in the world, may excite in the minds of many, among discontented with their lot in marriage" (1800: 15). The tone of this legal treatise may recall that of a review of *Posthumous Works* in *The History of Literature for 1799*: Robert Bisset expresses the same anxiety about Wollstonecraft's "teachings" for women that "if all women were to follow the example of Miss Wollstonecraft, universal profligacy and irreligion would ensure". As a whole, it is significant that the writer of *Thoughts on the Propriety of Preventing Marriages Founded on Adultery* relates the increase of divorce cases to the influence of Wollstonecraft, her writings and her feminism.

Despite the attacks of Wollstonecraft's opponents, who make moral judgments on her sexuality and marriage, during the debate on her posthumous reception, eighteenth-century writers, who support her feminist ideas, continue to have an influential impact on political and moral discourses on the subjects of matrimony and divorce. As I have suggested, these discourses can be seen in a wide range of genres from memoirs, novels, poems and even feminist treats or legal treatises. As I have also suggested, the influence of Wollstonecraft and her supporters, who fight against social and martial injustice, is anticipated in the prophecy of *The Analytical Review* that her writing and practice on marriage and divorce, given what they think about her feminist "instructions" for women, are indeed ahead of her time ("better time" will come).

To sum up, this chapter has enabled a greater understanding of the moral of Wollstonecraft's life stories, the ethical significance of her self-portrait as a wronged mother and wife, and finally the "instructions" of a philosophical ethics expressed through her critical discourses on sensibility, sexuality and marriage as understood by eighteenth-century readers. This close analysis of the posthumous reception of Wollstonecraft, by means of a different reading of the moral judgments of Wollstonecraft's sexual and married lives made by Godwin's reviewers, including Wollstonecraft's detractors and supporters, also reveals that her reputation is not as badly damaged as modern scholars have commonly supposed. Wollstonecraft's powerful influence helps to explain why Polwhele's satirical poem *The Unsexed Females* attacks her, among other public women, so forcefully for her "instructions" of "Jacobin morality" while citing her as one of the examples of "female advocates of Democracy" (1800: 12). This chapter thus reveals the poetics and politics of literature and ethics, in terms of rewriting a woman's life, but also the influence of Wollstonecraft's writings, especially the moral and legal discourses on social and marital injustice, upon eighteenth-century discourses on sensibility, Romanticism and feminism.

Notes

[1] See *The Emigrants*, where the wife Lady B— describes her misery: "I am bound to my Lord by the ties of matrimony, [in] which it is not possible to dissolve" (Imlay, 1964: 111). Her misery attracts the sympathy of the heroine Caroline's uncle P. P., who then quarrels with her husband Lord B— on her behalf. Lord B— falsely accuses them of adultery so as to divorce her and marry a wealthy heiress. Imlay's own sympathy towards unhappy wives is suggested by his marriage plot, which allows the "adulteress" Lady B— to marry P. P. when she is legally divorced from her husband.

[2] As discussed earlier, legitimate grounds for divorce in revolutionary France included "desertion for at least two years" in 1792. In 1794, the period of desertion was shortened, and "separation for six months or longer" became acceptable; this was "repealed in 1796" due to the cases of abuse (see Phillips, 1991: 60).

References

[Annet, P.] Archer, G. 1745. *Social Bliss Considered: in Marriage and Divorce*. London: Printed for and sold by R. Rose.

Anonymous. 1779. *Thoughts on Marriage, and Criminal Conversation [...]; Comprising Remarks on the Life, Opinions, and Example of the Late Mrs Wollstonecraft Godwin*. London: Printed for F. and C. Rivington *et al.*

Anonymous. 1800. *Thoughts on the Propriety of Preventing Marriages Founded on Adultery*. London: Printed for the Philanthropic Reform.

Bisset, R. 1800[?]. *The Historical, Biographical, Literary and Scientific Magazine*. London: Printed by G. Lawthron.

Godwin, W. 1987 [1798]. *Memoirs of the Author of the Rights of Woman*, collected in *Mary Wollstonecraft and William Godwin: a Short Residence in Sweden, Norway and Denmark and Memoirs of the Author of "The Rights of Woman"*. Ed. R. Holmes. London and New York: Penguin.

Imlay, G. 1964 [1793]. *The Emigrants*. Ed. R. Hart. Gainesville: Scholars' Facsimiles & Reprints.

Phillips, R. 1991. *Untying the Knot: a Short History of Divorce*. Cambridge and New York: Cambridge University Press.

Polwhele, R. 1798. *The Unsexed Females; a Poem, Addressed to the Author of the Pursuits of Literature*. London: Printed for the Author.

Tomalin, C. 1992. *The Life and Death of Mary Wollstonecraft*. London and New York: Penguin.

Tsai, L. H. 2010. "Mary Robinson's Self-Fashioning: Auto/biography and Visual Illustrations, 1780-2009", in Christina Ionescu (ed.), *Book

Illustration in the Long Eighteenth Century: Reconfiguring the Visual Periphery of the Text. Newcastle: Cambridge Scholars Publishing.

Turner, D. 2002. *Fashioning Adultery: Gender, Sex and Civility in England, 1660-1740*. Cambridge: Cambridge University Press.

Verhoeven, W. M. 2008. *Gilbert Imlay: the Citizen of the World*. New York and London: Pickering & Chatto.

Vogel, U. 1992. "Whose Property? The Double Standard of Adultery in Nineteenth-century Laws", in C. Smart (ed.), *Regulating Womanhood: Historical Essays on Marriage, Motherhood and Sexuality*. London and New York: Routledge.

Stone, L. 1990. *The Road to Divorce: England 1530-1987*. Oxford and New York: Oxford University Press.

Wollstonecraft, M. 1792. *A Vindication of the Rights of Woman: with Strictures on Political and Moral Subjects*. London: Printed for Joseph Johnson.

—. 1992 [1798]. *Maria or the Wrongs of Woman*, in *Mary Wollstonecraft: Mary and Maria; Mary Shelley: Matilda*. Ed. J. Todd. London and New York: Penguin.

—. 1798. *Posthumous Works of the Author of a Vindication of the Rights of Woman*, 4 vols. Ed. W. Godwin. London: Printed for Joseph Johnson.

Periodicals

Analytical Review 27 (March July 1798): 235-40
Anti-Jacobin Review 1 (July 1798): 94-102
Anti-Jacobin Review 1 (July 1798): 94-102
British Critic 12 (September 1798): 228-37; 234-5
Critical Review 22 (April 1798): 414-7
Monthly Review 27 (1798): 325-7
Monthly Visitor and New Family Magazine 3 (1798): 311-8
New Annual Register 19. 3 (1798): 315

HONEYDEW ETHICS:
THE DARK SIDE OF ROMANTIC INSPIRATION

LOUIS MARKOS

Though two centuries have passed since the fire of Romantic inspiration burned through the hearts and minds of Blake, Wordsworth, Coleridge, Byron, Shelley, and Keats, a strong argument could be made that we are still living in the Romantic Age. We still tend to view our poets and artists not as skilled craftsmen who imitate the beauties and mysteries of God, nature, and the human condition but as inspired bards through whom the power of creativity erupts like a volcano. For this reason, we often ascribe to them a prophetic role, hailing them as the modern, secular equivalents of Isaiah, Daniel, and Jeremiah.

In our celebration of the poet-as-prophet, however, we often ignore the moral and ethical danger that attends an over-reliance on Romantic inspiration. We ignore as well a second, more ironic danger: though the Romantics downplayed the neoclassical emphasis on the didactic nature of the arts, in their own poetry and literary theory they (arguably) substituted rational didacticism for a more emotional and intuitive form of prophetic instruction. Samuel Taylor Coleridge knew well these twin dangers, and, in arguably his greatest lyric, "Kubla Khan", he not only showcases the power of inspiration but explores its nature, its genesis, and its dark side.

I

Though most readers are familiar with the title of "Kubla Khan", far fewer could tell you the full title that Coleridge gave to his strangely beautiful (and beautifully strange) lyric: "Kubla Khan, Or, A Vision in a Dream. A Fragment". Each of the three nouns that make up Coleridge's subtitle is vital, not only for a proper understanding of the poem but of Romanticism itself. For each word points to the link between poetry and prophecy that lies at the heart of so many of the great Romantic poems.

When Coleridge published "Kubla Khan" in 1816, nearly two decades after he had composed it, he appended a note to it that must, I would argue, be read as an integral part of the poem. I quote the note at some length for it helps provide us with the key to understanding the relationship of the words "Vision", "Dream", and "Fragment" in Coleridge's subtitle:

> In the summer of the year 1797 the Author, then in ill-health, had retired to a lonely farm-house between Porlock and Linton, on the Exmoor confines of Somerset and Devonshire. In consequence of a slight indisposition, an anodyne had been prescribed, from the effects of which he fell asleep in his chair at the moment he was reading the following sentence, or words of the same substance, in Purchas's *Pilgrimage*: "Here the Khan Kubla commanded a palace to be built, and a stately garden thereunto: and thus ten miles of fertile ground were inclosed with a wall". The Author continued for about three hours in a profound sleep, at least of the external senses, during which time he has the most vivid confidence, that he could not have composed less than from two to three hundred lines; if that indeed can be called composition in which all the images rose up before him as *things*, with a parallel production of the correspondent expressions, without any sensation or consciousness of effort. On awakening he appeared to himself to have a distinct recollection of the whole, and taking his pen, ink, and paper, instantly and eagerly wrote down the lines that are here preserved. At this moment he was unfortunately called out by a person on business from Porlock, and detained by him above an hour, and on his return to his room, found, to his no small surprise and mortification, that though he still retained some vague and dim recollection of the general purport of the vision, yet, with the exception of some eight or ten scattered lines and images, all the rest had passed away like the images on the surface of a stream into which a stone has been cast, but, alas! without the after restoration of the latter! (Noyes, 1956: 391)

The anodyne to which Coleridge refers is opium, a drug whose harmful properties and addictive nature were not fully understood at the time. According to Coleridge, the opium cast him into a state which he describes as "a profound sleep, at least of the external senses". But what exactly was the nature of this state? The poet seems sure that his external senses were asleep, but what of his mind: was that asleep, awake, or in some strange middle state? Did Coleridge have a "Vision" or a "Dream"?

The great prophets of the Bible seem themselves to have been unclear as to the exact nature of the prophetic state. Surely when we read the writings of Isaiah or Ezekiel or John, it is not easy to say whether the Lord spoke to them while they were awake, asleep, or in some kind of a waking trance. For Romantic poets (and their heirs) the exact state of the inspired bard is itself a difficult thing to determine. In what category shall we place the poet who conceives his poem in a fit of inspiration? Is he active or passive, conscious or unconscious, awake or asleep? Does the origin of the inspiration (God, nature, drugs) determine the relative value of the prophecy? Should we embrace or avoid such prophecies?

One thing at least is clear. Those who receive such images, whether or not they originate in vivid dreams or prophetic visions or drug-induced reveries or flashes of inspiration, do not themselves have control over those images. That is why those who rely upon visions and dreams—whatever their source or the nature of their transmission—often end up producing "Fragments": either unfinished poems or works that, like Isaiah and Revelation, are fragmentary in nature. Or both. When Coleridge is interrupted by the businessman from Porlock, his reverie leaves him, and his would-be poetic masterpiece is put down, never to be taken up again. It will remain but the shadow of what might have been, in a disjointed, fragmentary form that has frustrated the attempts of two centuries of students and critics to arrive at a definitive interpretation—or, indeed, to determine what aesthetic or ethical value the poem can offer.

The poet-artisan, guided by the rules of decorum (both aesthetic and ethical) and his own sense of balance and harmony, works away at his poem until it has achieved the desired shape and form. The poet-prophet, guided by inspiration and by his own willingness to be a vessel *of* that inspiration, awaits the longed-for arrival of the vision (or dream) and then creates feverishly until it departs. The former trusts to his skill, while the latter trusts to his imagination; but it is an imagination that dwells in close proximity with the visionary states of the poet, the dreamer, the prophet, and, at least in "Kubla Khan", the opium eater.

For the Romantic poet, imagination is more than a tool for fashioning similes and metaphors; it is, rather, a kind of sacred energy: both a spell by which to conjure images from the depths of the soul, and a conduit for channeling, shaping, and fusing these images into new forms. Likewise, the poet is more than a dedicated craftsman; he is an intoxicated visionary, drunk on the spirit—whether that spirit be man-made or God-made. Just as the Oracle of Delphi breathed in the vapors from the earth before going into her prophetic trance, so the Romantic poet must open himself to the shattering force of the imagination before he can enter that visionary, dream-like state that is the very womb of poetry. As such, the Romantic poet is both closer and farther away from traditional, Judaeo-Christian ethics than his eighteenth-century predecessor. On the one hand, Coleridge, unlike, say, Alexander Pope, looks to revelation rather than reason as a source of aesthetic and moral instruction, an orientation that cleaves far more closely to traditional religion and ethics. On the other, by opening himself up so fully to the force of inspiration, he betrays a potential lack of discernment that would have horrified Pope as much as

Moses or St. Paul. Walter Jackson Bate was correct, I believe, when he identified the theme of "Kubla Khan" as "the hope and precarious achievement of the human imagination itself" (Bate, 1968: 78).

II

Those, as I see it, are some of the glories and dangers of the aesthetic and ethical stance that Coleridge adopts in his note to "Kubla Khan". And yet, having stated them, I must now pause and make a somewhat stunning confession. I do not think that we can necessarily believe everything that Coleridge says in his note. In saying that, I no more accuse Coleridge of bald-faced lying than one would a romantic lover who tells everyone that he and his wife fell madly in love at first sight when that really was not the case. The question is not one of sincerity but of the power of illusion and wish-fulfillment to shape our memories of past events. For you see, whether or not the composition of "Kubla Khan" occurred in exactly the way Coleridge says it did, what he does describe in his note is nothing less than the ultimate Romantic fantasy. Any of the Romantic poets would have sacrificed much to experience firsthand a "composition in which all the images rose up before him as *things* . . . without any sensation or consciousness of effort". Which is not to say that Romantic poets are like lazy college students who hope and pray that inspiration (or God!) will write their paper *for* them. It was because the Romantics valued so highly fresh, direct, unmediated spontaneity that they yearned to feel the force of inspiration flow through them in all its purity, and, by means of that inspiration, to break forth into what Shelley (in "To a Skylark") calls "profuse strains of unpremeditated art" (Noyes, 1956: 1064).

And they yearned for something else as well, something that Coleridge claims to have experienced in composing "Kubla Khan". Not only did "all the images [rise] up before him as *things*"; they rose up "with a parallel production of the correspondent expressions". What Coleridge is here suggesting is that inspiration fashioned through him an at once mystical and aesthetic incarnation of image and word, content and form. In a series of three essays known collectively as "Essays Upon Epitaphs", Wordsworth seeks for just this kind of incarnation, for a language that will not be "what the garb is to the body but what the body is to the soul". Indeed, Wordsworth goes so far as to assert that if "words be not [...] an incarnation of the thought but only a clothing for it, then surely will they prove an ill gift" (Owen and Smyser, 1974: I. 84).

As it offers direct insight into the nature of Coleridge's Romantic fantasy, Wordsworth's subtle but incisive distinction is worth drawing out.

Before I headed to work this morning, I covered my body with a red shirt and a pair of navy slacks. Both the shirt and the slacks were so designed as to conform to the rough contours of my arms, legs, and torso. There exists, however, no organic relationship between my body and my clothes. Before going to bed, I tossed both articles of clothing into the hamper without compromising in any way my arms, legs, or torso. Not so the relationship between my body and my soul. My flesh is more than a mere covering for my soul. My soul expresses itself through my flesh even as my flesh is animated—and, I hope, guided—by my soul. To use the language of Christian theology: I am not a soul trapped within a body (as Plato and the neo-Platonic Gnostics would have it), but an enfleshed soul.

What is so wonderful about Coleridge's description of the composition process of "Kubla Khan" is that he suggests that flesh-like words rose up together with soul-like images to produce, albeit in fragmented form, a perfect incarnation of the two. So often when a poet attempts to write a poem, his words prove a woefully inadequate medium for embodying his thoughts, feelings, and images. But what if he could find words that would not only express but externalize and give concrete shape to those thoughts, feelings, and images? That is what Coleridge celebrates in his note to "Kubla Khan", what Wordsworth calls for in his "Essays Upon Epitaphs", and what all Romantic poets yearn to achieve as the end product of their dream-visions, their visionary dreams, and their prophetic utterances.

If a traditional, neoclassical critic like T. E. Hulme were to read the last several paragraphs, he would no doubt be horrified by the arrogance of the claim to be able to effect an incarnation and the juvenile folly of the claim that a spontaneity which overcomes careful moral and rational reflection can in any sense be thought of as pure. And his horror would, in part, be justified, for these twin Romantic claims *do* smack of Faust-like pride and Rousseau-like primitivism. But let us not forget that Christian theology and ethics rest squarely upon the possibility of incarnation and the related desire of God to write the Law "not in tables of stone, but in fleshy tables of the heart" (2 Corinthians 3:3), and that Jesus himself honoured childlike faith, heart-based devotion, and spontaneous praise. The gospels assert that Jesus taught with authority, not like the Scribes and Pharisees, and though his teachings are expressed in parallelisms that are as concise and well-polished as neoclassical couplets, the teachings themselves bespeak an incarnational freshness and decorum-shattering spontaneity that is not so far removed from Coleridge's précis on Romantic inspiration.

III

Before moving on to analyze the poem itself, one more theoretical distinction that is central to Coleridge's aesthetic theory must at least be broached—particularly as it seems to contradict the very aesthetic theory laid out in the note to "Kubla Khan". I speak of the distinction between active and passive, a distinction that is central to Coleridge's influential definition of the primary and secondary imagination. In Chapter XIII of his *Biographia Literaria*, Coleridge defines these two types of imagination thus:

> The IMAGINATION then, I consider either as primary, or secondary. The primary IMAGINATION I hold to be the living Power and prime Agent of all human Perception, and as a repetition in the finite mind of the eternal act of creation in the infinite I AM. The secondary Imagination I consider as an echo of the former, co-existing with the conscious will, yet still as identical with the primary in the *kind* of its agency, and differing only in *degree*, and in the *mode* of its operation. It dissolves, diffuses, dissipates, in order to re-create; or where this process is rendered impossible, yet still at all events it struggles to idealize and to unify. It is essentially *vital*, even as all objects (*as* objects) are essentially fixed and dead. (Adams, 1992: 478)

In parsing Coleridge's difficult distinction between primary and secondary imagination, James Engell highlights the relative degree of involvement on the part of the poet: "The function of the primary imagination must precede that of the secondary. Otherwise the higher degree would lack perception to recombine and to shape into new relations [...] The secondary imagination is part of a self-conscious and willful apperception; the primary degree exercises involuntary or 'automatic' perception" (Engell, 1981: 344-45).

The essential passivity of the primary imagination, though not stated directly in the passage, is strongly implied by Coleridge's assertion that the secondary imagination co-exists with the "conscious will". Likewise, although he does not define the mode of perception that accompanies the primary imagination, he carefully distinguishes it from the "re-creative" mode of the secondary imagination and associates it with forces (living Power, eternal act of creation, infinite I AM) that the finite mind is incapable of comprehending. As forces that defy human containment in either time or space, they can only be taken in by a receptive mind in tune with the natural (and supra-natural) world. The secondary imagination, on the other hand, actively creates. By a process of dissolution and recombination it invents new forms into which and through which (the passage implies) the powers apprehended by the primary imagination may be incarnated. So great, in fact, is its passion for incarnation that when it is unable to create a suitable form to embody the previously apprehended force or feeling, it strives at least to unify that force or feeling into a comprehensible idea.

In the context of Coleridge's definition, the two levels of imagination are treated equally; however, Coleridge makes it clear that the creative genius of the poet lies finally in the power of his secondary imagination. Engell argues, convincingly, that when Coleridge uses the word imagination in a discussion of poetry, criticism, or the fine arts (as opposed to philosophy or psychology), he invariably means the secondary imagination (Engell, 1981: 344). This position is supported by the fact that, whereas his definition of the primary imagination finds no real echo in his literary criticism, his definition of the secondary imagination serves as the foundation of his aesthetic theory. For Coleridge, it is the secondary, not the primary, imagination that is the essentially vital one, and it is so precisely because of its link to the conscious will. In contrast, in the aesthetic theory of his friend and fellow Romantic poet William Wordsworth, true vitality is found in those mystical moments of apprehension when the mind, passive to the forces around it, is arrested and penetrated.

R. D. Havens has summed up nicely the stances adopted by the two poets *vis-à-vis* the active/passive nature of the imagination: "Coleridge thought of the imagination chiefly as it relates to poetry and thus regarded it as a conscious activity of the mind; Wordsworth, on the other hand [...] even when he considered the imagination in connection with poetry [...] was so deeply conscious of its independence of the will that he tended to think of its operations as spontaneous 'visitings of imaginative power', over which the conscious self had little control" (Havens, 1941: 220). Martin Greenberg, who explores this same Coleridge/Wordsworth dichotomy on more biographical terms, argues that Coleridge was plagued by a sense of moral guilt and despair over his passive, slothful nature. He further argues that while Coleridge felt obliged to counter his passive nature by championing the active powers of the mind and the will, Wordsworth was content to depress his will and receive (Greenberg, 1986).

What bearing has this on "Kubla Khan"? A great deal, I believe. As a poet and theorist who both privileges activity over passivity and who feels morally guilty when he gives in to his slothful, Hamlet side, Coleridge cannot finally embrace (as Wordsworth could have) the passive mode of inspiration that he seems to champion in his note to "Kubla Khan". This tension between an ethical-aesthetic mandate to work and to shape and a Romantic desire to be swept away, if not possessed by inspiration (via an opium-induced dream state), should alert the reader from the start that what the poet yearns for will carry both the promise of imaginative power and ethical danger—Romantic wish-fulfillment, with a dark side lurking in the shadows.

IV

The opening lines of "Kubla Khan" possess the rare, incantatory power to instantly sweep us away from the mundane world of our daily lives to the dream world of the imagination: to plunge us, that is, into the very tension that I just described above. We want to lose ourselves in this world, to be passive to whatever beauty and power it offers, even as we know that we should be more guarded, more discerning.

> In Xanadu did Kubla Khan
> A stately pleasure-dome decree:
> Where Alph, the sacred river, ran
> Through caverns measureless to man
> Down to a sunless sea. (Noyes, 1956: 391; future references to "Kubla
> Khan" will be by line number)

The strange yet somehow familiar names and places, the flow of the verse, the sound of the words: all work on us their fairy magic and make us feel as though we have been physically transported to Xanadu. We are invited not so much to read Coleridge's poem as to participate in his reverie.

At first we enter willingly into Coleridge's vision, but as we move through the poem, we become confused and unsettled. Things are not what they seemed at first to be:

> So twice five miles of fertile ground
> With walls and towers were girdled round:
> And there were gardens bright with sinuous rills,
> Where blossomed many an incense-bearing tree;
> And here were forests ancient as the hills,
> Enfolding sunny spots of greenery.
>
> But oh! that deep romantic chasm which slanted
> Down the green hill athwart a cedarn cover!
> A savage place! as holy and enchanted

As e'er beneath a waning moon was haunted
By woman wailing for her demon-lover! (6-16)

I argued above that the author of "Kubla Khan" is a poet, dreamer, and prophet in one, and indeed, the passage just quoted shares the vivid, disjointed, symbol-laden qualities of those enigmatic, often terrifying episodes that populate both the prophetic books of the Bible (Daniel and Revelation in particular) and our own personal nightmares. The symbols and episodes of the poem come at us, as they do in our dreams, in a swirl of sights and sounds that defy logical arrangement. As the poem proceeds, all sense of continuity and transition breaks down: opposites are juxtaposed and fused; places and figures appear, disappear, then appear once again. It is as if the binding of a book had snapped and the leaves, like those of the prophetic Sibyl in Virgil's *Aeneid*, had become loosened and detached, left to scatter and float on the wandering breeze. The critic who would make sense of "Kubla Khan" must, like a Freudian psychoanalyst, reassemble the fragments of the poem into a psychic narrative whose structural key is more emotional than intellectual, more intuitive than rational. We must leave behind the walled and ordered polis of Apollo (the "Enlightenment" god of order, balance, and harmony) and enter into the holy, savage forest of Dionysus (the "Romantic" god of intuition, intoxication, and excess). Or, to use the terms of Nietzsche's *The Birth of Tragedy from the Spirit of Music*, we must allow the "Apollonian dream artist" to give way to the "Dionysiac ecstatic artist" (Adams, 1992: 631). We need not leave ethics and instruction behind, but we must redefine the terms in which we receive them.

For the poem *does* seem to be leading us somewhere. Past the encircling walls, the fragrant gardens, and the ancient forests, we are led inexorably to the "deep romantic chasm", a sacred, primal place haunted by man's deepest passions and fears. The chasm is a volcano, but it is also a titan in labor:

And from this chasm, with ceaseless turmoil seething,
As if this earth in fast thick pants were breathing,
A mighty fountain momently was forced:
Amid whose swift half-intermitted burst
Huge fragments vaulted like rebounding hail,
Or chaffy grain beneath the thresher's flail:
And 'mid these dancing rocks at once and ever
It flung up momently the sacred river. (17-24)

Coleridge's fragmentary dream-vision carries us to the very birthing-place of Romantic energy, to the fiery abyss out of which inspiration flows like a mighty fountain. Here, we learn, is the source of all that the poet most desires; here may we gaze with awe and dread on the imagination in its rawest form. Here is the source of the wisdom that we seek, a wisdom that carries with it the power to shatter the old and birth the new.

But there is a dark side, a danger that awaits any poet (or reader) who receives passively without engaging active discernment:

> Five miles meandering with a mazy motion
> Five miles meandering with a mazy motion
> Through wood and dale the sacred river ran,
> Then reached the caverns measureless to man,
> And sank in tumult to a lifeless ocean:
> And 'mid this tumult Kubla heard from far
> Ancestral voices prophesying war! (25-30)

Just as the phantasmagoric burst of creativity that opium inspires in its user is quickly followed by an almost existential deadness of emotion and spirit, so the poet who opens himself too fully to the power of this unrestrained Romantic energy may find himself in the end drained of all will and desire, his dreams and visions sunk in a "lifeless ocean". Those who are lifted most high by inspiration suffer the most when inspiration leaves them. With the knowledge, the joy, the rapture, there comes as well the danger of slipping into the abyss. We may at first think it odd that when Kubla hears the tumultuous explosion of the chasm he does not hear in it the sound of imagination or inspiration but the dread prophecy of a coming war. That is, until we realise that the healing, life-giving power of creativity and the destructive, apocalyptic force of revolution both emanate from the same Romantic energy. Indeed, the Blakean Harold Bloom has suggested that "Kubla Khan" is not a "fragment but a vision of creation and destruction, each complete" (Bloom, 1961: 230).

Romantic inspiration is not so much a good force as it is a neutral one that can be channelled for good or for ill. It is like the fire that Prometheus stole from the heavens to give to man—it can both protect and devour, create and destroy, teach and lead astray. To give oneself over fully and without discernment to Romantic inspiration is truly to play with fire; too often, in our folly or arrogance, we account ourselves the master of something over which we have little final control. Many of the "Romantic" hippies of the 1960s and 70s who experimented with psychotropic drugs as a way to release their creative energies found in the end that their true creativity was stolen rather than enhanced. Worse yet, many found that their personality and self-identity were sucked out of them by their flirtation with the dark side of Romantic inspiration. Rather than shape the chaos around them, they found themselves being shaped, passively, by a darkness they did not understand.

V

For a moment, this loss of self threatens to afflict the poet of "Kubla Khan". Inspiration and its attendant vision have been swallowed by the lifeless ocean, leaving him empty and dry. And then, softly, gently, like the still, small voice that Elijah hears when the wind and earthquake and fire have died away (see 1 Kings 19:11-13), an image of pure beauty and romance drifts before the mind's eye of the poet:

> The shadow of the dome of pleasure
> Floated midway on the waves;
> Where was heard the mingled measure
> From the fountain and the caves.
> It was a miracle of rare device,
> A sunny pleasure-dome with caves of ice! (31-36)

For both Coleridge and Wordsworth one of the key functions of the imagination was to discover similitude in the midst of dissimilitude and thus effect a new incarnation out of previously discordant elements. Something similar happens in our dreams when we find ourselves in the bedroom of our home, but, when we look out the window, we see not the landscape behind our house but the backyard, say, of our grandmother's house. Or perhaps we meet people or visit places that are a combination of various people and places we have known in our lives. In the world of logic and rationality, there can be no traffic between sunny domes and caves of ice, but in the beautiful and terrible world of Romantic inspiration such things can happen and such things can *be*. Most people today hail Freud as the discoverer of the unconscious, when, in fact, it was Romantic poets like Coleridge (and William Blake) who first explored—often via the "royal road" of dreams—the internal landscape of the unconscious mind. What Freud did was to seize hold of the unconscious realm already mapped by the Romantics and give to it a scientific nomenclature.

Fast on the heels of Coleridge's lovely if paradoxical vision of the sunny domes and caves of ice, there arises a second vision that seems to have no logical connection to the first:

> A damsel with a dulcimer
> In a vision once I saw:
> It was an Abyssinian maid,

And on her dulcimer she played,
Singing of Mount Abora. (37-41)

Coleridge is possibly alluding to one of the nine muses that the ancient Greeks believed inspired poetry and the arts, but he resuscitates this well-worn allusion by his use of magical place names and the delicious liquidity of his phrasing and diction. Through our participation in Coleridge's fragmented reverie, we catch a glimpse of an ethereal, Apollonian inspiration to balance the violent, Dionysian energy of the deep romantic chasm.

As quickly as the two visions come, they depart from before the eyes of the poet. But not before he gives voice to a desire that all Romantic poets nurture within their hearts:

Could I revive within me
Her symphony and song,
To such a deep delight 'twould win me,
That with music loud and long,
I would build that dome in air,
That sunny dome! those caves of ice!
And all who heard should see them there . . . (42-48)

What if, the poet asks, I could "revive within" myself that initial burst of inspiration in all its freshness and purity? What if I could hold on to it until it yielded up all its wonder-working powers? Then, truly, could I build poetic castles in the air; then could I bring to shimmering life whatever lurks in the caverns of my mind's eye.

In his essay, "A Defence of Poetry", Percy Bysshe Shelley, while expressing the same desire as the speaker of "Kubla Khan", explains why such a desire cannot be realised in our world:

Poetry is not like reasoning, a power to be exerted according to the determination of the will. A man cannot say, "I will compose poetry". The greatest poet even cannot say it; for the mind in creation is as a fading coal, which some invisible influence, like an inconstant wind, awakens to transitory brightness; this power arises from within, like the colour of a flower which fades and changes as it is developed, and the conscious portions of our natures are unprophetic either of its approach or its departure. Could this influence be durable in its original purity and force, it is impossible to predict the greatness of the results; but when composition begins, inspiration is already on the decline, and the most glorious poetry that has ever been communicated to the world is probably a feeble shadow of the original conception of the Poet. (Noyes, 1956: 1109)

The problem, laments Shelley, is that we have no control over the winds of inspiration; we cannot even say for sure when they will come or when they will depart. The creation of poetry is not something we can will into existence as a carpenter might a table or a potter a vase. We must simply wait for the inspiration to fall, knowing all along that even when it does fall, the poem that results will be but a shadow of what was intended. Worse yet, when the power comes and inspiration begins to burn like fire in our bones, the very act of tapping that fire will hasten its extinction. Like a "fading coal", the more fiercely it burns, the more quickly it burns out.

There is, however, one thing of which both Shelley and Coleridge are sure. *If* they could hold on to that inspiration in its "original purity and force", then would they be able to do and create anything they desired. Then could they build in air a true dome of poetry that all would see and all would praise. Then would they truly become Romantic poet-prophets. But, of course, they cannot, and that "cannot" lies at the core of so much Romantic angst and despair. Romantic inspiration, even when it does not devour the poet's inner vitality and creative energy, has a way of leaving him stranded at the very moment when poetic triumph seems in his grasp. Neither personal nor purposeful, Romantic inspiration cares little for those who channel it, lifting them up in one moment and dropping them in the next. It makes no promises or covenants and is as likely to exalt as to abandon. What I have referred to in this essay as the dark side of Romantic inspiration is simply the danger that follows when we entrust the deepest part of ourselves to an energy or a force or an idol that lacks the power or the will to draw us upward toward true goodness and perfection.

VI

Here then, we expect, Coleridge will end his poem, with frustration at his inability to sustain the intensity of inspiration that promises to make him a poet-prophet. But instead he surprises us with an ending that takes Romantic wish-fulfilment to its final, triumphant, dreadful extreme. As the poem rushes to its close, the poet suddenly gets what he has so long desired. He builds that dome in air, and the people who hear his words see the dome for themselves. But their reaction, far from one of praise, is one of sheer panic and horror:

> And all who heard should see them there,
> And all should cry, Beware! Beware!
> His flashing eyes, his floating hair!
> Weave a circle round him thrice,

And close your eyes with holy dread,
For he on honey-dew hath fed,
And drunk the milk of Paradise. (48-54)

For the second time in the poem, the dark side of Romantic inspiration snares the poet. Too late he learns a terrible truth: if someone could embody in himself all the force of inspiration, if he could truly evolve into a divine poet-prophet, then would he become a contagion to the earth. People would shun his wild eyes and his mad gaze. He would become, at best, a border figure, unable to join in the life around him, condemned to wander, lonely and isolated, from land to land. At worst, he would cease to be human. He might possess the wisdom to instruct and embody in himself a higher ethic that transcends the mundane, but he cannot share that wisdom or that ethic. He cannot get close enough to his fellow man to do so. Like the Faustian Byronic hero, he has plucked forbidden fruit, tasted of wisdom not intended for mortal man, and it has made him an outcast.

Romantic inspiration, then, has both a dark side and a darker side. The poet experiences the first when, after being lifted high on the wings of inspiration, he finds himself left stranded in a dead, passionless, disenchanted world. He experiences the second when inspiration returns to lift him into that higher world that he yearns for, leaving him to learn, too late, that he cannot dwell in such a world, that no human can dwell in it without forfeiting his membership in the human community. Those who pluck forbidden fruit gain wisdom, but with it come despondency, despair, and madness. There are some things man was not meant to know. Or, to quote the old proverb: beware of what you wish for; you may have the misfortune to get it.

As far back as ancient Greece and Rome, Plato and Horace had warned against the dangers of divine madness. In his dialogue, *Ion*, Plato has Socrates assert that poets do not write by art or skill. Far from understanding (rationally) what they create, they are carried away (irrationally) by a divine inspiration that literally possesses them:

> For all good poets, epic as well as lyric, compose their beautiful poems not by art, but because they are inspired and possessed. And as the Korybantian revelers when they dance are not in their right mind, so the lyric poets are not in their right mind when they are composing their beautiful strains: but when falling under the power of music and meter they are inspired and possessed; like Bacchic maidens who draw milk and honey from the rivers when they are under the influence of Dionysus but not when there are in their right mind. . . . the poet is a light and winged and holy thing, and there is no invention in him until he has been inspired

and is out of his senses, and reason is no longer in him: no man, while he
retains that faculty, has the oracular gift of poetry. (Adams, 1992: 14)

Though Coleridge's references to "honeydew" and "milk of paradise" in
the last two lines of his poem are meant, I would argue, to refer to
opium—hence the necessity of reading the note as an integral part of the
poem—they are strongly reminiscent of Plato's *Ion*. Of course, whereas
Plato meant his words as a critique of poetry, Coleridge, as a Romantic
poet, celebrated the fact that poetry relied more on inspiration than on
reason and was essentially oracular, or prophetic, in nature.

Still, both Plato and Coleridge were aware of the dangers of Dionysus.
The Bacchic maidens to whom Plato refers—known also as Bacchae or
Maenads—were wild women who followed in the train of the Greek god
of the grape. Intoxicated by the physical and spiritual wine of Dionysus,
they abandoned the polis and lived in the woods among ferocious beasts.
They represent the breakdown of Apollonian order and rationality and the
primal, enthusiastic embrace of instinct and intuition. On one level they
embody the very heart and soul of nature; in Euripides' play, *The Bacchae*,
they are even described as offering their breasts to suckle fawns. But here
too there is a dark side. When the protagonist of Euripides' play
(Pentheus) spies on their Bacchic rites, they go insane and, with the
superhuman strength given them by the god, tear him limb from limb. The
ancient world's greatest musician, Orpheus, also learned the danger of the
Maenads. After losing his beloved Eurydice for a second time, Orpheus
was approached by the Maenads with offers of love. When he scorned
their approaches, however, they turned on him in fury and tore him to
pieces. As Ovid tells the story in *Metamorphoses* XI, Orpheus's lyre holds
back their irrational fury for a space, but eventually even the sweetness of
his lyre succumbs to the dark energy of the Maenads.

Shelley argues in his "Defence" that the imagination is "the great
instrument of moral good" (Adams, 1992: 520). That is partly because the
imagination, like love, is an incarnational force that privileges synthesis
over analysis and draws opposites together into new forms. As such, it
draws us toward the other person, even allowing us to put ourselves in the
place of the other. Once again, however, the madness that comes with
inspiration often has the opposite effect of cutting us off from the other
and turning us radically inward. Inspiration may not make the poet bad (as
some might argue that it did to Shelley), but if it makes him mad, it will
certainly compromise his ability to instruct others and to convey a vision
that will make men moral.

Nearly four centuries after the Greek Plato compared the poet to a
Bacchic reveler, the Roman Horace added his own touch to Plato's portrait

of the mad poet. In Horace's more satirical *Art of Poetry*, he playfully describes the reaction that such poets elicit from society:

> As people avoid someone afflicted with the itch, with jaundice, the fits, or insanity, so sensible men stay clear of a mad poet. Children tease him and rash fools follow him. Spewing out verses, he wanders off, with his head held high, like a fowler with his eyes on the blackbirds: and if he falls into a well or ditch, he may call, out, "Help, fellow citizens!"—but no one cares to help him. . . . He is mad, at any rate; and like a bear that has been strong enough to break the bars of its cage, he frightens away both the learned and the ignorant by reciting his verses. If he catches a victim, he clings to him and reads him to death, like a leech that will not leave the skin until it is filled with blood. (Adams, 1992: 74)

This remarkable passage adds to Plato's portrait a sense of the poet as one who is so diseased that people must avoid him lest they be infected themselves. One can almost hear Horace advising his readers to "Weave a circle round him thrice / And close your eyes with holy dread". However, what Horace says mostly in jest, Coleridge echoes with gravity and fear. He understands the risks of playing with fire. Those who feed on wild milk and honey cannot simply return to the farm when the fit of intoxication leaves them. Either they are driven to irrational behavior (like the Maenads), destroyed (like Pentheus and Orpheus), or cast out of society (like the poet of "Kubla Khan", the Ancient Mariner, and all the other Byronic heroes that populate the poetry and prose of the Romantic age).

Aside from the beauty of its lyricism and the power of its images, "Kubla Khan" must be read as both an invitation and a warning to the would-be Romantic poet. Inspiration offers gifts most precious to the poet-prophet, but beneath its divine promises lurk satanic dangers. Let us not, in seeking to rise above our human capacity for wisdom and understanding find that we have sunk below it. Let us not, in seeking to become an angel, find we have become a beast. Let us not tread the path of Satan and of Nebuchadnezzar (see Daniel 4).

Harold Bloom, writing, as always, in Blakean mode, criticizes Coleridge for renouncing "his own demonic version of the Romantic quest" and of allowing his "wavering Prometheanism" to be defeated by the "fear of his own imaginative energy" (Bloom, 1970: 20). As is often the case, Bloom is right, but refuses himself to learn from Coleridge's wisdom and discernment. Coleridge is afraid indeed for he knows the dark side of demonic, Promethean energy. He knows, as Bloom does not, that that way madness lies.

References

Adams, H. 1992. *Critical Theory Since Plato*. Rev. edn. New York: Harcourt Brace Jovanovich.

Bate, W. J. 1968. *Coleridge*. New York: Macmillan.

Bloom, H. 1961. *The Visionary Company: A Reading of English Romantic Poetry*. Garden City, New York: Doubleday.

Bloom, H. 1970. "The Internalization of the Quest-Romance", in H. Bloom (ed.), *Romanticism and Consciousness: Essay in Criticism*. New York: Norton.

Engell, J. 1981. *The Creative Imagination: Enlightenment to Romanticism*. Cambridge, MA: Harvard University Press.

Greenberg, M. 1986. *The Hamlet Vocation of Coleridge and Wordsworth*. Iowa City: University of Iowa Press.

Havens, R. D. 1941. *The Mind of the Poet: A Study of Wordsworth's Thought with Particular Reference to the Prelude*. Baltimore: Johns Hopkins University Press.

Noyes, R. 1956. *English Romantic Poetry and Prose*. New York: Oxford University Press.

Owen, W. J. B. and J. W. Smyser (eds) 1974. *The Prose Works of William Wordsworth*. 3 vols. Oxford: Clarendon Press.

KEEPING COMPANY WITH DICKENS

ROBERT MCPARLAND

Charles Dickens has had a significant place in the discussion of ethics and literature in recent years, appearing as a key figure in Richard Rorty's *Contingency, Irony and Solidarity* (1989), and Martha C. Nussbaum's *Poetic Justice: The Literary Imagination and Public Life* (1995). Dickens writes a kind of book that Rorty says is "relevant to our relations with others, to helping us to notice the effects of our actions on other people. These are the books which are relevant to liberal hope, and to the question of how to reconcile private irony with such hope" (141). Martha Nussbaum examines Dickens's *Hard Times* (1854) for its ethical imperative and call to sympathy and rejects "the economists' habit of reducing everything to calculation" and seeing only "abstract features of people and situations" (44). Both these thinkers underscore the continuing ethical relevance of Dickens's fiction for us. Their insights into the moral fiction of Dickens are tempered with an awareness of contemporary pluralism. However, they also reflect a perception of Dickens's ethical merit that was held by Dickens's own Victorian readers. Like Rorty and Nussbaum, these readers also saw that Dickens's quality of sympathy speaks loudly of human values and ethical principles. As Josiah Gilbert Holland wrote:

> He had a heart which brought him into sympathy with all those phases of humanity which were intellectually interesting to him. He loved the rascals whom he painted, and enjoyed the society of the weakest men and women of his pages; and it is this sympathy which gives immortality to his novels. (1872: 71)

It is this sympathy in Dickens that Nussbaum pointed to in her advocacy of ethical fiction in *Poetic Justice*. Some philosophers have criticized Nussbaum's early work as too attached to a principle of realism, or as too focused upon our affective response to literature. One might add that Nussbaum and Rorty both have notions about how a work of literature should be read. Readers do read in many different ways. They may or may not read in the manner that Rorty or Nussbaum anticipate that they will. Even so, it is clear that reading can have consequences, including moral and political ones. Imaginative literature from Homer to Dickens to our day conveys ideas, often with considerable power. Something happens when we keep company with literature.

Wayne C. Booth, in his book *The Company We Keep* (1998), argued for a re-centering of ethics in our contact with literature.[1] Booth, who spoke of "friendship with books" and of "the exchange of gifts," proposed that we who are concerned with ethics are interested in any effect on the *ethos*: in this case, on that of a reader or listener (46). Powerful stories, he said, may contribute toward a conversation among us. So we are led to ask, what happens as we read? With what quality do I accompany these authors and these characters, plots, and scenes? Who am I as I read and with whom am I keeping company?

Charles Dickens was quite aware of the ethical power of fiction upon his audience and he consciously sought connection with his readers through an appeal to *ethos*. Indeed, for Charles Dickens, his relationship with his readers constituted the greatest love affair of his life (Butt and Tillotson, 1957). They, in turn, kept company with this author. Keeping company with Dickens offered them connection with each other: a means of sympathetic identification that they shared. They were a community of readers engaged month to month with a serial publication that urged them to be attentive to issues of justice and to an ethics of care.

We can gain some insight into how deeply Dickens's fiction affected his readers by looking for their responses in their journals, letters, and autobiographies. The comments of common readers tend to support the view that Dickens was able to weave bonds of human sympathy among them. The "vast sympathetic participation in the daily life of mankind" that George Santayana saw in Dickens (60) is echoed by Dickens's contemporaries like James Nack, a poet who was a clerk at New York's City Hall, who began his poem on Dickens with the words "Friend of my heart! Friend of the human race" (72). It is sounded by Lydia Marie Child, an American abolitionist, who wrote in a letter to her friend Sarah Shaw on March 23, 1856: "I have admired several of Bulwer's heroines, but I never loved one of them and hugged them to my heart as I do Little Nell, and Esther, and Little Dorrit. Dickens is the great Apostle of Humanity" (96). The sympathetic responses of these readers to Dickens's writings testify to the fact that the multiple voices we meet in the author's works sound the plurality among us, as these texts call us to ethical reflection. As John Bowen observes, within Charles Dickens's lyricism, we hear the voices of people of all classes that are "suddenly and overwhelmingly blown back toward us in the form of an ethico-political responsibility" (255-69). Dickens's stories continue to play a role among us today as a point of reference in our efforts to construct a responsive society of mutual respect and ethical integrity.

Critics engaged in the ethical turn in fiction, such as Wayne C. Booth or J. Hillis Miller, have viewed Dickens's novels as among the great books that are our common cultural property. As philosopher Richard Rorty has pointed out, in the event of a disaster, novels like those of Dickens would preserve values (141). Books like those of Dickens are the kind of books that can sustain us. Dickens is, for Rorty, "a sort of anti-Heidegger" who is "paradigmatic of the West" and its commitment to democratic pluralism, freedom and liberty (Bowen, 2006: 255-69).

The cultural work done by Dickens in creating ethical appeal through pathos and sympathy is significant, say these critics. Of course, since these may be only the attitudes of these critics, we must look to Dickens's readers to better empirically ground these observations. We may look to contemporary readers like Andrew Kennedy Hutchison Boyd (1825-99), who wrote in a sermon:

> Your returning good for evil must be a real thing. It must be done heartily and without reservation, or it is nothing at all. Uriah Heep, in Mr. Dickens's beautiful story, forgave David Copperfield for striking him a blow. (207)

In readers' comments we can see that from the first appearance of *Oliver Twist* in 1837-38, Dickens's novels drew sympathy from his readers. Jane T. H. Cross, a writer from the American south, remarks in 1860, "I will read now, I will lose, in the pathetic story of Oliver Twist, a sense of my own miseries. It is one of the few novels I can read; there are some touches of deep feeling in it" (155). In Cross's comment we see how greatly Dickens possessed a rhetorical talent for pathos. Among his gifts was his capacity to evoke from his readers sympathetic identification with his characters. As Thomas Wentworth Higginson observed, Dickens

> can take a poor wretch like Fagin, whose emotions neither he nor his reader has experienced, and can paint him in colors that seem made of the soul's own atoms, so that each beholder feels as if he, personally, had been the man. (26)

Dickens's sympathetic power in creating Little Nell, in *The Old Curiosity Shop* in 1840-41, prompted even greater public response from his readers. Readers wrote to Dickens to spare Little Nell. Mothers wrote to him to tell him of their own children who had died, writing to him, as Edgar Johnson tells us, about "how good she was, and how, in this or that respect, she resembled Nell" (Collins, 1971: 114).

Many contemporaries of Charles Dickens proposed that his novels made important contributions to ethical reflection. As *Fraser's Magazine* suggested in April 1840: "he has always espoused the cause of the humble, the persecuted, the oppressed" (400). Or, we may look to readers like Bishop Martin John Spalding of Louisville, who wrote in 1875: "He is the friend and advocate of the poor and distressed, and he strikes at tyranny and avarice in high places. Besides, he leaves a good moral impression in most of his works" (526).

A reading of Dickens's texts shows that they address issues of justice and injustice in institutions and among individuals and also continually speak of the "connection" between human beings. The first concern may remind one of John Rawls's emphasis in *A Theory of Justice* (1971). The latter may remind one of Carol Gilligan's notion of an ethics of care in *In A Different Voice* (1982), as she targets an individualistic Kantian framework and the Piaget-based developmental notions of the moral psychologist Lawrence Kohlberg. Dickens's sense of a human community of "connection" was part of his insight into the nature of reality. He pointed to the fictive community of his characters and his readers when he wrote:

> It struck me that it would be a new thing to show people coming together, in a chance way, as fellow travelers... as happens in life; and to connect them afterwards, and to make the waiting for that connection part of the interest. (Forster, 1872-74: I: 624)

Dickens's widely-read fiction itself created connections. His stories provided a language of life for those nineteenth-century readers who were puzzled by the incomprehensibility of the modernizing world. Meanwhile, his texts presented a challenge to individualism, to the desirability of each individual pursuing the good in his own way, constrained only by legality or social contract. Much as in Carol Gilligan's ethics of care (1982), they presented a sense of "connection" between persons, a deep social web of interrelationship that calls for helping, nurturing, and mutual respect. For Dickens, social progress has to do with what Gilligan calls the "progress of affiliative relationship" (170) in which "the concept of identity expands to include the experience of interconnection" (173).

Martha Nussbaum in *Cultivating Humanity* (1997) writes: "A novel that recognizes the struggle of working class people—as up to a point the novels of Dickens do—may have little sensitivity to the lives and experiences of many types of women" (101). While this may be so, Michael Slater makes a strong case in *Dickens's Women* that the author hardly slighted them, or lacked sensitivity. Indeed, the cases of Sissy Jupe,

Esther Summerson, and Florence Dombey argue against any proposition that Dickens lacked sensitivity to the lives of middle class or working women. Given this, this mention of Dickens by Nussbaum may not be the best example. Even so, she points to a larger phenomenon. While sensitivity toward women is present in industrial novels like Charlotte Bronte's *Shirley* (1849) and Elizabeth Gaskell's *North and South* (1854), it is not everywhere present in the British fiction that depicts working class women. Nussbaum's point is to suggest how this can affect one's disposition toward reading. If a reader is sensitive to the plight of these women and the text is not this will affect one's sympathetic reading of the novel, Nussbaum observes. "If we are reading with democratic ideals of equal concern and respect of mind we sense an incompleteness" she argues (102). Clearly, this is true: we each bring attitudes and experience to our reading and so did Dickens's contemporaries.

Like many of Dickens's contemporary readers, Nussbaum points to the "experience of sympathy" as central in our reading. The novels of Charles Dickens and George Eliot are cited for their awakening of this sympathy. There is in these authors a "commitment to the making of a social world" and a "deliberative community" (104). Considering Dickens and Eliot's characters, Nussbaum asserts that it is impossible to care about these characters "without having some very definite political and moral interests awakened in oneself" (104). This sympathy, which permeates Dickens's work, was also a significant aspect of George Eliot's approach to fiction. Eliot wrote: "If Art does not enlarge man's sympathies, it does nothing morally" (Letter to Charles Bray, July 5, 1859. *Letters* 3: 111). Eliot and G. H. Lewes, often pondering the Darwinian evolutionary scheme and natural selection, reflected upon altruism, human sympathy, and the ethical. For Joseph Jacobs, who called Eliot an ethical artist, there is "an extension of sympathy" to all her characters and "her whole work is imbued with ethical notions" (39-41).

Middlemarch (1871-72) is one of Eliot's many novels that testify to this search for connection through sympathy. In the prelude we read of the desire for an epic life of noble ambition, high ideals, and self-sacrifice. There is a sense that "provincial life" will offer some challenges to this: A person of "spiritual grandeur" is "ill-matched with the meanness of opportunity" in this world (xiii). Dorothea could become a "St. Theresa", or she might be the "foundress of nothing". In contrast with Dorothea's "spiritual ardour" and principled ambition is Rosamond Vincy's shallowness and "frippery." We are brought into the life of a reformer, an idealist who imagines "generous schemes" and wishes to grow and to be useful: "to do something". As Bert Hornback observes, while Lydgate's,

Causabon's, and Will's ambitions in this novel "are not always bad, when they make mistakes it is because their values are wrong, and their ambitions are to serve themselves" (21-2). Dorothea, in contrast, seeks to serve the world. The novel explores ways to overcome egotism, as Hornback points out, to escape the egotism of a restricted point of view, to suppress desires, and to enlarge our sympathies, which is what Dorothea does, learning a kind of self-assertion and openness to others (100).

Dickens, in his novels, satirizes those characters who are deficient in this openness. A classic example is Jacob Marley and Ebeneezer Scrooge in *A Christmas Carol*. Nussbaum regards Dickens's character Jacob Marley as an image of poor citizenship. He drags the chains of all of the people he has injured and all the corrupt acts he has engaged in. Nussbaum writes, "[w]e produce all too many citizens who are like Marley's ghost, and like Scrooge before he walked out to see what the world around him contained" (14).

The work of Dickens and Eliot implies that by making the social world vivid and involving readers, fiction can help to produce citizens who leave those chains behind. Nussbaum notes that readers of a realist novel "do all that tragic spectators do—and something more. They embrace the ordinary" (95). This was true of Dickens's readers who clearly embraced his Sissy Jupe, David Copperfield, and Oliver Twist. These were sympathetic, common characters rather than princes and kings as Nussbaum points out (95) and Dickens joins his common readers in sympathy with them. To what extent does such sympathy, promoted by the novel, prompt action? In keeping company, we have an immersion experience of these fictional social worlds. Nussbaum's view that this may be an experience that moves a reader to ethical awareness and action is borne out by the experience of Dickens's contemporary readers, who personally and culturally held his books to be a form of moral fiction.

Indeed, Dickens insisted upon the passion of generosity. He wanted to change social organizations for the betterment of persons. His social critique aimed at the reform of institutions and the support of individuals whose lives were beset, rather than aided, by those institutions. His stories point to the loss of self to abstractions; the absorption of lives in the fog of *Bleak House* (1852), the workhouse of *Oliver Twist*, the Chancery and Mrs. Jellyby's telescopic philanthropy in *Bleak House*, and the Marshalsea Prison and Circumlocution Office of *Little Dorrit* (1856), all pose ethical claims. Dickens sees through illusions of mastery. He is paradigmatic of a commitment to human freedom and integrity and the right to equality. Indeed, Dickens's work underscores the capacity of language to engage clearly and truthfully with the world, not in circumlocution, not in evasive legal jargon or bureaucratic double-speak, and not in abstract reason or Gradgrindian fact.

Charles Dickens was fundamentally concerned with ethical action and believed that novel writing and reading was a practice that was fully engaged with life. We read at the conclusion of *Hard Times*, Dickens's narrator's final words: "Dear Reader! It rests with you and me, whether in our two fields of action, similar things shall be or not. Let them be" (266). Dickens here calls us here to create a just world—even where the Coketown of *Hard Times* or the London of *Bleak House* are unjust and characters like Stephen Blackpool or Jo the crossing sweeper die without justice.

In this sense, Dickens's novels may remind one of John Rawls, *A Theory of Justice* (1971), in which he writes that "justice is the first virtue of social institutions" (3-4). Justice is about fairness and Rawls sought to develop a series of principles that could be applied to our institutions, to judge whether they are just or unjust. Like Dickens, Rawls holds that laws and institutions must be reformed if they are unjust. Dickens provides a narrative and a different language for this same idea: a person has an inviolable dignity founded upon this justice. An interesting aspect of Rawls's theory is how he invites us to imagine. Rawls writes, "[t]hus we are to imagine that those who engage in social cooperation choose together, in one joint act, the principles which are to assign basic rights and duties and to determine the division of social benefits" (3-4). He also says that if we can imagine people in some initially unfair situation and determine what they would view as principles of justice then we would have some valid principles. We are also welcomed to imagine a "principle of redress" that would provide equality of opportunity and allocate resources to those who are disadvantaged. Rawls believes that there must be a concern in justice to provide for the least advantaged.

This concern for the disadvantaged appears throughout Dickens's novels. In his panoramic cross-section of London, Dickens shows us people in poverty and in need. He prompts his audience to ask where justice is when bad things occur in this world. How can innocent Little Nell of *The Old Curiosity Shop* (1840) die so miserably? Why are there Poor Laws that send Oliver Twist out onto the streets? Why must Tiny Tim be handicapped and perhaps die so young? Why do villains get away with murder? Why does justice get tied up in interminable cases before the courts of Chancery?

Dickens appealed to a Victorian audience seeking moral grounding in a changing world. Critiquing institutions, bureaucracies, and legal systems, he sounded the call to make these institutions responsive and responsible.

With *Oliver Twist* and *Nicholas Nickleby* (1839), he criticized institutions responsible for the plight of poor children. With *Bleak House*, he examined the legal system. With *Hard Times*, he assessed the educational and personal losses of imagination to utility and fact.

Beyond this, he expressed a kind of virtue ethics, urging the humanization of his characters. His characters, from David Copperfield and Pip to Sidney Carton and Eugene Wrayburn (and his readers) are led to ask the question, what ought I to be? In Dickens, the moral life is about discovering the ideals for human life and learning to embody them in one's life. He finds virtue and the wellsprings of life in sympathy.

The sympathetic and moral challenges of Dickens's fiction were an important resource for Victorians, who responded to the changing world around them: a crowded, diversified environment caught up in the engine of modernity.[2] Dickens and his readers met at this busy intersection of their world. Serial fiction was alive in periodical rhythm that has been likened by some to the train and its movement. It held a sense of the suspense and passage of time. Its readers were living in history and creating a home, as Linda K. Hughes and Michael Lund (1991) have pointed out. They too were heroes and heroines in danger of being pulled by the speed of the city, as we are pulled today by the rhythm of globalization and technologies. Reading fiction was, in a sense, performed in a space apart from history, or at least in a moment of reflection and respite from the challenges of the commercial world. As Anne C. Rose has pointed out, Victorians "read to each other to build bonds of sentiment by savoring literature together" (1992: 123). Dickens's serialized stories participated in this reflective and often communal moment, before people plunged back into change and the rhythms of their industrial world. For in these moments in the family circle, or the reading group, there was companionship between the book and its readers and between the readers, or listeners, and each other.

When the novelist John Gardner wrote *On Moral Fiction* several decades ago, he rested his argument upon a tradition of the book that has been important in Western culture: the belief that fiction can point to significant issues and can have a moral effect upon readers. However, much literary theory has not been comfortable with ethical criticism.[3] It has been argued that the value of art cannot be ethical: some art is good although its ethics are bad. Oscar Wilde wrote, "There is no such thing as a moral or immoral book. Books are well-written or badly written" (1891: 1). More recently, Suzanne Keen, considering fiction alongside neurology, recognizes "affective transaction" and immediate "feeling" but is sceptical that ethical action follows (2007: 145-68). Then there are those who think that ethical judgments about stories are merely subjective opinion. So what can we say about literature's presumed salutary effects upon the reader? Some critics have held the moral consequences of art to be "unresearchable" and impossible to predict. Who knows whether an author helps people to empathize with others or makes people perceptive of others' states, these critics will say. Who knows whether reading novels is good or bad for one's character? The Puritans certainly thought novel reading was one of the worst things a person could do in life.

These critics could stand to do a little work in the archival records left by ordinary readers. Recently developed methodologies for the empirical study of actual readers can indeed suggest the moral consequences that reading fiction may have had in their lives. For example, the circulation records of the New York Society Library demonstrate that one reader, George Pierce, checked out Dickens's *Oliver Twist* twice in 1854. Not long afterward, he created two orphanages in upstate New York. As his own journal shows, there appears to be a correlation between his reading and his action.

Gauging whether a work of fiction has an ethical appeal for a reader may be problematic because of the many variations of reader response to a literary work. Thus, critics from Paulette Kidder to J. Plotz (1996) and D. Z. Phillips (1998) will say that for Martha Nussbaum to assert that reading Dickens's *Hard Times* moves readers in a particular way and has social, ethical benefits may express *her* way of reading more than theirs. However, Nussbaum's reading of Dickens's *Hard Times* appears quite similar to the readings produced by Dickens's contemporaries. Some of them did not like the novel, saying that they preferred the comical Dickens. However, in their letters and journals these readers regularly point to the moral quality of his stories. Meanwhile, in Victorian journals we can see abundant comment that Dickens is widely recognized for his social sympathy and the ethical core of his writing. The experience of these readers affirms that Dickens's fiction, in its "complex psychological and moral motives" is full of possibilities and these include the possibility of an ethical reading. His books include an appeal to the ethical, not only an aesthetic appeal. His books are "good," in part, because they did affect their readers.

There may, of course, be some other objections to turning to Dickens for an ethics of fiction. Dickens has been soundly criticized by writers on aesthetics, from Mill to James, as popular, vulgar, and low. John Stuart Mill, after reading Dickens's *Bleak House* in 1852 complained about "that creature Dickens," who was "neither philosopher nor human" (Letter to Harriet Taylor, March 20, 1854, in Collins, 1971: 297-8). The narrator of

Justin McCarthy's 1874 novel *Massie—A Romance* writes of the Reverend Eustore Massie:

> Dickens he endured because of his generally commendable morals, although he thought several of his characters terribly vulgar, but he supposed that certain natures needed such entertainments. (60)

One may also trot out several *ad hominem* arguments against Dickens, the man. Dickens challenged Utilitarians while sometimes being utilitarian and he disparaged political economists while making a lot of money. He apparently enjoyed creating the sinister criminals and villains in his books and got quite excited enacting murder in his public readings. In the mid-1850's, he divorced his wife of several decades, leaving her for a younger woman. So this is the author Martha Nussbaum and Richard Rorty will turn to for *ethical fiction*? How are we to read Dickens? As a centre of narrative control and surveillance, as D. A. Miller sees him? Or as a source for the promotion of empathy and understanding for disadvantaged people, as Nussbaum sees him? Is it not so that, as the American philosopher George Santayana said, Dickens expressed "sympathetic participation in the daily life of mankind"? (60). Research into the response of his readers to his novels suggests that his contemporary readers felt this sense of sympathetic participation. Dickens's contemporary reading audience appears to offer us some accounts that Dickens's writings touched sympathetic chords in them.

The energy and excess that critics like John Kucich see in Dickens's texts communicates sympathetic relationship within the human condition. As the Russian critic Mikhail Bakhtin once wrote in his reflections on Fyodor Dostoevsky, "[t]o be means to communicate [...] I cannot become myself without the other" (Todorov, 1984: 96). Dickens became an author of worldwide importance in connection with his audience. In his novels he offered his readers a dialogism of voices of all classes in which the claims of abstract reason and power discourse are deposed and people are allowed to speak. Through his writing we are invited into a mutual engagement in life. Dickens's texts enact human connection through sympathy. It is through the details of his characters' lives that we enter the material circumstances and meet his narrative mobility and strangeness, and what John Bowen calls "the ways in which the works make an ethical claim upon or call to us" (208).

Dickens's appeal was not to conventional Victorian morality. His novels emphasize the necessity of making moral choices and life choices. For example, Pip in *Great Expectations* has to mature and learn to see his place in the world, to choose authenticity. It is in characters like Pip that

Dickens speaks to us still, as he spoke to his contemporaries, through his universal sympathy. We respond to Oliver Twist or Esther Summerson as they seek a kind of liberty and wholeness.

The characters and settings that Dickens portrayed point outward, beyond the page, to sites of the search for liberty and dignity in the world. To put liberty into practice, in the 1830s-70s or today, requires responsive institutions: ones anchored in values. Conveying the quest for human sympathy and dignity within a broad and pluralistic social panorama, Charles Dickens's novels help us to map today's ethical turn in fiction. They call us to responsibility and continue to speak to the heart of the humanities, which today is very alive on the margins of a world that is largely absorbed in commercial and techno-scientific activity.

To see how Dickens's novels continue to speak to the inner life of people and to the crisis of modernity, we must look at the reader as well as at text. The voices of readers suggest how they thought and felt about Dickens's stories. To listen to them can lend some further support to the view that Dickens's novels perform cultural work, including evoking sympathy and a sense of ethical responsibility from his readers. What do Dickens's stories do for us? What do his different modes of narrative invite us to in our reading? Can they prompt us toward ethical reasoning, or perhaps encourage ethical conduct? How can Dickens's novels be useful in probing what is right or wrong, good or bad, just or unjust? Can his stories help people to understand the nature of an ethical problem? Can they provide conceptual tools to enable students to think critically or to feel and reason about ethical matters? What happens when we see fiction, like that of Dickens, not so much as a mimetic reflection of its times but as an active and dynamic part of history?

From his first appearance with *Sketches by Boz* and *The Pickwick Papers*, Dickens made his readers laugh. He caught the popular imagination and his characters became topics of discussion. They invited readers to keep company with them in what Patricia Okker has called "social stories" in which "reading magazine novels provided individuals with an opportunity to connect with a community of disparate members and, at the same time, to reshape the community itself" (159).

Considering this manner of "keeping company" with Dickens's fiction, we may agree with George Santayana that

> what he had was a vast sympathetic participation in the daily life of mankind; and what he saw of ancient institutions made him hate them, as needless sources of oppression, misery, selfishness, and rancor. His one political passion was philanthropy, genuine but felt only on its negative, reforming side. (59-60)

Notes

[1] See W. C. Booth, 1998. *The Company We Keep*, Chicago: University of Chicago Press.
[2] Catherine Waters remarks, "Dickens's writing is a constitutive element of Victorian history: his writings played a significant role in shaping that culture's sense of reality" (2005: 157).
[3] Ethical criticism, however, has had many proponents: Judith Butler, Irving Babbitt, Tobin Siebers, Lillian Furst, Christopher Clausen, Martha Nussbaum, and J. Hillis Miller among them.

References

Booth, W. C. 1998. *The Company We Keep: An Ethics of Fiction.* Chicago: University of Chicago Press.

Bowen, J. 2006. "Dickens and the Force of Writing", in J. Bowen and R. Patten (eds), *Charles Dickens Studies*. London: Palgrave. 255-272.

Boyd, A. K. H. 2007. *Autumn Holidays of a Country Parson*. Boston: Ticknor and Fields.

Butt, J. and Tillotson, K. 1957. *Dickens at Work*. London: Methuen.

Collins, P. (ed.) 1971. *Charles Dickens: The Critical Heritage*. London: Routledge and Kegan Paul.

Dickens, C. 1836. *Sketches By Boz*. Oxford: Oxford University Press.

—. 1836. *The Pickwick Papers.* Oxford: Oxford University Press.

—. 1837. *Oliver Twist.* Oxford: Oxford University Press.

—. 1838. *Nicholas Nickleby.* Oxford: Oxford University Press

—. 1840. *The Old Curiosity Shop.* Oxford: Oxford University Press.

—. 1850. *David Copperfield.* Oxford: Oxford University Press.

—. 1852. *Bleak House.* Oxford: Oxford University Press.

—. 1854. *Hard Times* New York: Books Inc., 1956, 266.

—. 1856. *Little Dorrit.* Oxford: Oxford University Press.

—. 1861. *Great Expectations.* Oxford: Oxford University Press.

—. 1865. *Our Mutual Friend.* Oxford: Oxford University Press.

Eliot, G. 1985 (1871). *Middlemarch*. New York: Penguin.

—. 1885. Letter to Charles Bray, July 5, 1859. In *George Eliot's Life as Related in Her Letters and Journals*. Vol 3. Tauchnitz: Leipzig.

Forster, John. 1872-74. *Life of Charles Dickens*. 3 vols. London: Chapman and Hall.

Fraser's Magazine. 1840. 21 (April 1840): 400.

Gardner, J. 1979. *On Moral Fiction*. New York: Perseus.

Gilligan, C. 1982. *In A Different Voice*. Cambridge: Harvard University Press.

Higginson, T. W. 1863. *Out of Door Papers*. Boston: Ticknor and Fields.

Holland, J. G. 1872. "Topics of the Time," *Century Magazine*, 5 (1): 763.

Hornback, B. 1988. *Middlemarch: A Novel of Reform*. New York: Twayne, 1988.

Hughes, L. K. and Lund, M. 1991. *The Victorian Sequel*. Charlottesville: University Press of Virginia. 11.

Jacobs, J. 1891. *Essays and Reviews*, London: Macmillan. 39-41.

Johnson, E. 1952. *Charles Dickens: His Tragedy and Triumph*. 2 vols. New York: Simon and Schuster.

Keen, S. 2007. *Empathy and the Novel*. Oxford: Oxford University Press,

Kidder, P. 2009. *Philosophy and Literature* 33.2 (October 2009): 417-26.

Kohlberg, L. 1981. *Essays in Moral Development*. San Francisco: Harper and Row.

Kucich, J. 1981. *Excess and Restraint in the Novels of Charles Dickens*. Athens: University of Georgia Press.

Marx, K. 1854. "The English Middle Class," in *New York Tribune* (August 1, 1854): 4.

McCarthy, J. 1874. *Massie—A Romance*. New York: Sheldon and Company.

Mill, J. S. 1854. Letter to Harriet Taylor. March 20, 1854. Collins, P. (ed.) 1971. *Charles Dickens: The Critical Heritage*. London: Routledge and Kegan Paul.

Miller, D. A. 1983. "Discipline in Different Voices: Bureaucracy, Police, Family and *Bleak House*", *Representations*, 1: 58-89.

Miller, J. H. 1958. *Charles Dickens: The World of His Novels*. Cambridge, MA: Harvard University Press.

—. 1998. *Reading Narrative*. Norman: Oklahoma University Press. 158-77.

Nack, J. 1859. *Poems*. New York: Delisser and Procter.

New York Society Library. Circulation Registers.

Nussbaum, Martha. 1995. *Poetic Justice: The Literary Imagination and Public Life*. Boston: Beacon Press.

Okker, P. 2003. *Social Stories*. Charlottesville: University of Virginia Press.

Phillips, D. Z. 1998. *Studies in Philosophy and Education*, 17: 193-206.

Plotz, J. 1996. "A Sympathetic Social Science", *Novel: A Forum on Fiction*, 30 (1): 132-34.

Rawls, J. 1971. *A Theory of Justice*. Cambridge: Harvard University Press.

Rilke, R. M. 2001. *Letters to a Young Poet*. New York: Random House.

Rorty, R. 1989. *Contingency, Irony and Solidarity*. Cambridge: Cambridge University Press.

Rose, A. C. 1992. *Victorian America in the Civil War*. Cambridge: Cambridge University Press.

Santayana, G. 1921. *Soliloquies in England and Later Soliloquies*. New York: Charles Scribner's Sons.

Spalding, J. 1875. E*ssays and Reviews*. New York: Catholic Publications Society.

Todorov, T. 1984. *Mikhail Bakhtin: The Dialogical Principle*. Trans. W. Godzich. Minneapolis: University of Minnesota Press.

Waters, C. 2005. "Reforming Culture", in R. L. Patten and J. Bowen (eds), *Charles Dickens Studies*. London and New York: Palgrave.

Wilde, O. 1891. Preface to *The Picture of Dorian Gray*. London: Folio.

Wilson, E. 1941. *The Wound and the Bow: Seven Studies in Literature*. Boston: Houghton Mifflin.

LITERATURE, THEORY AND THE BEATIFIC EFFECTS OF READING

BECKY MCLAUGHLIN

Growing up in the 1970s in the southern United States, or the "Bible Belt", I was exposed to a Christian coffeehouse scene whose Friday night meetings involved musical entertainment by rock groups such as God's Power and Light Company, followed by a sermon with a big emotional wind-up, the grand finale of which was an altar call. During one such meeting, I was moved to raise my hand in response to the preacher's inevitable question, "Do ya wanna be saved?" Oh, yes, I thought, for I was sure that my twelve-year-old soul was as black as the hell I envisioned every night as I tried desperately and generally unsuccessfully to escape into sleep. And so overcoming my timidity, I found myself making the trek to the altar and joining hands with the preacher. After we had "prayed together" (which really amounted to his praying and my listening in a kind of cloyed awe), I was asked to commit to reading the Bible every day. I kept my promise for the next several years, dutifully beginning on page one and proceeding through the text without skipping a word. But I must confess that what I called "reading" degenerated into merely allowing my eyes to pass over the black marks on the page, and the number of black marks grew fewer and fewer as the years passed. At this point, I found myself in a dilemma. Although I had begun to doubt that reading the Bible in this mechanical way was the key to salvation, I was afraid that breaking my promise would only make slimmer my already slim chances of avoiding hell. And thus I had become the most pathetic of readers, bound to the book, clinging solely to the letter of the law.

What this anecdote illustrates is a pedagogical failure on the preacher's part, which I began to intuit as I continued with his curricular directive. Although he may have chosen the proper textbook for a course on salvation, he had failed to instruct me in the proper way to read it. His certainty regarding the location of the salvific effects—i.e., in the words on the pages of a sacred text such as the Bible—blinded him to the possibility that these salvific effects might be located elsewhere—i.e., in the kind of engagement a reader brings to bear on the text. Perhaps it is not too far off the mark to say that while the preacher had not yet gotten wind of the death of the Author, I was beginning to give birth to myself as a Reader. Here, then, is a perfect illustration of that old critical controversy in which texts and selves, or Authors and Readers, fight for control of meaning.

I begin with this rather humorous anecdote drawn from my childhood in order to set the stage for what I will be attempting to do in this paper: that is, to show a connection between reading literature and behaving ethically. Can literature teach readers to be better people? The answer to this question, for me, has always been an unqualified *yes*; in fact, my firm belief in the beneficial effects of reading literature is probably what led to my becoming an English professor. But despite this strongly-held belief, I have never been able to satisfactorily articulate *why* literature has the power to teach readers to be better people. Of course, it is easy enough to argue that reading has beneficial intellectual effects. But does reading have beneficial ethical effects? Does it have the power to make us fly in the face of contemporary capitalist society to embrace a beatific ethic that values difference as much as sameness, humility rather than hubris, generosity rather than greed, love rather than hate, and, maybe most importantly in our increasingly global community, accountability rather than irresponsibility?

It was only after I began teaching critical theory and, of necessity, having repeated encounters with what might be called a set of tutor texts that I began to find a fruitful way to frame an answer to this question. But in beginning to frame an answer, I also found myself having to qualify my previously unqualified, purely affirmative *yes*. What I now find myself wanting to argue is that not only are certain reading practices more ethical than others (i.e., it is not simply *reading* that makes us better people but a certain *practice* of reading) but also certain types of reading material may be more likely to lead to ethical behavior than others.

It is probably accurate to say that most of the literate world, with the exception of those who teach and study literature, takes reading for granted, not seeing anything particularly profound in the act of reading, merely viewing it as a useful tool, a means of collecting the information one needs when one finds oneself confronted with a certain set of circumstances—reading a road map in order to get from point A to point B; reading a service manual in order to assemble a new electronic device; reading a recipe in order to bake a cake—or of passing the time when one is bored. There are, however, situations in which reading is given a unique power not usually assigned it, and in these situations we see the potentially profound effects of reading: its ability to save or damn depending on how it is used.

Take Claude Chabrol's 1995 film, *La Cérémonie*, for example. Although reviewers have described the film as "a tale of murder, violence, and betrayal", I would argue that it is a meditation on the ethics of reading. An inability to read, a corrupt and careless reading practice, and a naïve misreading: each position is represented in the film *vis-à-vis* a character, and when the three come together, the result is murder and mayhem. (As early as Roland Barthes's publication of *S/Z* in 1970, we knew that a failure to re-read could lead to one's demise, but this is obviously a lesson that Chabrol's characters failed to learn in the intervening twenty-five years.)

When the wealthy Lelievre family hires Sophie as their maid, they think they have found in her a domestic gem, for Sophie quietly and efficiently goes about the household work of cleaning, cooking, and grocery shopping with not so much as one complaint. What the Lelievres do not know, and what will be the death of them quite literally, is that Sophie cannot read and that keeping this fact a secret is far more important to her than correcting the problem by learning to read. (In this respect, she is not unlike the cheating student whose act of plagiarism and attempts to cover the act exhaust just as much energy and as many resources as writing an original paper might have done.) Once Sophie has settled in with the Lelievres, she becomes fast friends with Jeanne, the local postmistress, who makes it a habit to open and read her postal customers' mail and who steals a book from the Lelievres' library, confusing O'Neill with Celine.

If Sophie's character represents an inability to read, which is a source of shame great enough to cause her to commit murder, then Jeanne's character represents a corrupt and careless reading practice, which makes her just cavalier enough to join in the carnage. As for the Lelievres, they are wealthy and educated, but they are not sophisticated readers, for they read one part of the Sophie-Jeanne text and ignore the other. If we were to use terms supplied by phenomenologist Wolfgang Iser, we might say that the loquacious Jeanne represents the written part of a text, which gives the Lelievres knowledge, and that the laconic Sophie represents the unwritten part, which allows the Lelievres to use their imagination in order to picture things. In short, Jeanne represents the words, sentences, and paragraphs, while Sophie represents what Iser refers to as the gaps or blanks between, *all* of which are essential to the reading process and to the creation of the literary work, which, in Iser's model, resides in a virtual space between the artistic and aesthetic poles of text and reader. Or, to put it in Sartrean terms, we might say that Jeanne represents "the hundred thousand words aligned in a book [which] can be read one by one so that the meaning of the work does not emerge" (Sartre, 1965: 38), while Sophie represents the silence, the inexpressible, the void between the landmarks set up by the author of a text. If the Lelievres had given the same amount of attention to reading the taciturn Sophie as they gave to reading the garrulous Jeanne, they might have saved themselves from slaughter in their own home.

Let us say, then, that Chabrol's film can be read as a cautionary tale about the necessity of careful, sophisticated reading. But how does one go about becoming such a reader, especially when the "educational package" has assumed the shape of a consumer product to be delivered as efficiently and cheaply as possible to a student population? It has been over thirty years since Walker Percy published *The Message in the Bottle* (1977), but what he was saying then seems even more apropos of today, for his biggest gripe, at least in the chapter entitled "The Loss of the Creature," is that we have become consumers who purchase pre-packaged knowledge rather than knowledge-seekers who exercise intellectual sovereignty, an exercise allowing us to stake a claim in our world and thus to care about it. Although Percy does not explicitly say so, the troubling implications of his argument are clear: when we give up our sovereignty, we also give up accountability for our actions and their effects. Using the example of a tourist at the Grand Canyon, Percy argues that in a modern technical society, the tourist is deprived of an authentic encounter with the Grand Canyon because of the way in which this natural wonder has been packaged and sold: "The very means by which the thing is presented for consumption, the very techniques by which the thing is made available as an item of need-satisfaction, these very means operate to remove the thing from the sovereignty of the knower" (1977: 62). This same type of deprivation occurs in the classroom, argues Percy, because of the educational package in which something such as a dogfish or sonnet is presented. The teacher, the textbook, and even the classroom itself are part of the package and thus obscure rather than reveal the object of study.

Perhaps this deprivation goes unnoticed by the tourist and the student because of its very nature, for what the tourist and the student are being deprived of is meaning that emerges from "*a reading encounter*, and in an interpretive moment within that encounter" (Bloom, 1979: 5). In other words, the tourist and the student are no longer involved in the work of reading and thus of interpreting the Grand Canyon, the dogfish, or the sonnet; they are simply purchasing and consuming an already-prepared reading and interpretation made by the experts and planners. But as Jean-Paul Sartre points out in "Why Write?",

It has often been observed that an object in a story does not derive its density of existence from the number and length of the descriptions devoted to it, but from the complexity of its connections with the different characters. The more often the characters handle it, take it up, and put it down, in short, go beyond it towards their own ends, the more real will it appear. (1965: 55)

Because tourists at the Grand Canyon believe they are there to get away from their jobs and students of English or biology think themselves clever in finding ways to avoid their assignments, it would never occur to either that in failing to "handle" the object (whether it be the Grand Canyon, a dogfish, or a sonnet), they have given up the very thing they have come in search of, ceasing to be sovereign wayfarers and becoming instead consumers of prefabricated experiences. Although Percy is somewhat pessimistic about reclaiming the "creature" in the "preformed complex" of the traditional classroom, he does make some suggestions as to how this might be accomplished, one of which is the surprise encounter. He suggests, for example, that the biology teacher place a Shakespeare sonnet on his students' dissecting boards and that the English teacher startle her students with a dogfish.

According to Percy, the surprise encounter interrupts the operation of the symbolic complex, which mediates or, worse yet, obstructs any encounter between sovereign knower and thing-to-be-known, and thus a girl who squats in the azalea bushes outside someone's window, drawn there in order to listen to the strains of Beethoven issuing from within, will be more likely to hear the music than the people seated comfortably around the record-player. An example of the squatting girl is the experimental artist, musician, philosopher, and poet John Cage, who made getting lost a way of life. According to Joan Retallack, Cage was at his happiest when he "genuinely [did] not know where the processes he had set in motion would lead. This was not in order to produce the market value of an 'original' commodity, but to move into a zone of unintelligibility, the only place where the possibility of discovery lies, where the future is not at the outset already a thing of the past" (1996: xxvi).

If we were to speak in slightly different but nevertheless related terms about what Percy calls the "symbolic complex" and what Cage calls the "zone of unintelligibility," we might assert that the machinations of the symbolic complex give rise to belief, while a traversal of the zone of unintelligibility leads to thought. Although belief "is frequently assumed to turn upon conscious assent, or [...] upon 'the acceptance of a proposition, statement, or fact as true, on the ground of authority or evidence'" (Silverman, 1992: 17), Kaja Silverman argues that belief "is granted not at the level of consciousness, but rather at that of fantasy and the ego or *moi*" (1992: 16), and thus it is based on illusion rather than reality. We find an excellent illustration of the opposition between belief and thought in Henrik Ibsen's play *Ghosts*, during a conversation between Pastor Manders and Mrs. Alving about unchallenged belief and reading as its corrective:

> MRS. ALVING. [...] It's not just what we inherit from our mothers and fathers that haunts us. It's all kinds of old defunct theories, all sorts of old defunct beliefs, and things like that. It's not that they *live* on in us; they are simply lodged there, and we cannot get rid of them. I've only been to pick up a newspaper and I seem to see ghosts gliding between the lines. Over the whole country must be ghosts, as numerous as the sands of the sea. And there we are, all of us, abysmally afraid of the light.
> MANDERS. Aha! So there we see the fruits of your reading. And a nice harvest it is, I must say. Oh, these disgusting, free-thinking pamphlets! Revolting!
> MRS. ALVING. You are wrong, my dear Pastor. You were the one who goaded me into doing some thinking. And I shall always be grateful to you for that.
> MANDERS. *I* did!
> MRS. ALVING. Yes, when you forced me to submit to what you called my duty and my obligations. When you praised as right and proper what my whole mind revolted against, as against some loathsome thing. It was then I began to examine the fabric of your teachings. I began picking at one of the knots, but as soon as I'd got that undone, the whole thing came apart at the seams. It was then I realized it was just tacked together. (1981: 126-27)

Yet another illustration of the opposition between belief and thought turns up in George Bernard Shaw's *Man and Superman* when Roebuck Ramsden forbids his young ward to read *The Revolutionist's Handbook*, while Jack Tanner encourages her to read it and make up her own mind about its contents. What these plays suggest is that one must be allowed to examine and challenge inherited belief in order to determine what one thinks and, in turn, how one should behave. Because one must be allowed to not know before one knows, adopting doubt as both a pedagogical and philosophical stance opens up a hole or gap through which knowledge can emerge, a hole or gap that certainty clogs up. Just as religious faith is based on doubt, so too is knowledge. So, too, is the beatific ethic for which I am arguing.

When students or teachers work from a position of certainty rather than of doubt, the goal in the study of literature becomes absolute mastery of the text, the presentation of the final word or definitive reading. But if anything kills or deadens a text, it is the drive for mastery on the part of a reader. For mastery does not delight in difference or oddity; it seeks to dominate and subdue, to bring power to bear on knowledge. An example of how occupying the position of "Master" or "subject presumed to know" can lead to destructive consequences is eloquently articulated in George Orwell's famous essay, "Shooting An Elephant," in which he tells the story of killing an elephant that has rampaged through a Burmese village. As a British police officer in a colonized country, Orwell is called to intervene when an elephant gets out of control, and although he knows as soon as he sees the elephant that its attack of "must" is over, he feels compelled, against his better judgment, to shoot the elephant because of the large crowd of Burmese who have turned out to watch:

> Here was I, the white man with his gun, standing in front of the unarmed native crowd—seemingly the leading actor of the piece; but in reality I was only an absurd puppet pushed to and fro by the will of those yellow faces behind. I perceived in this moment that when the white man turns tyrant it is his own freedom that he destroys. He becomes a sort of hollow, posing dummy, the conventionalized figure of a sahib. For it is the condition of his rule that he shall spend his life in trying to impress the "natives," and so in every crisis he has got to do what the "natives" expect of him. (1990: 292)

If we transfer this narrative into the classroom, it is easy to see what the implications are. In the master-slave dialectic as Orwell has depicted it, we teachers become the British police, our students the expectant Burmese, and whatever text we are studying, the elephant. Given this scenario, we can only assume that the student masses hope to see us shoot the text by aiming one unequivocal reading at its great, pulsing heart. We can only assume that our students want us to suppress the surplus energy of the text (its "must") and that the only way to avoid their contemptuous laughter is by shutting down the large and complex machinery through which a text operates. But everyone loses when the elephant sinks down into the mud and trumpets no more.

One of the theorists I have found most useful in keeping the elephant alive and trumpeting is Roland Barthes. In fact, his ideas and Barbara Johnson's lucid and generous gloss of them have become central to my understanding of what constitutes an ethical reading practice. With writing he describes as "controlled accident," Barthes embraces doubt and uncertainty as well as otherness. In fact, he runs along a track parallel to Percy and Cage when he argues in *S/Z* that it is only through rereading one can escape consumerism and move beyond the status quo of what one already knows:

> Rereading, an operation contrary to the commercial and ideological habits of our society, which would have us "throw away" the story once it has been consumed ("devoured"), so that we can then move on to another story, buy another book which is tolerated only in certain marginal categories of readers (children, old people, and professors), rereading is here suggested at the outset, for it alone saves the text from repetition (those who fail to reread are obliged to read the same story everywhere). (1974: 15-16)

Johnson's gloss of this passage in "The Critical Difference: BartheS/ BalZac" (1980) implies that Barthes's take on rereading is useful for combating narcissism and its hostility toward alterity.   As Johnson explains, for Barthes, "difference" means difference *within* a single book, not difference *between* two or more books: "Far from constituting the text's unique identity, [difference] is that which subverts the very idea of identity, infinitely deferring the possibility of adding up the sum of a text's parts or meanings and reaching a totalized, integrated whole" (1980: 4). And thus one could say, as Johnson does, that reading a text only once is a narcissistic experience because "what we can see in the text the first time is already in us, not in it" (1980: 3).   When we read a book only once, it becomes a mere echo or reflection of ourselves.   We see what we already know; the text we read is none other than our own.   In order to see the text as "other," as well as to see the text's otherness from itself, we must reread it rather than throwing it away and consuming a new one.   It may sound stupidly hyperbolic to say that a failure to reread leads to death, and yet it is precisely our narcissism, our failure to reread, that leads to the death of many a relationship. Certainly, this is the case for Balzac's character, the sculptor Sarrasine, who meets his death because he is unwilling to read the Italian castrato, La Zambinella, in terms other than his own narcissistic fantasies.   In other words, Sarrasine's passion is based on ignorance rather than knowledge, misrecognizing a castrated man for a woman, and on his deluded image of the opera singer as his binary opposite, the Galatea to his Pygmalion.   Sadly, when his foolish illusion is shattered and he threatens his "beloved" with bodily harm, La Zambinella's bodyguards rush in and kill him.

   If we were to understand difference as Barthes does and read as he suggests, the implications for our interpersonal relationships are great. I cannot but think that the application of these theoretical insights could actually help us read friends, family members, lovers, and everyone we encounter more effectively and magnanimously, for we would return again and again to the same friend, family member, or lover in a gesture of fidelity that engages the more rigorous practice of the art of understanding as laid out by nineteenth-century theologian Friedrich Schleiermacher: "The more lax practice of the art of understanding [...] proceeds on the assumption that understanding arises naturally. [...] The more rigorous practice proceeds on the assumption that misunderstanding arises naturally, and that understanding must be intended and sought at each point" (Gadamer, 1976: xiii). We would also cease to assume that people can be summed up or stereotyped, for we would know that people are always greater than the sum of their parts since something (what Jacques Lacan might call *objet petit a*; R. D. Laing, the "no-thing"; or Barthes, difference) always eludes observation and thus remains unsymbolizable.

One of the insights Barthes and Johnson allow us to grasp is that "difference" and "identification" are fraught with problems when understood as absolute terms or thought of separately rather than as part of a dialectical process through which we move beyond the narcissism of our personal text to engagement with another or the other. As I have examined these terms more carefully, it has begun to seem to me that housed within each is a dialectical operation already at work. For example, "identification" has in itself the possibility of difference in that identification is a metaphorical gesture involving the bringing together of disparate objects. One begins not by saying this *is* that but this is *not* that, and yet, with some effort, points of comparison can be found, and so even though love is an abstract concept and the flower a material thing, one can compare the two in a metaphorical gesture of identification. Likewise, in "difference" is housed identification, for when we want to emphasize difference, we say, "it's like comparing apples and oranges," and yet both are fruits and both round. In order to see difference, there must be a starting point of sameness from which we begin to elaborate how this is *not* that. Understanding these sometimes (or perhaps all too frequently) divisive terms as part of a dialectic could, I think, allow us to find common ground with those different from ourselves and to find something different in those we assume to be just like us.

Johnson also calls attention to the "major polarity" Barthes uses to evaluate a text, "the readerly versus the writerly":

> The readerly is constrained by considerations of representation: it is irreversible, "natural," decidable, continuous, totalizable, and unified into a coherent whole based on the signified. The writerly is infinitely plural and open to the free play of signifiers and of difference, unconstrained by

representative considerations, and transgressive of any desire for decidable, unified, totalized meaning. (1980: 5-6)

In regard to this polarity, what comes to mind is Simone de Beauvoir's chapter on myth and reality in *The Second Sex* (1968). A readerly approach poses Woman as the Eternal Feminine, a Platonic Ideal by which flesh-and-blood women are measured and of which they always fall short. A writerly approach, on the other hand, poses the "dispersed, contingent, and multiple existence of actual women" (1968: 253). The readerly assumes texts (and people) to be static, while the writerly assumes texts (and people) to be dynamic. If we were to adopt a writerly rather than a readerly approach, we would "no longer [be] a consumer, but a producer of the text" (Barthes, 1974: 4). What this means when applied to interpersonal relationships is that we would understand our reading of others as part of a dialectical exchange, a situation in which the attitude and behavior with which we approach other people help shape not just how we view them but who they are and how they view us. Thinking about reading as part of a dialectic is both frightening and wonderful because it puts squarely on our own shoulders a tremendous amount of responsibility for how we treat and, in turn, are treated by others.

Although Barthes is not always recognized as a phenomenologist, what he says about the writerly text and rereading sounds akin to the phenomenology of someone such as Iser, author of *The Implied Reader*, who argues that the "moment we try to impose a consistent pattern on the text, discrepancies are bound to arise. [...] And it is their very presence that draws us into the text, compelling us to conduct a creative examination not only of the text but also of ourselves" (1974: 290). While we tend to think of discrepancies, inconsistencies, or contradictions as undesirable, they are, from this perspective, what draw us to a text (or a person) and bring it to life. To be in perfect accord with oneself, to have no split, other, seam, gap, or pucker, would make one an automaton. And if discrepancies are cause for self-examination, surely discrepancies are all to the good. Iser further argues that the "efficacy of a literary text is brought about by the apparent evocation and subsequent negation of the familiar. [...] And it is only when we have outstripped our preconceptions and left the shelter of the familiar that we are in a position to gather new experiences" (1974: 290). Here, Iser is articulating something very similar to Lacan's notion of occupying a position of non-mastery, for Iser, like Lacan, is advocating an acceptance of the unfamiliar, the new experience not yet mastered, the landscape of otherness.

What I find most appealing about the phenomenologist's approach to reading is that it generally involves an interest in and embracing of alterity (whether the altern is represented as an "alien consciousness" or unfamiliar experiences and ideas does not really matter), which is articulated in terms of collaboration rather than opposition between reader and writer and/or text. Again, if we were to adopt the model offered by phenomenology for reading people, no doubt our interpersonal relationships would take a turn for the better. In fact, in a passage that sounds downright utopian, Georges Poulet argues that the ideal of criticism is represented by the street celebration or rustic feast: "There is a milieu or a moment in the feast in which everyone communicates with everyone else, in which hearts are open like books. On a more modest scale, doesn't the same phenomenon occur in reading? Does not one being open its innermost self? Is not the other being enchanted by this opening?" (2001: 1329).

When one first encounters Poulet's "Phenomenology of Reading", one may be put off by the title, which suggests nothing if not a musty, old philosophical tome out of step with today's concerns. And yet when one moves beyond the title into the first paragraph, one is immediately drawn into Poulet's essay—one is "gripped", to use Poulet's language—by the charming description he gives of the book's plight. Comparing books to animals in a pet store, Poulet says,

> When I see them on display, I look at them as I would at animals for sale, kept in little cages, and so obviously hoping for a buyer. [...] Made of paper and ink, they lie where they are put, until the moment some one shows an interest in them. They wait. Are they aware that an act of man might suddenly transform their existence? They appear to be lit up with that hope. Read me, they seem to say. (2001: 1320)

Because one enters Poulet's phenomenological world by way of a pet store, one immediately gets the sense that mysterious and magical phenomena lie just ahead, round the bend of the next paragraph. The experience of reading Poulet is not unlike what I imagine the experience of entering Narnia through the Professor's wardrobe must be like for C. S. Lewis's Pevensie children. The wardrobe, like Poulet's title, seems musty with its ancient fur coats and smell of mothballs, and yet it is the gateway to a land of fauns, talking beavers, witches, and black dwarves. And like the good and evil the Pevensies encounter in Narnia, one encounters both *heimlich* and *unheimlich* language in Poulet's articulation of what happens when one reads a book. Like Narnia, Poulet's phenomenological world of the book can be understood as an analogue of the split subject, as Lacan refers to the concept traditionally called the "self." For what the Penvensie children encounter in Narnia is the opportunity to confront themselves in the guise of the other. For example, Edmund's encounter with the White Witch in *The Lion, the Witch, and the Wardrobe* allows him to get acquainted with his selfish and gluttonous double, which would have remained a shadowy but profoundly influential stranger had it not been hauled out into the light during Edmund's stay with the White Witch. Poulet's reader is like Edmund in that the reader allows himself or herself to be inhabited by the other and thus to transform unconscious belief into conscious thought.

As one reads of Poulet's encounter with a book, one can feel him both marveling at the happy miracle of reading and struggling to accurately describe the nature of the relationship between perceiving subject (the reader) and perceived object (the book), and perhaps it is his simultaneous marveling and struggling that accounts for the uncanny nature of his description, his strange oscillation between language cozy and friendly on the one hand, hostile and predatory on the other. For instance, when he holds a book in his hands, he says,

> I am aware of a rational being, of a consciousness; the consciousness of another, no different from the one I automatically assume in every human being I encounter, except that in this case the consciousness is open to me, welcomes me, lets me look deep inside itself, and even allows me, with unheard-of license, to think what it thinks and feel what it feels. (2001: 1321)

What Poulet describes, here, is a kind of human communion or contact that many long for but few, if any, ever achieve. And yet, according to Poulet, it is possible to experience such closeness, such at-one-ness, with the consciousness that emerges from a book. But when he begins to disclose where this consciousness resides—i.e., in one's innermost self— the world he describes becomes strangely claustrophobic. Because an "interior object" such as a book depends upon the consciousness of a reader to provide shelter for its mental entities or significations, it takes up residence, makes itself at home in the mind of the reader: "As soon as I replace my direct perception of reality by the words of a book, I deliver myself, bound hand and foot to the omnipotence of fiction. [...] I surround myself with fictitious beings; I become the prey of language. There is no escaping this take-over. Language surrounds me with its unreality" (2001: 1322). He reconciles what appear to be opposing views of the relationship between perceiving subject and perceived object, however, when he says, "[b]ecause of the strange invasion of my person by the thoughts of another, I am a self who is granted the experience of thinking thoughts foreign to him. I am the subject of thoughts other than my own" (2001: 1322). The implications of Poulet's statement are profound and radical in the same way Christ's command that we love our enemies and turn the other cheek are, for Poulet is suggesting that there are benefits to be gained when we allow ourselves to be invaded by the thoughts of another. There is in Poulet's moving account of reading a generosity on the part of the reader, who acts as host or shelter for the homeless "alien consciousness" of the writer: "Reading is just that: a way of giving way not only to a host of alien words, images, ideas, but also to the very alien principle which utters them and shelters them" (2001: 1323).

No discussion of ethical reading practices would be complete without giving attention to Sartre's beatific "Why Write?", for it is with Sartre's existential version of phenomenology that we see generosity and cooperation at their height. Although he argues that "[o]ne of the chief motives of artistic creation is certainly the need of feeling that we are essential in relationship to the world" (1965: 33), this need to feel essential does not result in egoism, narcissism, or solipsism; for, according to Sartre, the art object one creates is not created for oneself but for others: "the operation of writing implies that of reading as its dialectical correlative and these two connected acts necessitate two distinct agents. It is the joint effort of author and reader which brings upon the scene that concrete and imaginary object which is the work of the mind" (1965: 37). If in Poulet's articulation of reading, one loses any sense of barriers or borders between oneself and the book, in Sartre's articulation the two agents remain separate but in relationship. And for the relationship to operate as it should, there must be generosity and tact on the part of both agents:

> If I appeal to my reader so that we may carry to a successful conclusion the enterprise which I have begun, it is self-evident that I consider him as a pure freedom, as an unconditioned activity; thus, in no case can I address myself to his passiveness, that is, try to *affect* him, to communicate to him, from the very first, emotions of fear, desire, or anger. [...] Freedom is alienated in the state of passion [...]. The writer should not seek to *overwhelm*. (1965: 43)

Sartre is not arguing here or elsewhere that a writer should have no passion; he is simply arguing that when one writes, one must step back from one's feelings in order to avoid manipulating one's reader. In fact, he speaks of reading as

> a Passion, in the Christian sense of the word, that is, a freedom which resolutely puts itself into a state of passiveness to obtain a certain transcendent effect by this sacrifice. The reader renders himself credulous; he descends into credulity which, though it ends by enclosing him like a

dream, is at every moment conscious of being free. [...] Thus, the reader's feelings are never dominated by the object [...]. And just as activity has rendered itself passive in order for it better to create the object, conversely, passiveness becomes an act; the man who is reading has raised himself to the highest degree. (1965: 44-45)

In Sartre's articulation of the dialectical relationship between writer and reader, there is joint responsibility for the universe created in and/or by the world of the novel. And here we begin to move beyond a consideration of what constitutes an ethical reading practice to what constitutes ethical reading material. For Sartre, "there are only good and bad novels," the former an "act of faith" and the latter an act of flattery (1965: 57). "It would be inconceivable," says Sartre, "that this unleashing of generosity provoked by the writer could be used to authorize an injustice, and that the reader could enjoy his freedom while reading a work which approves or accepts or simply abstains from condemning the subjection of man by man" (1965: 57). The kind of literature Sartre is advocating is one that would stir readers to action rather than support an unexamined belief system or allow for complacency. One would not be able to walk away from a novel about injustice but would be forced to work toward correcting it. In words that sound more akin to poetry than prose, more akin to the words of a benediction or marriage vow than literary criticism, Sartre argues thus:

the writer's universe will only reveal itself in all its depth to the examination, the admiration, and the indignation of the reader; and the generous love is a promise to maintain, and the generous indignation is a promise to change, and the admiration a promise to imitate; although literature is one thing and morality a quite different one, at the heart of the aesthetic imperative we discern the moral imperative. (1965: 56-57)

As for me, I can speculate only very tentatively about what form an ethical literature might take. If we believe as Poulet does that ideas "pass from one mind to another as coins pass from hand to hand" but that during their sojourn in my mind, "I assert myself as subject of these ideas; I am the subjective principle for whom the ideas serve for the time being as the predications" (2001: 1322-23), then we have before us the possibility of entering the identity and thus the predicament of the abject or downtrodden other: William Faulkner's Benji (*The Sound and the Fury*), Jamaica Kincaid's Xuela (*The Autobiography of My Mother*), Clarice Lispector's Macabéa (*The Hour of the Star*), and Yukio Mishima's Kochan (*Confessions of a Mask*), to name but a few. For those of us who are part of mainstream middle-class society, perhaps it would be an ethical act to choose books narrated by those with whom we seldom have reason to identify, much less rub shoulders. Perhaps occupying the position of the other, at least during the act of reading, would make it possible for us to behave more charitably, mercifully, or lovingly toward those whose lives are different from our own.

Although I am much less confident about the validity of what I shall say last, I want to propose it merely as food for thought. In John Berger's *Ways of Seeing*, he points out that the convention of perspective established during the early Renaissance "centres everything on the eye of the beholder" (1991: 16) as if to suggest that the beholder is the unique centre of the world. With the convention of perspective, the "visible world is arranged for the spectator as the universe was once thought to be arranged for God" (1991: 16). The problem with perspective, however, is that it contains an inherent contradiction, structuring "all images of reality to address a single spectator who, unlike God, could only be in one place at a time" (1991:16). Once the camera was invented, this contradiction became apparent, and with the movie camera, in particular, it became possible to demonstrate that there was no centre (1991: 18). The question I would like to pose is whether novels and/or works of literature that make use of something other than a Renaissance perspective—for example, Cubism—might constitute an ethical literature. As Berger argues, "For the Cubists the visible was no longer what confronted the single eye, but the totality of possible views taken from points all around the object (or person) being depicted" (1991: 18). A literature that allows one to operate under the illusion that one is the centre of the universe might support egoism, narcissism, and perhaps even solipsism, while a literature that engages not just the single view (or eye) but multiple views (or eyes) might just lead to a "possible felicity in history" to use the words of Luce Irigaray (1996): an understanding of as well as compassion and sympathy for those who occupy a point of view different from our own.

References

Barthes, R. 1974. *S/Z*. Trans. Richard Miller. New York: Hill and Wang.

Beauvoir, Simone de. 1968. *The Second Sex*. Ed. and Trans. H. M. Parshley. New York: Alfred A. Knopf.

Berger, J., *et al.* 1991. *Ways of Seeing*. London: British Broadcasting Corporation and Penguin Books.

Bloom, H., *et al.* 1979. *Deconstruction & Criticism*. New York: Seabury Press.

Faulkner, W. 1993. *The Sound and the Fury*. New York: Norton.

Felman, S. 1985. *Writing and Madness (Literature / Philosophy / Psychoanalysis)*. Ithaca, NY: Cornell University Press.

Gadamer, H-G. 1976. *Philosophical Hermeneutics*. Ed. and Trans. David E. Linge. Berkeley: University of California Press.

Ibsen, H. 1981. *Four Major Plays*. Trans. James McFarlane and Jens Arup. Oxford: Oxford University Press.

Irigaray, L. 1996. *I Love to You: Sketch of a Possible Felicity in History*. New York: Routledge.

Iser, W. *The Implied Reader: Patterns of Communication in Prose Fiction from Bunyan to Beckett*. Baltimore: Johns Hopkins University Press.

Johnson, B. 1980. *The Critical Difference: Essays in the Contemporary Rhetoric of Reading*. Baltimore: Johns Hopkins University Press.

Lispector, C. 1986. *The Hour of the Star*, Trans. G. Pontiero. New York: New Directions.

Kinkaid, J. 1996. *The Autobiography of My Mother*. New York: Penguin.

Mishima, Y. 1958. *Confessions of a Mask*. Trans. M. Weatherby. New York: New Directions.

Orwell, G. 'Shooting an Elephant' in D. Hunt (ed.), *The Dolphin Reader*. Boston: Houghton Mifflin Company.

Percy, W. 1975. *The Message in the Bottle: How Queer Man Is, How Queer Language Is, and What One Has to Do with the Other*. New York: Farrar, Straus and Giroux.

Poulet, G. "Phenomenology of Reading" in V. Leitch (ed.), *The Norton Anthology of Theory and Criticism*. New York: Norton.

Retallack, J. 1996. *Musicage: Cage Muses on Art Music Words*. Hanover: Wesleyan University Press.

Sartre, J-P. 1965. *What Is Literature?* Trans. Bernard Frechtman. New York: Harper & Row.

Silverman, K. 1992. *Male Subjectivity at the Margins*. New York: Routledge.

"Familiar Hearts":
Metaphor and the Ethics
of Intersectionality
in Contemporary Women's Fiction

Susan Alice Fischer

Influenced by feminist and other progressive social movements, contemporary women's fiction often envisions a more just world. Such writing draws upon the concept of intersectionality—the recognition of the non-hierarchal and relational nature of identity and the need to oppose oppression in all its forms—as it presents the possibility of justice. That contemporary women's novels concern themselves with ethical issues has been seen most obviously recently in *On Beauty* (2005), as Zadie Smith takes her title from philosopher Elaine Scarry's *On Beauty and Being Just* (1999), which highlights, as does Smith's novel, the connection between beauty and ethical behaviour. While Scarry posits that beauty can and does lead to more just action in the world, Smith illustrates this premise through images of paintings and of music which induce empathy in the viewer or listener and in so doing evoke action which is more just in terms of attempting to redress social inequities. In her novel, Smith opposes a worldview based on hierarchical binary oppositions in favour of one that, in recognising beauty in all ethnic, sexual, gender, class and national identities, brings us closer to justice. In contemporary women's fiction more generally, the notion of justice is often rooted in a feminist struggle towards a more equitable social, economic and political system which takes into account the intersections of diverse aspects of identity.

A feminist ethics emphasising intersectionality also underpins texts with less obvious philosophical references. Numerous contemporary women's novels base their ethical vision on empathy and connection across difference and attempt to ensure that diverse voices are heard. This tendency surfaces in contemporary fiction by authors of various backgrounds, from Andrea Levy, Maggie Gee, Hanan al-Shaykh and Sarah Waters in the UK to Gloria Naylor, Dorothy Allison and Toni

Morrison in the US, all of whom are influenced by and represent a concern with intersectionality in their work. That they are of different backgrounds and nationalities underscores the transnational nature of contemporary feminist discourse. The ethical and political stance of such writing determines in part the rhetorical choices these writers make, in particular with regard to metaphors of connection and revised notions of community and through the extensive use of narration which draws on a multitude of voices and points-of-view.

During the 1980s and 1990s, discourses associated with intersectionality began circulating in feminism in response to the failure of "second-wave feminism" to consider the complexities of women's identities and experiences, and especially in reaction to the assumption that all women's experiences were like those of the mostly white, middle-class, Christian (in background, if not practice), heterosexual, able-bodied women whose voices dominated the movement in the 1960s and 1970s. Considerable tensions arose as women with other experiences made their objections heard and argued that they had to struggle against racism, classism, homophobia and other forms of oppression as well as against misogyny. Indeed, gender inequality plays out differently according to one's social positioning with regard to all aspects of identity. While in more recent years a body of scholarship has arisen around the term "intersectionality"—a politics and an ethics that recognises, among other things, the non-hierarchal nature of oppression and the need to oppose it in all its forms—earlier iterations show that this concern has been high on the agenda for some time, coming to the fore in the 1980s. For instance, in her 1984 essay "Age, Race, Class, and Sex: Women Redefining Difference", Audre Lorde refers to herself as "a forty-nine-year-old Black lesbian feminist socialist mother of two, including one boy, and a member of an interracial couple" (2004: 854) to highlight that different contexts shift the terrain of the complexities of multiple social locations. Lorde does not use the term "intersectionality" here, but her point of view contributes to the theoretical perspective.

The idea of intersectionality emerged more fully with such authors as Kimberly Crenshaw, whose critical race theory recognises "the production and reproduction of inequalities, dominance, and oppression" in the legal arena (Shields, 2008: 303). And indeed the idea, if not always the term, has been key to feminist thought in the past few decades as writers from a range of disciplines have adopted it in an attempt to move away from a gender-dominant feminism and towards the general notion of what Andersen and Hill Collins term "interlocking categories of experience [which] emerged out of a growing recognition that it is not possible to separate out the categories of gender, race, class, and sexuality, nor to explain inequalities through a single framework" (Valentine, 2007: 12). Stephanie A. Shields (2008) defines intersectionality as "the mutually constitutive relations among social identities" that "has become the central tenet of feminist thinking" and one that has become "the most important contribution of feminist theory to our present understanding of gender" (301). Intersectionality keeps a focus on multidimensional relations of power that can otherwise get lost with a focus on only one aspect of identity, such as gender or race (Shields, 2008: 302).

In her poetry and prose, Lorde argued early on that the future "may depend upon the ability of all women to identify and develop new definitions of power and new patterns of relating across difference" (2004: 859), and in so doing, one must not mistake the "need for unity [...] as a need for homogeneity" (857), but rather make connections and form coalitions across difference. In literature, the idea has presented itself as part of various authors' visions for a more just society. In her essay "Metaphor and Memory" (originally published as "The Moral Necessity of Metaphor"), Cynthia Ozick (1996) makes a case for the regenerative power of a literature which fosters connection by focussing on its ethical (and political) dimensions:

> Through metaphor, the past has the capacity to imagine us, and we it. Through metaphorical concentration, doctors can imagine what it is to be their patients. Those who have no pain can imagine those who suffer. Those at the center can imagine what it is to be outside. The strong can imagine what it is to be weak. Illuminated lives can imagine the dark. Poets in their twilight can imagine the borders of stellar fire. We strangers can imagine the familiar hearts of strangers. (328-29)

This simple, yet powerful evocation of empathy is significant to the ways in which many contemporary women authors writing in a variety of contexts envisage a world in which women thrive by making connections across differences and imagine how they might redraw community based on a shared ethical vision for humanity. In so doing, they often cross temporal and other boundaries and reconstruct communities located outside the confines of time and space as they create metaphorical communities of affiliation. Indeed, metaphor is the primary figure of speech which represents this connection and this ethical position. Metaphor is a bearing of meaning across obvious boundaries. It functions because of association with what may often be more unlike than alike, but for one aspect which allows the metaphorical association of meaning to function. As such, it requires a leap of faith, what Gloria Anzaldúa (1987) calls a "tolerance for ambiguity". Made possible through shared, socially constructed associations, metaphor can also reconfigure those associations and posit new ones. While making new links, metaphor holds together the similar with the disparate. It is a connection necessary to creative thinking and to being able to move the mind, and often the heart and soul, beyond the expected. Metaphor thus changes thinking.[1] Ozick (1996) maintains "that metaphor is one of the chief agents of our moral nature, and that the more serious we are in life, the less we can do without it" (315).

Ozick (1996) argues for metaphor grounded in memory with "a base in a community model or a collective history" (322). She finds the "will to [...] harness metaphor for the sake of a universal conscience" (322) in the story of the Jews who, as a nation of former slaves, conceptualise, through metaphor, the most basic tenet of conscience in the sentence, "[l]ove thy neighbor as thyself" (324). This concept emerges, she argues, "because a moral connection has been made with the memory of bondage", epitomised in the phrase "[b]ecause you were strangers in the land of Egypt [...] a stranger you shall not oppress [...] for you know the heart of a stranger, seeing you were strangers in the land of Egypt" (325). She continues: "Without the metaphor of memory and history, we cannot imagine the life of the Other. [...] Metaphor [...] makes possible the power to envision the stranger's heart" (325).

Many contemporary women writers use this empathetic metaphor of boundary crossing as an underlying ethical vision for their work. For instance, in her award-winning 2004 novel, *Small Island*, Andrea Levy centres on the ability of characters to cross boundaries of difference as they imagine and begin to create a more ethical vision. A novel about the exclusionary treatment that Jamaicans of the Windrush Generation experienced upon migrating to England, it is also a novel which exposes and connects various sorts of discrimination—classism, anti-Semitism in Nazi Germany, racism in Britain and in the US, colonialism and sexism— in order to provide an alternative ethical vision of community and nation. Thus some of her characters are able to connect across the socially constructed boundaries that separate them. We see this perhaps most obviously in the unnamed white English woman who appears on a cold night to extend a kind hand to the black Jamaican character, Gilbert Joseph, just as he is feeling most weighed down by the racism he encounters in post-war London. In this allusion to the biblical story of the Good Samaritan, Levy suggests that empathy—the active manifestation of the metaphor of connection—is the first step in envisioning a more ethical and inclusive world. As feminism attempts to alter relations of power in society and as women writers articulate this desire through metaphors of connection, they are able to engage fully the dialectic—that is the social, political and transformative—nature of language. Metaphor—bearing across—not only enables them to "find their voices" but to imagine an ear —an interlocutor—receptive to their metaphors of shifting paradigms.

Engaged women writers and their protagonists struggle to straddle at least two worlds. They attempt to hold on to what is valuable in their worlds of origin through a metaphoric or symbolic connection to that world. The idealised vision of community is relegated to the realm of symbolic connection. Metaphors of connection enable a straddling between what is of value in traditional or lost communities and newly envisioned communities in which women can survive and even thrive. Writers thus develop metaphors of connection which allow them to create and tap into imagined communities which cross temporal boundaries. In this way, a literature which presents itself as profoundly ethical and transformative has emerged and recognised the "familiar hearts of strangers". For Ozick, memory—"because we were slaves in Egypt"— engenders metaphor:

> The great novels transform experience into idea because it is the way of metaphor to transform memory into a principle of continuity. By "continuity" I mean nothing less than literary seriousness which is unquestionably a branch of life-seriousness. (328)

In her novel, Levy draws not only on metaphor, that is on the ability to make connection across difference, but also on memory, here that of the Windrush Generation's experiences of Otherness—Ozick's "stranger"— upon arrival in London to imagine a more just world and a more inclusive sense of community and, specifically, of national identity. She does this, in part, through the novel's temporal shifts and most especially through the use of four different narrators whose stories interconnect: two heterosexual couples, one black Jamaican, one white-English. Through their interactions, she is able to alter the balance of power, to allow each character to tell his or her own story and to suggest ways in which "strangers" may connect.

Though writing from a very different place and sensibility, the white, working-class, Southern US, lesbian writer Dorothy Allison shares an ethical vision with both Ozick and Levy. In "A Question of Class", from her collection of essays, *Skin: Talking About Sex, Class and Literature*, Allison discusses her early perception of marginalisation, which she terms "the politics of *they*" (1994: 35) and which she understood because she was poor and abused. She sensed the objectification of the Other: "They're different from us, don't value human life the way we do" (13). As a child, she recognised early on that her people "were the *they* everyone talks about—the ungrateful poor. [...] I did not know who I was, only that I did not want to be *they*, the ones who are destroyed or dismissed to make the 'real' people, the important people, feel safer" (Allison, 1994: 13-14).

In an interview with Minnie Bruce Pratt, Allison talks about two communities: the one into which one is born and "the community in which you see yourself as a child" (Pratt, 1995). She explains the difference:

> The community I saw myself in—at the edge of the world—hated me. [...]
> But the community of affinity for me was the queer community—that
> outlaw community. And it was clear to me [...] by the time I was a
> teenager that I had more in common with black people who were in the
> civil-rights movement than I did with my stepfather. Especially when I got
> the shit kicked out of me. (Pratt, 1995)

Allison's "queer community" comprises more than sexual outsiders; it refers to the marginalised generally. Her creation of a place elsewhere is to be found at the points at which various marginalised groups overlap: it is a community of affiliation where "familiar hearts of strangers" can meet.

This ethical vision emerges clearly through the search for connection and community in Allison's first novel, *Bastard Out of Carolina* (1992). Autobiographical in emotional impact if not in all specifics, it tells the story of the struggle of a girl to survive in an abusive home and to keep what is left of herself intact. The protagonist, Ruth Anne Boatwright, better known as Bone, is essentially exiled and silenced by her miserable abuse at the hands of her stepfather, Daddy Glen. She senses that her mother, Anney, desperately needs Glen. "She needs him, needs him like a starving women needs meat between her teeth" (41), says one of Anney's sisters. Another replies, "He loves her like a gambler loves a fast racehorse or a desperate man loves whiskey" (41), thus completing this picture of dysfunctionalism. Because Bone cannot bear the thought of shattering her mother's illusions—and because she is afraid her mother will choose between them—she seeks outlets for her rage. In part, she enters a world of fantasy through her masturbatory dreams of fire, fury and control, through her desire to become a gospel singer and find her voice, cracked though it may be, through her continuous, but failed attempts at religious salvation, and through her story-telling, reading and imaginary games.

But in the outside world, Bone also attempts to ally herself with other Others, and it is through this insistence on connection with other oppressed people that Allison's feminist ethics become apparent. One of the first instances occurs in a short, but significant scene, when Bone visits her Aunt Alma, who had moved into an apartment building downtown where black people lived, and she sees herself in one of the children. Allison writes of a time which saw the rise of the Civil Rights Movement, yet she writes from a poor, white Southern child's perspective. Thus African American people remain shadow figures who are nonetheless extremely important to her sense of self. Race figures indirectly in the novel and racism is presented as analogous with the other forms of abuse with which the book deals directly. [2] Bone's mother, Anney, hates certain words and does not allow them to be used (32). These words—"bastard", "trash", "nigger", "ugly"—all denigrate the marginalised who make up the shadow community. Throughout the novel, the associations with others' experiences of marginalisation allow Bone to imagine survival. Without metaphor, Bone's isolation would have been complete. Without the metaphor of connection, Allison's ethical vision could not have emerged.

In a crucial scene in the novel, Bone is caught stealing candy from the local Woolworth's. Assuming that "trash" not only steals, but that Anney is incapable of disciplining her child properly, the store clerk augments Bone's punishment by telling her she "can't come back in here for a while" (97). Writing of a time and place in which African Americans were "barred from the Woolworth's [lunch] counters" (97-98), Allison again underlines Bone's affiliation with the marginalisation of the oppressed and in so doing presents an ethics of connection.

Allison makes these connections through literary references as well. She has said that "nothing ever hit [her] as hard as" Toni Morrison's *The Bluest Eye* (Pratt, 1995). Also about a young girl, Pecola, who is abused and thought to be ugly, Morrison's novel is "written with love and respect" (Pratt, 1995). In *The Bluest Eye*, Pecola wonders why a dandelion is considered an ugly weed:

> The dandelions at the base of the telephone pole. Why, she wonders, do people call them weeds? She thought they were pretty. But grown-ups say, "Miss Dunion keeps her yard so nice. Not a dandelion anywhere." [...] Outside, Pecola feels the inexplicable shame ebb. Dandelions. A dart of affection leaps out from her to them, but they do not look at her and do not send love back. She thinks, "They are ugly. They are weeds". (Morrison, 1985: 2092, 2094)

Similarly, in *Bastard Out of Carolina*, Bone hears her Aunt Ruth say that she likes the plant known as Wandering Jew, despite the fact that "[p]eople says it's a weed" (130). Within the community that Allison reconstructs, the specific name of the plant is significant as Jews are also despised. Both novels pose ethical questions about the arbitrary nature of beauty and ugliness and present the rage that both Pecola and Bone harbour at being made to feel ugly and unloved. In Bone's relationship with the unattractive Shannon Pearl, we find both of Pecola's impulses: on the one hand, a desire to protect what others have defined as ugly because of her identification with ugliness, on the other, a conflicting impulse to project all the hatred she has absorbed onto another object of contempt.

At various points of their discordant friendship, Bone is most drawn to Shannon when the latter is most obviously despised for being physically repugnant. When it is obvious that Shannon is well loved by her parents, Bone likes her less. In the argument that ends their friendship, Bone lashes out at Shannon for saying "nigger": "The way Shannon said 'nigger' tore at me, the tone, pitched exactly like the echoing sound of Aunt Madeleine sneering 'trash' when she thought I wasn't close enough to hear" (170). Bone is justly angry, but her words lock her into the same unethical paradigm. Bone hurls at Shannon all the hatred she herself has garnered: "You ugly thing […]. You monster, you greasy cross-eyed stinking sweaty-faced thing! […] You so ugly your own mama don't even love you" (171-72). When Shannon literally ignites and combusts the next time Bone sees her, all the rage in the book has finally exploded.

Bone's connection with Shannon helps her to shed light on her own despair and its origins and also teaches her that she can either continue the cycle of rage and abuse that she herself experiences or she can develop an ethics that allows her to see into the "familiar hearts of strangers", as she did with her fascination with the young black girl who reflected her own sense of illegitimacy and marginalisation. Hence, too, the ban from the Woolworth lunch counters: Bone's individual outcast status is after all interconnected with larger issues of power and powerlessness, of oppression and violence visited upon her merely because she is a "bastard", a child, poor and "trash", and therefore not worthy, she feels, of salvation.

Because Bone's mother has also internalised this view of herself, she is unable to extricate herself or her daughter from this situation. Through references to Morrison's work, through the words Anney detests, through Shannon and through the unnamed black child, Allison insists on making these connections. All these elements evince the need to conceive a community of affiliated Others to recognise one's own reality and reconstruct the self. At the end of the novel, Bone's mother gives her an unmarked birth certificate, from which the red-stamped word "illegitimate" has been excised. Meagre though it is, this gesture symbolises the hope that Bone will be able to reclaim herself. Her new-found connection to her Aunt Raylene (significantly, for Allison's vision, a lesbian and an outsider) and to the strength of generations of Boatwright women before her give her a sense of the woman she will become and the ethical vision she will hold.

An ethical vision based on connection also pervades Gloria Naylor's novel *The Women of Brewster Place* (1982) which draws on diverse points-of-view and imagines a world where women nurture one another, often taking on a role of surrogate mother (cf. Christian, 1990). Naylor's ethics are also rooted in the intersecting social struggles against racism, classism, sexism and homophobia. The novel is a series of interweaving stories of individual African American women's lives framed by the relationships they form with one another. Despite the failures of wider society that have created the ghetto which is Brewster Place, the intense connections between the women, the similarities of their experiences and the community that issues from their bond keep these women and their dreams alive. While each woman has her own story, the women's interconnectedness also blurs their individuality and blends their lives, demonstrating the link between their struggles. Naylor ably braids their stories together so that the particularity of each strand remains, yet entwines with the others to make something larger than itself. Thus the structure becomes the metaphor of connection which underscores the ethical vision of the novel as it suggests social equality based in community building.

Crossing spatial and temporal boundaries, the novel centres on interconnection as the female characters support one another. Stretching the novel's parameters, Naylor connects her creative process to writers who have preceded her. The epigraph to the novel is the well-known portion of Langston Hughes's poem of 1951 "Harlem" which asks "What happens to a dream deferred?" This initiates the dream imagery that pervades the entire novel. In a sense the novel is a gloss on this text. The quotation also recalls Lorraine Hansberry's *A Raisin in the Sun* (1960), a reference developed in various points in the novel. When we first meet Mattie Michael, the central mother figure in Naylor's novel, it is moving day. In Hansberry's play, the Younger family's move from Chicago's Southside to the suburbs begins the hopeful process of integration, made possible by the father's legacy, the mother's nurturance of a dream and the ultimate ability of the son, Walter Lee, to stand up and become "a man". Despite the lack of good sunlight in her apartment, Mrs. Younger has nurtured her plant—symbolic of the dream—on her apartment windowsill. In the final moment of the play, on moving day, she returns alone on stage to retrieve her plant and bring it to her new sunlit home in the hope that her dreams for a better life will flourish. Mattie's move is a mirror image. She leaves a nice home with "an entire sun porch" (97) for the dilapidated

Brewster Place because of a son unprepared to take on adulthood and responsibility. While Hansberry's Walter Lee foolishly gives part of the money for the new house to a crooked associate, he does not fully jeopardise the family's future and more importantly, he learns from his mistake. Conversely, Mattie's son Basil jumps bail and forces his mother to forfeit her house. He thus sets Mattie's reverse move in motion, from a home of her own to life in the ghetto. Mattie also brings her plants, but she knows they will struggle to survive in Brewster Place. She puts them on the ill-lit windowsill facing north, yet keeps her dream alive.

By placing Mattie's story with its references to *A Raisin in the Sun* first, Naylor immediately locates herself within a tradition of African American and women writers. Naylor further associates herself with her creative community through an oblique reference to Virginia Woolf's *A Room of One's Own* (1929). After seeing *A Midsummer Night's Dream*, which continues the theme of the dream, Cora Lee's son Sammy asks his mother if "Shakespeare's Black". She replies, "not yet". This recalls Woolf's imaginary Judith Shakespeare who could not have emerged in Shakespeare's time because of the restrictions of female creativity (Woolf, 1929). As Alice Walker's "In Search of Our Mothers' Gardens" (1996) shows, hindered creativity does not always die, but manifests itself in other ways. Just as slave women's creativity materialised through the scraps of cloth they pieced together into quilts, Naylor's Cora Lee recognises that her son's creativity emerges through the "writing of rhymes on her bathroom walls" (127). And just as the characters' survival depends on connection to the community of the women of Brewster Place and their tradition of caring for one another, Naylor suggests that the writer must locate herself within her artistic community based on her multiple identities. Thus the metaphoric connection is multi-layered, being both inside and beyond the text.

Naylor's feminist ethics of intersectionality and inclusion also emerges through the way she shows the community's failure to recognise the experiences of her lesbian character, Lorraine, who is gang-raped. Naylor seems to be suggesting that the dream of acceptance has not only been deferred for her characters, but that it requires a more complex response: in the Hansberry play, the Younger family asserts their place in Clybourne Park, whereas in Brewster Place, Lorraine's pleas for acceptance go unheard. Naylor's story shows the destructive forces of racism, sexism, classism and homophobia and the necessity of making connections across boundaries of difference if they are all to survive.

Indeed, in *The Women of Brewster Place*, Gloria Naylor posits connection and community as the most powerfully regenerative force. She imagines a world in which women care for one another and in which, despite the impoverished life Brewster Place offers, they form a community. While the women have their own stories, they are often able to cross the boundaries that divide them—structurally across the stories themselves—to see into the "familiar hearts of strangers".

When a young, pregnant Mattie Michael leaves town to escape her father's wrath, she survives because Miss Eva Turner helps her. Mattie's relationship with Miss Eva sets the tone for the connection amongst women. Named for the biblical mother, Miss Eva is Everywoman: though black, she looks white, she is "partial to" men of all hues and shades, and just as she encompasses all women's lives, eventually her life and Mattie's become intertwined: "The young black woman and the old yellow woman sat in the kitchen for hours, blending their lives so that what lay behind one and ahead of the other became indistinguishable" (34). Through her relationship with Miss Eva and through her own mistakes, Mattie in turn takes on this nurturing role, particularly with Miss Eva's granddaughter who also finds her way to Brewster Place. Involved with a man who will not be tied down, Ciel has an abortion to appease him. The tragic irony is that she not only loses him, but when she is distracted by an argument with him, her untended daughter sticks her finger in an outlet and is electrocuted. At her unbearable loss, Ciel enters a depression of catatonic depths. Mattie saves her and "rocks" her back to life,

> past Dachau, where soul-gutted Jewish mothers swept their children's entrails off laboratory floors. They flew past the spilled brains of Senegalese infants whose mothers had dashed them on the wooden sides of slave ships. She rocked her into her childhood and let her see murdered dreams [...] to the nadir of her hurt, and they found it—a slight silver splinter, embedded just below the surface of the skin. [...] the splinter gave way, but its roots were deep, gigantic, ragged, and they tore up flesh [and] left a huge hole, which was already starting to pus over, but Mattie was satisfied. (103-4)

The ethical vision of Naylor's work comes most clearly to light in this passage as Ciel heals. In bringing Ciel back to life, Mattie focuses on the connections with other women's lives and tragedies, centring especially on women belonging to oppressed groups—victims of slavery and the Holocaust—and on women whose dreams have been shattered and whose children slaughtered. Through connection with the pain other women have endured, Ciel can begin to feel her own and emerge from it. By recognising the "dream deferred"—and the "pus" in this passage is reminiscent of the "festering sore" in Hughes's poem—she can begin to heal. Mattie brings Ciel back to life, baptising her anew and letting her cry to dream again.

Barbara Christian (1990) has analysed the theme of "mothering" in the novel and noted that it extends to all but "the two", Lorraine and Theresa, the lesbian couple. They do not survive because of homophobia and the failure of the women of Brewster Place to include them in their community. Through the destruction of Hansberry's namesake, Lorraine, Naylor shows us the explosion of a "dream deferred". Lorraine, who pleaded for acceptance, is attacked by young men whose power has been denied and thus twisted by a racist, sexist and classist society because they are black and poor, thus alluding to the complexities of intersectionality. Ultimately, dreams do not die, as the dream sequence in which all the women pull down the wall in Brewster Place shows. The epilogue also recognises the enduring spirit of these women, who "still wake up with their dreams misted on the edge of a yawn" (192). Naylor's most rare vision is one in which women are connected to each other across time, space and social divides. Hence the connection made between Ciel's tragedy and those of enslaved Senegalese women who dashed their children to their deaths rather than see them taken across the sea and sold into slavery and of Jewish women at Dachau who killed their children with their own hands, rather than permit them to meet a crueller death at the hands of the Nazis. Hence, the insistence on what Toni Morrison (1994) refers to as the "ancestor" or collective memory—Miss Eva who passes the mantle on to Mattie in turn. Hence, too, the warning of the destructive failure of both hegemonic and non-hegemonic communities which exclude "the two". Naylor places her characters into a context which acknowledges the collective memory of women and their ability to see into the "familiar hearts of strangers" as essential to the survival of self and community. Her own artistic vision thrives, in part, because she is able to locate herself within an artistic community with a shared ethical vision.

Many other contemporary women novelists writing from a range of cultural perspectives propose an ethical vision by looking at the connections across difference and by connecting memory to current realities. Some authors retrieve memory to imagine the struggles that earlier generations of marginalised people have endured as they envisage a more ethical future, as seen in Andrea Levy's *Small Island* (2004). Such a future posits a society in which the ethical ideals of feminist intersectionality are honoured and all people, regardless of ethnicity, nationality, class, gender and sexuality, are accorded equal respect and justice. Allison and Naylor also draw on memory and metaphorical connection through the trope that Henry Louis Gates, Jr (2004) calls "signifying" by alluding to other texts with the purpose of developing a community of writers who share an ethical or political stance. Similarly, Zadie Smith's *On Beauty* (2005) alludes both to E.M. Forster's *Howards End* (1910) and his "only connect", which forms a large part of her novel's ethical vision, and to Zora Neale Hurston's *Their Eyes Were Watching God* (1937), which asserts a black woman's quest for identity and connection (Fischer, 2007). Andrea Levy's *Small Island* (2004) refers back to Sam Selvon's *The Lonely Londoners* (1956), as does Sarah Waters's *The Night Watch* (2006) to Radclyffe Hall's *The Well of Loneliness* (1928), as these authors develop black or lesbian identities. Gloria Naylor's *The Women of Brewster Place* (1982) is an early example of a long line of contemporary women novelists who use a narrative structure that draws on a plurality of perspectives or voices. More recent examples include Maggie Gee's *The White Family* (2002), which explores the effects of racism, classism and homophobia through narratives using diverse points of view, Hanan al-Shaykh's *Only in London* (2002), which gives voice to Arab women and a gay man, Sarah Water's *The Night Watch* (2006), which presents London during the Blitz mostly through the eyes of two lesbians, a gay man and a heterosexual woman, as well as Andrea Levy's *Small Island* narrated in four voices. This structure decentres established hegemonic narratives and gives voice to a range of perspectives in a way that mirrors a politics of intersectionality and an ethics of connection across difference. In these various ways, contemporary women authors continue to be engaged in exploring the possibilities of envisioning a more just world as they recognise the "familiar hearts of strangers" and imagine more ethical communities.

Notes

[1] While Ozick argues that "[m]etaphor uses what we already possess and reduces strangeness" (234), it should be noted that this suggests an idealistic slant in the ethical posture of many contemporary women writers. Metaphor can also increase strangeness, as Ozick notes elsewhere and hence also can be used negatively (e.g. the Nazis comparing Jews to a cancer). Moreover, this emphasis on "community" runs the risk, as Alan Sinfield points out, of presenting an ethical view with "cosy, togetherness connotations" (1994: 206). He prefers the notion of "subculture" as it underlines the separateness necessary to retaining a sharper political edge and producing a full-fledged culture of opposition.

[2] One could also see this use of African American shadow figures in terms of Toni Morrison's notion of "black surrogacy" that she explores in *Playing in the Dark* (1992), except that Allison does treat the black characters and struggles with respect despite not fleshing them out. In this sense, perhaps the allusions to African

American experience might be seen more along the lines of the trope that Henry Louis Gates, Jr. defines as part of "signifying", in which "black writers read and critique other black texts as an act of rhetorical self-definition. Our literary tradition exists because of these precisely chartable formal literary relationships" (Gates, 2004: 992). In the world of feminist intersectionality, some of these allusions for "self-definition" cross ethnic divides.

References

Allison, D. 1992. *Bastard Out of Carolina*. New York: Dutton.

—. 1994. *Skin: Talking About Sex, Class and Literature*. Ithaca: Firebrand.

Anzaldúa, G. 1987. *Borderlands La Frontera: The New Mestiza*. San Francisco: Aunt Lute.

Christian, B. 1990. "Gloria Naylor's geography: community, class and patriarchy in *The Women of Brewster Place* and *Linden Hills*", in H. L. Gates, Jr (ed), *Reading Black, Reading Feminist: A Critical Anthology*. New York: Penguin. 348-73.

Fischer, S. A. 2007. "'A Glance from God': Zadie Smith's *On Beauty* and Zora Neale Hurston", in *Changing English: Studies in Culture and Education*, 14 (3): 361-371.

Forster, E.M. 1910. *Howards End*. London: Edward Arnold.

Gates, Jr, H. L. 2004. "The blackness of blackness: a critique on the sign and the signifying monkey", in J. Rivkin & M. Ryan (eds), *Literary Theory: An Anthology*. 2nd edn. New York: Blackwell. 987-1004.

Gee, M. 2002. *The White Family*. London: Saqi.

Hall, R. 1928. *The Well of Loneliness*. London: Jonathan Cape.

Hansberry, L. 1960. *A Raisin in the Sun: A Drama in Three Acts*. London: Methuen.

Hurston, Z. N. 1937. *Their Eyes Were Watching God*. Philadelphia: J. B. Lippincott.

Levy, A. 2004. *Small Island*. London: Review.

Lorde, A. 2004. "Age, Race, Class and Sex: Women Redefining Difference", in J. Rivkin & M. Ryan (eds), *Literary Theory: An Anthology*. 2nd edn. New York: Blackwell. 854-860.

Morrison, T. 1985. *"The Bluest Eye"*, in S. M. Gilbert & S. Gubar (eds), *The Norton Anthology of Literature by Women: The Tradition in English*. New York: W. W. Norton.

—. 1992. *Playing in the Dark*. Cambridge, MA: Harvard University Press.

—. 1994. "Rootedness: the ancestor as foundation", in D. Soyini Madison (ed), *The Woman That I Am: The Literature and Culture of*

Contemporary Women of Color. New York: St. Martin's Press. 492-497.

Naylor, G. 1982. *The Women of Brewster Place*. New York: Penguin.

Ozick, C. 1996. *Portrait of the Artist as a Bad Character and Other Essays on Writing*. London: Pimlico.

Pratt, M. B. 1995. "Dorothy Allison", in *Progressive*, 59 (7): 30.

Scarry, E. 1999. *On Beauty and Being Just*. Princeton: Princeton University Press.

Selvon, S.D. 1956. *The Lonely Londoners*. London: Allan Wingate.

al-Shaykh, H. 2002. *Only in London*. Trans. C. Cobham. London: Bloomsbury.

Shields, S. 2008. "Gender: an intersectionality perspective", in *Sex Roles*, 59 (5/6): 301-11.

Sinfield, A. 1994. *The Wilde Century: Effeminacy, Oscar Wilde and the Queer Moment*. New York: Columbia University Press.

Smith, Z. 2005. *On Beauty*. London: Hamish Hamilton.

Valentine, G. 2007. "Theorizing and researching intersectionality: a challenge for feminist geography", in *Professional Geographer*, 59 (1): 10-21.

Walker, A. 1996. "In search of our mothers' gardens", in S. M. Gilbert & S. Gubar (eds), *The Norton Anthology of Literature by Women: The Tradition in English*. New York: Norton. 2314-22.

Waters, S. 2006. *The Night Watch*. London: Virago.

Woolf, V. 1929. *A Room of One's Own*. New York: Harcourt Brace.

ETHICS, VIOLENCE AND THE SELF IN J.G. BALLARD'S *CONCRETE ISLAND*

LAWRENCE PHILLIPS

> To this war of every man, against every man, this is also consequent; that nothing can be unjust. The notions of right and wrong, justice and injustice, have there no place. Where there is no common power, there is no law, no injustice. (Thomas Hobbes, *Leviathan*, 1651)

The conjoining of "ethics" and "violence" would seem to be inimical to Hobbes's argument for communal order. More so the work of J. G. Ballard where expressions of violence can superficially appear to be a gratuitous exercise nihilistically signalling the breakdown of community. Yet Ballard is actively exploring a social ethic based on a misconception of "common power" that leads to banality, conformity, repression, fear, and the sort of fascistic politics conducive both to the destruction of the individual and a tolerant society. Ballard's interrogation of modern life is resonant in Baudrillard's characterisation of contemporary society as "whitewashed": "Violence is whitewashed, history is whitewashed, all as part of a vast enterprise of cosmetic surgery at whose completion, nothing will be left but a society for whom all violence, all negativity, are strictly forbidden" (Baudrillard, 1993: 45). This is not a naive argument that violence is in and of itself somehow "good" and transformative akin to Spencer's social reconfiguration (and misuse) of Darwin in the phrase "survival of the fittest". Rather, a society solely premised on control, on the restraint of difference, on the denial of historical change, is far from the ethical commonwealth envisioned by Hobbes, but is in many ways a logical development of an over emphasis on "common power". Authoritarian regimes claim legitimization on just such a premise: that power is wielded for the "common good" by a tiny stratum of the population, or outright by an all powerful demagogue. Perhaps the greatest modern historical example—and perhaps the most distressingly ironic since its origins are well intentioned as a stepping stone to a classless society—is Marx's notion of a transitional "dictatorship of the proletariat" which in the post-revolution Soviet Union soon elided its transitional purpose to quickly become the legitimization of state-sponsored control. The violent misuse of Marx's notion of a transitional order to wield in trust "common power" to facilitate the transfer of government to a new communal society, nicely encapsulates the risk inherent in the prior establishment of power and order as the necessary prerequisite for an ethical society. Ballard's fiction consistently explores this margin of risk where a "common power" which creates a framework for an ethical community slips into a repressive banality openly hostile—if not violently opposed—to change and progress that is more about the Right than doing right, the point at which rectitude becomes reaction.

In this chapter I will focus on Ballard's *Concrete Island* (1973) one of three novels from the mid-1970s which along with *Crash* (1973) and *High Rise* (1975) can be seen, if not as a trilogy, then as an interlinked series. All three novels are thematically and conceptually linked: in each the central protagonist is a middle-class professional man brought to a realisation of the vacuity and repetitiveness of their lives; they are tested in physically confined and indistinguishable environments that are creations of the very social planning their class dominates—a traffic island, a high rise residential block, the motorway system around London; and in each instance the defamiliarisation of their existence brings to the fore ethical questions which in their fracturing release an excess of violent energy that is implicit in their roles, but generally disguised or displaced. As Ballard observes in the introduction to *Concrete Island*: "Marooned in an office block or on a traffic island, we can tyrannise ourselves, test our strengths and weaknesses, perhaps come to terms with aspects of our characters to which we have always closed our eyes" (Ballard, 1994: 5). Their lives are expressions of the social violence articulated by Slavoj Žižek in the following terms:

> subjective violence [violence performed by a clearly identifiable agent] is just the most visible portion of a triumvirate that also includes two objective kinds of violence. First there is "symbolic" violence embodied in language and its forms, what Heidegger would call "our house of being" [...] this violence is not only at work in the obvious—and extensively studied—cases of incitement and of the relations of social domination reproduced in our habitual speech forms: there is a more fundamental form of violence still that pertains to language as such, to its imposition of a certain universe of meaning. Second there is what I call 'systemic" violence, or the often catastrophic consequences of the smooth functioning of our economic and political systems. (Žižek, 2008: 1)

Ballard's protagonists as middle-class professional men are embedded in this structure of objective violence; educated in the forms of language that enact it and the mainstay of the economic and political systems that sustain it.

In *Concrete Island* the protagonist is Robert Maitland, a successful architect who crashes his Jaguar off the Westway interchange in central London near the M4 motorway spur. Plunging down a high embankment which surrounds a traffic island waste land hemmed in by endlessly busy roads, injured he finds himself trapped: "The sequence of violent events only micro-seconds in duration had opened and closed behind him like a vent of hell" (Ballard, 1994: 8). The mention of hell is not just for emphasis since we are quickly offered details of his life that underline how he is morally compromised; he has been carrying on an affair with a doctor—Dr Helen Fairfax—with whom he has recently shared a holiday and yet before the crash he was on his way to pick up his son and return to his wife, Catharine. While the senior partner in his architectural practice his role seems rather abstract having trained his staff to accept his comings and goings without question. Much like his personal life, his immediate absence is unlikely to elicit alarm, suggesting his domination of both settings by his refusal to be constrained by his personal family or work, two moral frameworks to which he does "symbolic" violence to adopt Žižek's formulation. Clearly capable of acting amorally, he is able to operate outside the ethical framework created by "common power" over which his class wields disproportionate influence economically and socially. This seems to contradict the substance of Hegel's assertion that "when individuals are simply identified with the actual order, ethical life appears as their general mode of conduct" (Hegel, 1952: 90). There is most certainly a moral order implicit in these relationships; it is Maitland's symbolic power that both identifies him with "the actual order" as a middle-class professional, as a capitalist employer, and husband, but also enables him to subvert the ethical framework of which he is a pillar on many levels. The result is, of course, an institutionalised and personal hypocrisy.

His marooning on a modern day equivalent of Crusoe's island—a clearly signalled intertext for the novel (Ballard, 1994: 32)—is an opportunity to recreate the bourgeois society of which he is a dominant member. However, his wrecked ship is the now useless twisted hulk of expensive chrome "the decorative grille [...] meshed into the radiator honeycomb" (Ballard, 1994: 10); a status symbol, its only immediately useful component being a crate of wine in the trunk. But like Defoe's Robinson he soon finds that he is not alone. Physically injured in the crash and his subsequent attempt to attract attention from passing traffic proving fruitless and leading to further injury, he is unable to leave the island which is devoid of food. Unlike Defoe's Crusoe, he does not recreate a bourgeois order from the wilds of the island indicating the "right thinking" mind at one with both his class and his god (with a little help from the goods in the hold of the wrecked ship), but uncovers the community over which the traffic island has been "built" or, more accurately, a crumbling patch of demolition amidst the transfixing, bisecting, modern roads. In his halting exploration he variously discovers "building foundations, the ground plans of Edwardian terraced houses", "the entrance to a World War II air-raid shelter", "ruins [...] of a stucco Victorian house", "a former neighbourhood high street", "an abandoned churchyard", and "the ground plan of a post-war cinema" (Ballard, 1994: 38, 40, 42, and 69). The motorway system habitually used by Maitland travelling from his home to his office has obliterated a functioning community—roads, transitional/ transit structures, have replaced a moral order; a history has been erased or "whitewashed" to recall Baudrillard's expression, an obliteration to which Maitland, as an architect, is a party. As Marc Augé argues: "The installations needed for the accelerated circulation of passengers and goods (high-speed roads and railways, interchanges, airports) are just as much non-places as the means of transport themselves" (Augé, 2003: 34). The "abandoned landscape" of the Island (Ballard, 1994: 59), has been more of a "place" than the surrounding roads swarming with people in their cars.

His ultimate delirious identification with the site—"I am the island" (Ballard, 1994: 71)—reveals its symbolic import. Indeed, as Maitland identifies the physical remains of the community creates associations with his own childhood and his adult failure as a moral being:

> Maitland listened to the rain striking the galvanized iron. He remembered the house his parents had taken in the Camargue for their last summer together. The intense delta rain had fallen on the garage roof below the windows of the bedroom where he had happily spent most of the holiday. It was no coincidence that when he had first taken Helen Fairfax to the south of France they had gone straight to La Grande Motte, the futuristic resort complex on the coast a few miles away, Helen had quietly hated the hard, affectless architecture with its stylized concrete surfaces, nervous of Maitland's buoyant humour. At the time he had found himself wishing that Catharine were with him—she would have liked the ziggurat hotels and apartment houses, and the vast, empty, parking lots laid down by the planners years before any tourists would arrive to park their cars, like a city abandoned in advance of itself. (Ballard, 1994: 65)

Maitland's choice for his own holiday over his parents is instructive. The Camargue in the Arles region of France is a famous wetland now preserved as a natural site of international importance. From this natural landscape visited with his parents, Maitland chooses a contiguous site that is noted for its artificiality and repetitive (while striking) architecture erected in the 1960s and 1970s, virtually new at the time the novel was written and is set, but today the site of mass tourism. In the 1970s it is not an "abandoned landscape" but an artificially evacuated one anticipating a transitory mass-market population. In a novel based on one symbolic landscape, what do these psychic landscapes tell us about Maitland? Drawn to the same region as his last happy holiday with his parents, he rejects the naturalism the region associates with them for the superficiality of a forensically empty, architecturally alienating, holiday complex. As a purpose-built tourist site through which people simply pass, it is a certainly a candidate for one of Augé's "non-places". Maitland's choice is a paradox. Drawn to a site with organic resonances of family he takes his mistress rather than his wife, but is nastily amused by her discomfort while noting how much it would appeal to his wife perhaps suggesting that his most significant relationship is itself "like a city abandoned in advance of itself". His capacity for casual cruelty is hardly surprising since it is necessary to maintain his position within the ruling caste, and while he does not quite reject his parents, he prefers to pervert his memory of them.

It is worth reflecting further on the nature of this "perversion" through Kant's notion of moral law. For Kant, on the one side there is our natural physical self driven by desires, while on the other there is our intellectual or spiritual self from which moral law drives. On the one hand natural desire draws him back to this landscape, but the prevailing intellectual self rather than drawing a moral conclusion accentuates desire by reflecting on his use of both his mistress, Helen, and his wife, Catharine. His pleasure and his power are derived from his use and manipulation of others. At the point of encounter with the other inhabitants of the Island, it is worthwhile developing this theme within Kant's ethical framework: "Act in such a way that you always treat humanity, whether in your own person or in the person of any other, never simply as a means, but always at the same time as an end" (Nozick, 1974: 33). Maitland's reflections on his two holidays and his personal relationships reveal much and provide a key pointer to his subsequent behaviour on the Island. However, he does not encounter his Man Friday; instead the literary frame shifts from the model of *Robinson Crusoe* to Shakespeare's *The Tempest* which also signals a more reflective analysis of his character. Unlike Crusoe, marooned as a consequence of a driving wanderlust mutating into an early parable of colonialism well able to assert the bourgeois order of things on his island, Maitland is incapable of mastering the physical environment himself and the novel becomes an examination of his ability (or inability) to master others and himself. A colonial ideology is present in both and is significant to the examination of power and domination in the novel, but whereas Crusoe's island is an empty landscape ripe for colonisation (even Friday and his fellow cannibals are visitors not residents), Prospero's island is pre-inhabited by the exiles Ariel and particularly Caliban. The moral question is therefore a shift from bringing order to and developing a god-given natural landscape into capitalist productivity, to the control, exploitation, and domination of other peoples signalling an ethical shift. The occupation and exploitation of a fecund natural landscape is, perhaps, an ethical endeavour akin to the original meaning of colonisation, or was certainly seen as such read through Crusoe's protestant moral framework. The exploitation of other people, which we might align with imperial power, falls foul of Kant's categorical imperative as the people become a means to further his ambition to leave the Island rather than a common good. Maitland proves incapable of the former, but rather more adept at the latter.

Prospero is of course an exile; the deposed ruler of Milan. The allusion gestures towards Maitland's position, power, and failure in the outside world and suggests that his "exile" to the traffic island has been brought on by himself. The fact that he was speeding in his car from an encounter with his mistress to meet his son leading to the accident that brought him to the Island, effectively signifies both his arrogance and its consequences. He is rescued by his Miranda (Jane Sheppard) and Caliban (Proctor). Unlike Maitland, they are the apparent victims of the hierarchy of which he is a member. Exploited and then marginalised they are forced to inhabit the Island, homeless, since that same society has little use for them. Indeed, they are terrified that Maitland's attempts to bring attention to his plight on the Island—by burning his car for example—might bring them to the attention of the authorities. Jane's attitude towards Maitland is contradictory; on the one hand she is caring, gentle, and respectful when she first rescues him but then hostile, defensive, and aggressive when he returns to strength and tries to persuade her to help him escape. As he learns her history and guesses more, he becomes aware of the source of her hostility while never quite associating it directly with his own behaviour and identity:

> Curious about her background, Maitland spread the photographs out on the bed. One showed a strong-faced adolescent girl, clearly Jane, standing protectively beside a faded middle-aged woman with glazed eyes on the frayed lawn of a small sanatorium. In another she was visiting a fairground, arm-in-arm with a heavy-set man twenty years older than herself. Maitland assumed that the man was her father, but a wedding

photograph showed Jane, proudly six months pregnant, standing beside the man, the fey-looking mother hovering in the background like a deranged ghost.

A second man appeared in the series, a dapper figure of about fifty in an old but well-made suit, posed beside a white Bentley in the drive of a large Victorian house. Her father, Maitland decided, or perhaps another middle-aged lover. What had happened to the child? (Ballard, 1994: 106-7)

Maitland's suppositions are open to dark insinuations. Is Jane's hostility fuelled by resentment against a wealthy father? Or is the latter man a lover who seduced and abandoned her? Had the earlier man seduced, married, and then abandoned her and, indeed, what happened to the child? Did it die, was it taken away from Jane, or has she abandoned it or, even, something worse? That she has learnt through experience to be wary of if not hate men of Maitland's class and wealth is undeniable, while there is enough in even the limited information he uncovers to suppose that she has a real reason to fear the authorities not least because we later learn that she has turned to prostitution.

Proctor's history is more straightforward but no less distressing: "he used to be a trapeze artist with some fly-by-night circus. That was before they had any safety legislation. He fell off the high wire and damaged his brain. They just threw him out. Mental defectives and subnormals are treated appallingly—unless they're prepared to go into institutions they have absolutely no protection" (Ballard, 1994: 98). Both these partial personal histories bring to mind Raymond Williams's reminder of the etymological relationship between the words "violence" and "violation"; the latter suggesting a breaking of custom or some dignity (Williams, 1983: 330). That both have suffered at the hands of those who "society" sets up as their traditional protectors by custom and in law—the middle-class male, a father, an employer—is a further reminder of how ethically compromised Maitland's social identity is as he is both. It also reaffirms the hypocrisy inherent in this traditional, paternalistic, structure. While entirely dependent on Jane and Proctor, he soon contrives to drive a wedge between them to further his own ends. Representative of women and the working classes in the micro-society of the Island, Maitland attempts to bribe Jane with money and when that does not work, brings Proctor over to his side by the promise of money and then by feeding him bottles of wine from the ruined car's trunk. Replicating his role in society, he attempts to use his companions as a means rather than an end in themselves. Increasingly enfeebled by his injuries and poor diet, he does so by using the force of his discursive and class prerogatives rather than his physical presence recalling Žižek's insistence on the violence inherent in the "social domination reproduced in our habitual speech forms" (Žižek, 2008: 1), although he also humiliates Proctor more directly by urinating in his face. Proctor is not quite so damaged as not to recognise this as is evident in his distrust of writing as Jane relates: "He never learned to read and write. He hates words of any kind" (Ballard, 1994: 102). The scene seems set for a violent confrontation by which Maitland gains his freedom at the expense, again, of Jane and Proctor as he resolves: "Determined to survive above all else, he would exploit this strain of cruelty in himself in the same way that he had earlier exploited his self-pity and contempt. All that mattered was that he dominate the senile tramp and this wayward young woman" (Ballard, 1994: 139). Yet this is not what occurs.

Maitland's new approach reveals more about Jane's background. A turning point comes immediately after he humiliates Proctor by urinating on him. This new aggression shocks Jane into submission as well and her earlier persona of carer comes to the fore again although not before she observes "[i]t was [...] a bastard thing to do. You must be a real shit" (Ballard, 1994: 137). Maitland's calculation is finely tuned since Jane responds to his overt aggression and domination by bathing him and then having sex with him. But why respond to Maitland's calculated and overt cruelty? We learn that she miscarried her child and wishes to avoid the law because she stole a large amount of money from one of her husband's friends. There remain intriguing complications such as how she gained access to such a large sum, but it reveals her to be less immediately a victim. However, it is the fate of her father that is the most psychologically intriguing:

> He's not my father any more. I don't think about him. [...] Suicide is [...] a suggestive act, it runs in families, you know. When someone in your family reaches the point where they cannot just kill themselves, but take a couple of years over it—really take their time, as if it was the most important thing they'd ever done—then it's difficult to stop seeing your own life through their eyes. Sometimes I'm nervous of my mind. (Ballard, 1994: 139-40)

While this is a subjective elaboration of her father's actions, Jane's interpretation of them is as a punishment for the living. A punishment she constantly carries within her. We are not told of the origin of the despair or mental illness that drove her father to this end, nor why the nature of the act directed such simmering resentment towards his family. One must allow that the situation as Jane recounts it may be coloured by her own sense of guilt towards her father, but the psychological violence is unanswerable whether deliberately caused by her father or self inflicted.

That Jane fears the same fate and the same responsibility for Maitland becomes evident in the penultimate section of the novel: "You're a shit. Are you dying? Don't die here" (Ballard, 1994: 164). It precedes a rant provoked by Maitland's suicidal course in which she relives a previous separation, perhaps from her husband: "I loved you dearly and you buggered it up. Just twelve hours and you'll be gone. Who wants relationships? You bore me right now. You never had any affection as a child. Don't commit any acts of violence tonight" (Ballard, 1994: 165-6). Does this event follow the emotional guilt of the loss of her child? is her husband violent and is that the cause of the miscarriage—"Don't commit any acts of violence tonight". What is clear within the confused concern for and antagonism towards Maitland is some sort of catharsis. The violence on the island is almost a stage for their competing psychological unwinding in which they both assume roles that strip away the social pressures that have crippled them as human beings. As Maitland reflects after they have sex: "He accepted the rules of the young woman's charade, glad of the freedom it implied, a recognition of their need to avoid any hint of commitment to each other" (Ballard, 1994: 142).

There is some truth for both of them in Jane's earlier utterance that "I was never very good at patching up quarrels—I wanted to go on simmering for days. That way you can really hate" (Ballard, 1994: 117). Indeed, there is a strong sense here of washing away sins to reveal an essential being. However, while in Jane's case it is festering psychological baggage, her debilitating hate the cause of her rage that is washed away, for Maitland what he sheds is far more profound and destructive:

> His relationships with Catharine and his mother, even with Helen Fairfax, all the thousand and one emotionally loaded transactions of his childhood, would have been tolerable if he had been able to pay for them in some neutral currency, hard cash across the high-priced counters of these relationships. Far from wanting this girl to help him escape from the island, he was using her for motives he had never before accepted, his need to be freed from his past, from his childhood, his wife and friends, with all their affections and demands, and to rove for ever within the empty city of his own mind. (Ballard, 1994: 142)

This desire is no less than to strip away everything that registers Maitland as a social being; it is profoundly anti-social in intent. Certainly, to recognise and shed the negative, ethically noxious, persona he occupies through his social position is no bad thing given the cruelty and hypocrisy to which it leads. But to strip away an emotional history, to reject "any hint of commitment" and social intimacy is to be less than human. The situation recalls what W.G. Sebald wrote about Jean Améry's confrontation with the trauma of the Nazi concentration camps: "Resentment, writes Améry in full awareness of the illogicality of his attempt at a definition, 'nails everyone one of us unto the cross of his ruined past. Absurdly, it demands that the irreversible be turned around, that the event be undone.' [...] The issue, then, is not to resolve but to reveal the conflict" (Sebald, 2003: 160-62). Of course Maitland's situation is not driven by anything comparable to the horror of the concentration camps, but his need does seem to be driven by resentment as does Jane's, but in her case the ultimate motivating source appears to be fuelled by guilt. There is much for Maitland to feel guilty about but in revealing the source of his resentment at least to himself, the affections and demands of friends and family and the need to be freed from his own past, there is little left to psychologically come to terms with. By giving in to this resentment, this desire, what is left of the man but "the empty city of his own mind"?

The novel does not, of course, end at that point but holds out the question: "Where does Maitland go from here?" Social erasure and emptiness is his desire; a figurative, social, if not literal death seems to await. The parallel with the mystery of the suicide of Jane's father, at least from her perspective, appears to be the most likely outcome. The penultimate chapter ends with Jane's attempt to persuade Maitland to leave with her and be taken to a hospital with him insisting "I don't want anyone to know I'm on the island"; Jane responds "Proctor wants to leave. He asked me to take him with me" (Ballard, 1994: 167). The physically damaged Proctor is ostensibly the least complex to understand of this trio. The fear that governs his self-exile to the Island is well founded and perfectly comprehensible. He is, in fact, far less complex as an entity than his model, Caliban. His fate is, however, loaded with symbolic weight. The dawn of the following day begins with a bolt of excitement. A repair vehicle arrives bringing engineers to work on one of the concrete overpasses and, in so doing, they dangle a cradle from the balustrade trailing ropes onto the Island proper. Despite his expressed desire not to leave the island, Maitland's mind myopically clings to the idea of attempting to do so. Before he can act, however, Proctor dressed in his trapeze artist leotard streaks towards the ropes, catches it and lifts himself onto the balustrade. Sensing the loss of his chief means of support on the Island, Maitland suspects him of wanting to leave by himself, but he soon realises that the tramp is trying to help him escape. Of course, contradictorily, Maitland calls him back; the prospect of genuine escape is not what he has in mind. Revelling in one last demonstration of the athletic powers his injuries had apparently cost him, the truck starts and pulls away with Proctor caught in the ropes:

> Trussed like a carcass in an abattoir, he hung above the cradle. Legs kicking as he grappled with the ropes, he was carried backwards through the air.
> The repair vehicle picked up speed, its engine drowning Maitland's shouts. Proctor hung helplessly as it moved above him, carrying him towards the nearest concrete pillar. When his body struck the pillar it thudded like a punchbag against the massive column. Unconscious now, he hung limply from the rope around his neck. (Ballard, 1994: 172)

Maitland recovers the body and resolves to bury it but rejects Jane's final plea to leave with her, which she does for good. Alone on the island he is exultant: "Already he felt no real need leave the island, and this alone confirmed that he had established dominion over it" (Ballard, 1994: 176). So what purpose does Proctor's death serve other than to open the way to Maitland's unchallenged domination of the Island?

Proctor's death is suggestively sacrificial recalling Girard's observation that,

> Violence is frequently called irrational. It has its reasons, however, and can marshal some rather convincing ones when the need arises. Yet these reasons cannot be taken seriously, no matter how valid they may appear. Violence itself will discard them if the initial object remains persistently out of reach and continues to provoke hostility. When unappeased, violence seeks and always finds a surrogate victim. (Girard, 2005: 2)

Within the narrative logic of the novel, does this scene deflect the repressed violence that Maitland unleashes in his nihilistic desire "to rove for ever within the empty city of his own mind" (Ballard, 1994: 142); should that logic dictate that it is he who is released by death given his desire for social death inherent in self-imposed exile from family and friends and the demands of their reciprocal bonds? His self exile on the Island denies his social obligations replaced, instead, by chimerical plans for escape which will, presumably, never reach fruition. Does Proctor's sacrifice preserve Maitland but because of his own self-erasing proclivity only lead him into an ephemeral quest for selfhood—escape from the Island and assumption of his social obligations—or has Maitland really found his "place", himself?

The Island becomes the physical manifestation of the "city of his mind"; a microcosm of the encompassing city that in its modernity has erased and buried its past traced through the building foundations scarring the Island, the residue of an erased community. Is Maitland's self-effacing retreat onto the Island chasing the dust of his old life really the logic of the society and city that spawned him where the fixation, the obsession, denotes the evacuation of the self to then tantalise oneself with what one has left? With violence deflected meaning seems to evaporate as well— "violence is whitewashed, history is whitewashed" (Baudrillard, 1993: 45). As Girard goes on to argue: "society is seeking to deflect upon a relatively indifferent victim, a 'sacrificable' victim, the violence that would otherwise be vented on its own members, the people it most desires to protect" (Girard, 2005: 4). And yet in this offer of "sacrifice" Maitland evades the violence that he brings into the open on the Island, yet then rejects society itself in what appears to be an endless loop of planned but unachieved escape. The conclusion poses an ethical and moral question: the evasion, the denial, the elision of social ties, of community, of history, of pain, is to posit the end of the self. This is a challenge for modern, urban life which in a massive conglomeration promotes and creates the physical possibility of isolation and disconnection. While Maitland was a nodal point of what Žižek identifies as objective violence and through this power was able to renege on obligations and resort to casual cruelty; completely self-ripped from this social complex is to embrace nullification. Unethical behaviour within an ethical structure is, at least, to remain a social being, to be human although it is certainly not to be "good"; but nor is it a social "good" to allow someone complete self-extraction from such a system and to, literally, dehumanise. The consequence is the psychosis that Maitland has reached. So, perhaps Hobbes's common power with an emphasis on "common" has a resonance here after all: it does not guarantee ethical behaviour, but to remain within the social structure is at least to subject yourself to ethical judgement.

References

Augé, M. 1995. *Non-Places: Introduction to an Anthropology of Supermodernity*. Trans. John Howe. London and New York: Verso.
Ballard, J.G. 1995. *Concrete Island*. London: Vintage.
—. 2004. *Crash*. London: Vintage.
—. 2000. *High Rise*. London: Flamingo.
Baudrillard, J. 1993. *The Transparency of Evil*. Trans. James Benedict. London and New York: Verso.
Girard, R. 2005. *Violence and the Sacred*. Trans. Patrick Gregory, London and New York: Continuum.

Hegel, G. W. F. 1952. *The Philosophy of Right*. Trans. T. M. Knox. Oxford: Clarendon Press.

Hobbes, T. 1914. *Leviathan*, London: Dent.

Kant, I. 1949. *The Foundations of Morals in the Philosophy of Immanuel Kant*. Trans. L. W. Beck. Chicago: University of Chicago Press.

Nozick, R. 1974. *Anarchy, State and Utopia*. New York: Basic Books.

Sebald, W. G. 2003. *On the Natural History of Destruction*. London: Penguin.

Williams, R. 1983. *Keywords: A Vocabulary of Culture and Society*. London: Flamingo.

Žižek, S. 2008. *Violence: Six Sideways Reflections*. London: Profile Books.

SPANDEX PARABLES:
JUSTICE, CRIMINALITY AND THE ETHICS OF VIGILANTISM IN FRANK MILLER'S *BATMAN: THE DARK KNIGHT RETURNS* AND ALAN MOORE'S *BATMAN: THE KILLING JOKE*

STEVE BRIE

> If the story tellers could ha' got decency and good morals from true stories, who'd have troubled to invent parables? (Thomas Hardy, *Under the Greenwood Tree*)

Since the late 1980s the graphic novel has attained academic acceptance as an important form of contemporary narrative.[1] Like the literary novel, many graphic novels employ a sophisticated range of narrative effects which challenge the reader intellectually in ways that early comic-books never did; consequently the graphic novel reader demographic is made up largely of adults.[2] Since the 1930s by far the most popular comic-books have been those operating within the superhero genre. These fictions offer the reader interrogations of a series of myths and archetypes, which are universally recognizable and, as Jeph Loeb and Tom Morris suggest, "speak to our nature as well as to our aspirations and fears" (Morris and Morris, 2005: 16). Since the 1980s the most intellectually and philosophically significant of these stories have been those involving Batman, or The Dark Knight as the character has come to be known. Since being introduced in *Detective Comics* #27 in May 1939, Batman has become an iconic figure, an instantly recognizable semiotic.[3] During his long crime-fighting career one opponent, or "villain" as comic convention dictates, has consistently threatened to be his nemesis—the Joker.[4] Contemporary story-tellers such as Frank Miller and Alan Moore have appropriated these long established characters and the myths that surround them in order to explore such concepts as criminality, duty, justice, retribution and the ethics of vigilantism. This chapter will contextualise and interrogate a series of philosophical perspectives pertaining to conventions of ethical behaviour as highlighted within Miller's *Batman: The Dark Knight Returns* (1986) and Moore's *Batman: The Killing Joke* (1988).[5] It will highlight the ways in which both Moore and Miller blur the boundaries between the traditionally Manichean concepts of good and evil and suggest that their seminal fantasy texts function as latter day parables, parables which present a series of thought provoking perspectives on what Thomas Hardy terms "decency and good morals" (1972: 64).

Unlike most superheroes, but in common with characters such as Captain America and Green Arrow, Batman is a superhero without superpowers, his crime-fighting abilities being centred upon a combination of highly developed martial arts skills and a razor-sharp mind honed in all aspects of criminology; his powers are rooted and contained within the conventions of realism. Tom Morris has labelled Batman "the Aristotle of the comic-book", describing him as a "worldly thinker interested in the natural sciences and immersed in the practical and the real" (Morris and Morris, 2005: 262). Indeed, within the pantheon of comic-book heroes, Batman, because of this close relationship with the conventions of realism, has become the most recognisably human and therefore the most open to moral and ethical interrogation. As David Seidman suggests, writers like Miller and Moore have made the character so convincingly human that it has become academically acceptable "to treat him as if he were real" in order to "see how his world matches up to reality" (O'Neil, 2008: 210). In contrast to characters such as Superman and Spider-Man who, since their introduction in 1939 and 1962 respectively, have remained relatively psychologically static, Batman has, via the revisionist storylines of writers like Miller and Moore, morphed into The Dark Knight, developing a complex and edgy psychological profile which has attracted significant critical analysis.

In a classic Freudian scenario, the Batman persona developed as the result of a traumatic childhood experience. After a night at the cinema, the young Bruce Wayne, son of a billionaire philanthropist, witnessed the murder of his parents by a petty criminal in Crime Alley, a notoriously dangerous location in the back streets of Gotham City. The boy, possibly suffering from Post-Traumatic Stress Disorder (PTSD) becomes the plaything of memory, persistently re-experiencing the murders during the states of both dream and daydream. Memory, as the Joker suggests in *Batman: The Killing Joke*, can be a cruel process which can take you from "a carnival of delights with poignant childhood aromas [and] the flashing neon of puberty" to "somewhere you don't want to go" (Moore, 1988: 21).

Memory can also, with the benefit of hindsight or what Freud termed *nachtraglichkeit* (translated as afterwards) confer specific meanings on experiences that did not initially possess such meanings, indeed as Mikhail Bakhtin argues, "[i]n the world of memory, a phenomenon exists in its own peculiar context, with its own special rules, subject to conditions quite different from those we meet in the world we see with our own eyes" (1981: 18). In response to the torments induced by the processes of secondary memory (long-term memory) and episodic memory (the memory of events in one's own life history), Bruce Wayne struggles to give meaning to what could be seen as a random act of violence. Irrationally believing that he contributed to the deaths of his parents due to what he considers to be an act of cowardice on his part, having simply watched the incident without making any attempt to intervene, he comes to experience, to varying degrees, bouts of schizophrenia, neurosis, paranoia and psychosis resulting in an inability to balance reason and passion. This inability becomes central to the narrative trajectory of all subsequent story lines as he comes to discover that, as Kahlil Gibran points out "Passion, unattended" can develop into "a flame that burns to its own destruction" (1988: 44). Tormented by his memories, Wayne vows to gain revenge for his loss by eradicating the criminal element of Gotham City. Struggling to realize an outlet for his torment, after witnessing the shadowy flight of a bat, he takes on the persona of the Batman, a crime-fighting alter-ego destined to dominate the rest of his life.

Batman's Gotham is a relatively faithful representation of New York City, constructed of desolate, concrete canyons and labyrinthine alley-ways where, as in classic *film noir*, the action always seems to take place in a rainy, night-time *mise-en-scène* which is dominated by shadows and canted structures clearly influenced by Gothic aesthetics and by the psychologically representative camera angles utilized in German Expressionist cinema. This is an ethically and morally bankrupt environment, a landscape in which Wayne's repressed memories habitually return to fuel his paranoia. His character has been forged over the years by the need to confront a world which he feels defies logic and often refuses to make sense. His foes tend to be socially inept outsiders—the Riddler, the Penguin, the Joker, Two Face, the Scarecrow, each a dysfunctional character, representing various forms of madness and deviation from reality. The relationships between Batman and his enemies can be seen to be symbiotic, the characters operating within a Saussurean binary axis; without the villains Batman would not exist and vice versa. While in terms of psychological representation the Riddler, Two-Face and the Penguin are interesting characters, the Joker is, and always has been, Batman's *bête noire*.

Both *Batman: The Dark Knight Returns* and *Batman: The Killing Joke* feature the Joker as the villain protagonist. Like all comic-book villains, the Joker has a back story, or rather an "origin" story as dictated by comic convention. The reasons for his descent into criminality depend on which version of the origin story one is dealing with. As is the case with many superhero characters, origin stories often change over time according to which writer happens to be working on the narrative. The first version of the history of the Joker goes like this: initially the character was positioned as a normal, reasonable, intelligent member of Gotham society; after falling into financial difficulty, he is forced into taking on the persona of the Red Hood by a gang of thugs. While attempting to rob the Ace Chemical Plant the gang are confronted by Batman. The character soon to become the Joker falls into a vat of chemicals and is disfigured, his skin bleached a blank white, his wild hair an extreme shade of emerald green, and his mouth permanently fastened into a vermilion-lipped manic smirk. From this point on he becomes a dangerous sociopath, persistently engaging in criminal activities which inevitably endanger the lives of the citizens of Gotham. Another version of the origin story suggests that far from being an upstanding member of Gotham society who falls on hard times, he becomes a dangerous sociopath as a child under the corrupting influence of an abusive, wife-beating father. In Moore's *Batman: The Killing Joke*, the suggestion is that in addition to his physical misfortunes, the Joker suffered a personal tragedy similar to Bruce Wayne's traumatic experience, when his wife and his unborn child died. In the first scenario the implication is that Batman played a significant part in creating the character of the Joker; in the second the Joker's character was to all intents and purposes already forged. In Moore's version the emotional and the physical are inextricably intertwined. As Terrence Wandtke points out, as comic-book characters are re-inscribed by different writers, they become "endlessly multiple with an identity that is quintessentially post-modern" (2007: 15). In *Batman: The Killing Joke*, in what can be described as a self-referential, device-bearing aside on the multiplicity of origin stories, the Joker quips "Sometimes I remember it one way, sometimes another…if I'm going to have a past, I prefer it to be multiple-choice" (39). The multiplicity of Joker origin stories together with the struggle for identity experienced by Batman in both *Batman: The Killing Joke* and *Batman: The Dark Knight Returns* ideally illustrate the concept of fragmentation of the "self" which has dominated literary fiction since the development of Modernist movements in the arts at the turn of the nineteenth century.

Having discussed the origins of the two characters, origins which play a central role in determining their motives and their actions, I now intend to focus on the moral and ethical issues explored by Miller in *Batman: The Dark Knight Returns* and by Moore in *Batman: The Killing Joke*.

In *Batman: The Dark Knight Returns*, Miller positions Batman as an ageing vigilante coming out of enforced retirement into a dystopian world on the brink of nuclear war. Batman sets himself the task of ridding Gotham City of a murderous, rampaging gang and of greater significance, the Joker, recently released from Arkham Asylum, Gotham's mental institution. Miller's narrative informs the reader that Batman had been forced to retire a decade earlier due to intense public protest against his vigilante *modus operandi*. He returns as The Dark Knight, an angry, disturbed shadow of his former self, mentally and physically damaged. Miller presents the Gotham authorities as weak and corrupt. Batman feels only contempt for the lawmakers, the judicial system and for what he deems to be pathetically ineffective liberal policies. It is for this reason that he feels forced to turn to what is deemed by the Gotham authorities to be fascist vigilantism; "I'm in charge now and I like it" he boasts as early as panel four on the first page of Miller's story (10), before going on to state defiantly "I am the law" (173). In contrast to the Platonic argument that reason should govern the soul (Grube, 1974: 98-104), and that justice "consists in minding your own business and not interfering with other people" (Plato, 1972: 178), under the influence of what Superman terms his "wild obsession" (Miller, 1996: 120), Batman's vision of justice becomes blurred as he develops an obsessive desire to personally institute a biblical form of retribution against Gotham City's criminal underclass, a desire which results in the formulation of a draconian ethical reference point against which he comes to judge society.

Ever since the Joker's first appearance in 1940 Batman has believed the character to be beyond the prevailing level of evil to be found within Gotham's criminal underworld. In *Batman: The Dark Knight Returns*, Batman sees the Joker as a representation of what Stephen King in *Salem's Lot* has termed "Evil with a capital E" (179), a demonic, biblical form of evil. In *The Man Who Laughs*, a story published in 2008, Batman articulates this perspective succinctly when, contemplating the prospect of once again having to renew combat with the Joker he confesses, "I never prepared for this. I planned for the killers, the muggers, the rapists. Desperate people doing desperate things. But I never imagined something like the Joker" (Brubaker: 53). It is possible to argue that in turning to retributive vigilantism in order to combat this capitalised Evil, an Evil "with its cerements of deception cast aside" (King, 1975: 179), an Evil beyond the understanding of contemporary society, Batman effectively operates like a spandex-clad fire and brimstone Old Testament God, a vengeful God seeking draconian justice.

Lawrence Kohlberg suggests that there are three levels of moral development: the "pre-conventional" stressing obedience to authority, the "conventional" based on the principle that one should act conventionally with respect to others and uphold the social order, and the "post-conventional level" whereby a citizen should act in accordance with the highest moral principles focused on justice (Singer, 1993: 465-6). Technically the vigilantism practiced by Miller's Batman does not fall within the boundaries of either pre-conventional or conventional moral development patterns. The post-conventional level, however, allows for criticism of society by a person or group acting in accordance with what they believe to be morally and ethically correct actions. Immanuel Kant has suggested that where "moral worth" is at issue, "what counts is not actions, which one sees, but those inner principles of action that one does not see" (1997: 62). In both *Batman: The Dark Knight Returns* and *Batman: The Killing Joke* Batman's "inner principles of action" cannot be "seen" but only surmised in relation to the narrative's internal and external character dialogue; it is possible, however, to argue that he is convinced that, irrespective of personal motives, he acts in an ethical and morally appropriate manner.

Friedrich Nietzsche offers the warning to those seeking to combat immorality that in fighting "monsters" they should "see to it that in the process [they do not] become a monster" (1989: 89). To the Gotham authorities, Batman has become a "ruthless monstrous vigilante, striking at the foundations of [...] democracy" (Miller, 1996: 65), as much of a danger to Gotham City as is the Joker. From the perspective of the authorities, in enforcing his own absolute model of justice, Batman disregards conventional concepts of ethical and moral behaviour and becomes, like the Joker, a "terrorist" (Miller, 1996: 88), a character deemed by the citizens of Gotham to be, in the words of a television news presenter, "a harmful influence on the children of Gotham" (59). In sharp contrast to the mutually tolerant and magnanimous relationship he had enjoyed with the authorities in the early years of his career, when *Batman: The Dark Knight Returns* begins Batman is a fugitive being chased by the police who have a warrant for his arrest, the links of moral alignment which had once bound citizens and crime-fighter clearly broken. In the past Batman was able to engage the passions of the Gotham public by positioning the Joker as a vicious, depraved maniacal criminal; in *Batman: The Dark Knight Returns*, however, this is no longer possible as he, once the hunter, now joins the Joker in becoming the hunted. Batman's position can be seen to emerge from the conflict between the drive to adhere to what might be termed his "positive" duties and obligations that is, to do things that aid people, and his "negative" duties, obligations to refrain from doing things that actually harm other people.

Søren Kierkegaard argues that those seeking to live an ethically and morally virtuous life should give up their "self-loving desires and cravings, their self-seeking plans and purposes" so that they can "truly work unselfishly for the good [and] put up with being abominated almost as a criminal, insulted and ridiculed" (1995: 194). Within the panels of *Batman: The Dark Knight Returns* Batman struggles to come to terms with his "desires and cravings" and becomes a criminal in the eyes of the people of Gotham. It is against this background of public and institutional hostility that Batman and the Joker play out their *danse macabre*.

In contrast to Batman, who comes to be universally derided as a social pariah, the morally elevated Superman operates within Miller's narrative with the full cooperation of the authorities who sanction him to enforce a conventionally acceptable form of justice. Articulating their different approaches to dealing with the authorities, Superman describes how, in exchange for giving them his "obedience" they gave him a "license" to "save lives" (139), a deal which results in both the authorities and the media refraining from criticism of his actions.

The self-regulatory Comics Code was set up by publishers in 1954 to ensure that the worlds and actions depicted in the American comic-book were ethically and morally acceptable. In line with the Code, Batman's mission statement has over the years been based upon the notion that in every instance good should triumph over evil and that the criminal be punished for his/her misdeeds. If, as Simon Blackburn argues, "the core of morality lies not in what we do, but in our motives in doing it" (2003: 102), then the retribution-driven force behind Batman's *raison d'être* may be brought into question. It can be argued that his devotion to the eradication of crime may be as much influenced by a need for personal revenge as it is by an altruistic sense of justice. Whilst he accedes to the maxim that the safety of the people *is* the supreme law in *Batman: The Dark Knight Returns* and *Batman: The Killing Joke* he also appears to operate under the assumption that justice should be done irrespective of the consequences.

Prefiguring some of the evolutionary ideas posited by Richard Dawkins in *The Selfish Gene* (Dawkins, 1989), Ayn Rand controversially posits the idea that selfishness is in fact a virtue and that altruism is a vice which should be eradicated (1964: 27-32). In direct contrast to consequentialist utilitarian ethics, a philosophy which looks forward to the consequences of actions in order to assess them, the aim of which should be to promote benevolence, solidarity and the advancement of the greatest good for the greatest number (Blackburn, 2003: 75), Rand posits the notion of "ethical egoism", a branch of ethics which focuses on the idea that a character should serve his/her own self interest by acting in such a way as to bring about their own personal happiness, even if this means causing harm to others (27-32). Batman does not attempt to use his talents to rectify the detrimental social conditions that produce endemic crime and poverty, his *raison d'etre* is individualistic rather than collective. In *The Amazing Transforming Superhero*, Terrence Wandtke argues that Batman lives in a "morally ambiguous world" in which he acts pragmatically rather than cruelly (94). If this is the case then Batman's actions may be rooted in a specifically egocentric desire for justice, a personal justice rather than a collective justice, and that in the words of the Joker he is "morally bankrupt" (Miller, 1996: 41). Can Batman's vigilantism be explained in terms of ethical egoism? Well, in extracting retribution for the death of his parents he does serve his own self interest, and he certainly does do harm to others. In *Batman: The Dark Knight Returns* for example, he is involved in a series of violent clashes with a criminal gang who seek to "taste Gotham's blood" (88); in one sequence he throws one of them from the top of Gotham Towers, the highest spot in the city (68). However, in another scene he has the chance to shoot a terrorist mutant; gun in hand, he struggles with his conscience:

> There's only one thing to do about him that makes any sense to me…just press the trigger and blast him from the face of the earth…Though that means crossing a line I drew for myself thirty years ago…I can't think of a single reason to let him live. (77)

Yet he does not kill the mutant. And of course, over the years, in a succession of battles with the Joker, when presented with the opportunity to kill his most dangerous enemy he refrains from doing so, refusing to cross a conventionalised ethical borderline. As he himself acknowledges in *Batman: The Dark Knight Returns*, throughout the history of their confrontations he has given the Joker "too many chances" (146). Over the years, this refusal to kill the Joker consistently comes back to haunt Batman.

If Batman can be deemed to be morally vindicated in terms of utilitarian philosophy, where does his behaviour stand in relation to the concept of virtue ethics? Most ethical theories focus on the concepts of duty-orientation or action-orientation, virtue ethics, however, focuses on the personality of the protagonist. Whilst action-based ethics centres on concept of doing, virtue ethics relates to the process of being. From the perspective of virtue ethics, the issue is not what Batman should do, but rather what he should become; in other words what sort of a person he should aspire to be, not how he should act. According to Aristotle, moral virtues are the central character traits of what he terms a "good" person (1987: book two). As Blackburn suggests it takes "education" to become virtuous (2003: 97); in the case of Batman his traumatic childhood experience can be seen to be educationally instrumental in the further development of what has consistently been portrayed as an inherently virtuous disposition. In both *Batman: The Dark Knight Returns* and *Batman: The Killing Joke*, Batman's past, present and prospective lives can be termed good or in the case of his future life potentially good and therefore, in line with Aristotle's argument, virtuous. The Joker, on the other hand, is positioned in both graphic novels as being devoid of any virtuous sensibility.

In addition to the plethora of crimes committed by the Joker during the long-running history of their confrontations, a list headed by more than 2,000 murders, in *Batman: The Killing Joke* he kills a series of characters including Sarah Essen, the wife of Gotham's Police Commissioner. In addition he shoots and paralyses Barbara Gordon, the Commissioner's adopted daughter. In Moore's dark narrative, the Joker photographs Gordon's daughter naked and forces him to look at the images (13-26). Within the narrative of *Batman: The Dark Knight Returns* the Joker is deemed to have committed or orchestrated more than six hundred murders. Miller consistently forces Batman to confront his past, with each murder that occurs the memories of Crime Alley come flooding back and the pain returns as "for the hundred thousandth time" his parents die (132). Still believing that he was responsible for the creation of the Joker, Batman, acknowledging what he deems to be causal responsibility, declares that he will "count the dead one by one [and] add them to the list", that is the list of people he, by association, believes he has murdered (117). He describes how he has "lain awake nights...planning it. Picturing it [...] considering every possible method...treasuring each imaginary moment" (142), and yet, despite having had numerous opportunities, he has never carried out his fantasy of killing the Joker. Batman's reticence seems paradoxical in the light of his deontological, Manichean belief that right is right and wrong is wrong, and that wrong should always be punished. Surely, if Batman's actions were motivated purely by Rand's concept of ethical egoism then he would have pulled the trigger at the first opportunity without suffering any moral or ethical remorse. From a purely utilitarian perspective, irrespective of his personal crusade, Batman's vigilantism can be seen to be quintessentially good, or even beyond good in that in sparing the life of a character positioned as beyond evil, he does act for the benefit of the greatest number, even if the greatest number, the citizens of Gotham, are no longer appreciative of his efforts.

Since his first appearance in the Batman narratives, the Joker has spent innumerable years as an inmate in Gotham's Arkham Asylum. Both the authorities and the citizens of Gotham City believe that the Joker is insane. Like Batman, the Joker can indeed be read as psychotic, creating, as he does his own ethically distorted milieu and suffering, as Reynolds suggests, from "a radical inability to function in the everyday world" (1992: 67). Throughout both graphic novels he exhibits extreme anti-social attitudes, appearing to inhabit an alternative world in which he is unable to distinguish right from wrong. From this perspective it is possible to argue that he is incapable of interpreting the real world or his actions within that world rationally. Of course it is often the case that any significant deviation from conventional morality is deemed to be a sign of madness as much as of immorality. From his distorted perspective, however, the Joker's nihilistic desire to undermine and disrupt what he claims to be mankind's "frail and useless notions of order and sanity" (Moore, 1988: 33) is perfectly rational because within ethical nihilism moral and ethical properties do not exist, the binaries good and bad are erased and therefore no behaviour can be deemed to be morally right or morally wrong.

The case for the Joker being insane is a strong one. In *Batman: The Killing Joke* he describes himself as a "loo-oo-oony", and as he himself suggests, "When you're a loo-oo-oony, then you just don't give a fig" (25). The Joker goes on to relate his madness to what he perceives to be an absurdist world, claiming that he went crazy when he saw what a "black, awful joke the world was" (39). Railing against "life and all its random injustice" (28), a rant presumably motivated by his experience of disfiguration, in a Beckettian reverie he describes the world as "a black awful joke", and proposes the notion that "everything anybody ever valued or struggled for…is all a monstrous, demented gag" (39). The Joker seems to view his own state of mind as just a step away from the psychotic shadows which exist on the periphery of "normality." All it takes, he suggests is "one bad day to reduce the sanest man to lunacy" (38).

Blackburn suggests that arguing about ethics is akin to "arguing about the place at the end of the rainbow, something which is one thing from one point of view, and another from another" (2003: 19), a belief which underpins the claim made by ethical relativists that morality can only be understood in relation to individual points of view. If this is indeed the case, then it can be suggested that from the Joker's perspective he simply operates logically within his own [distorted] moral and ethical parameters. In *Batman: The Killing Joke* he articulates the divide which he feels exists between himself and the rest of humanity; in one of his trademark polemics he questions the sanity of the "average man" who, he claims, works to "a deformed set of values" within what he terms a collective "club-footed social conscience" (33). The Joker sees the concept of adherence to conventional morality as nothing more than a blind collective obedience to custom. This paradigm allows the Joker, who clearly sees himself as superior to the rest of humanity, to rationalise and maximise his Nietzschean desire to "ride upon the backs of lesser beings" (Pearson and Large, 2007:82).

Childs suggests that myth is often used to create "a controlling narrative that could be mapped onto and make sense of [...] modernity" (2008: 209). Comic-book superheroes do just that, operating within the modern world as parabolic moral ambassadors, as latter-day Sampsons in Day-Glo spandex tights. The sequential-art narratives created by Miller and Moore utilise the Batman-Joker relationship to suggest that the righteous are not always innocent of the deeds of the wicked, that as Gibran argues, "the white-handed is not clean in the doings of the felon" (1988: 35), and that evil can be seen as "good tortured by its own hunger and thirst" (58). In *Batman: The Killing Joke* Moore argues that villainy and heroism proceed out of the same confrontation with absurdity as both Batman and the Joker struggle to make sense of their lives. In illustrating the way in which the citizens of Gotham rapidly transform Batman from a moral and ethical exemplar into a despised social pariah, Miller highlights the fine line that divides the hero from the villain. The ambiguous signifiers infused within these seminal texts allow the reader to construct Batman as either a heroic crime-fighter or as an egocentric fascist vigilante depending on the degree of moral alignment developed with the character. The Joker can be read as an irrational, nihilistic madman, or as a victim of fate and an uncaring society.

"Zap!" "Pow!" superhero comic-book narratives can insightfully highlight moral and ethical benchmarks and dividing lines which point us in the right direction in terms of developing an understanding of what constitutes both conventionally acceptable and conventionally reprehensible behaviour, and of how we might practise the former and avoid the latter. Paradoxically, a genre traditionally labelled escapist, as a medium for those who want to hide from reality, can, through the works of writers such as Miller and Moore, be seen to confront and interrogate some of the most important issues relating to the realities of the human condition. The stories contained within the pages of *Batman: The Dark Knight Returns* and *Batman: The Killing Joke* have already attained mythical status. These tales undoubtedly have important things to say about ethical behaviour, about what Thomas Hardy termed "decency and good morals" (1972: 64). It may be the case that today, as in Hardy's time, realism remains an inadequate genre for the contemplation of such important subjects and that perhaps superhero parables may well be a more effective means of stimulating interest in contemporary philosophical debate. Miller and Moore use their sequential-art narratives to tell stories which, whilst ostensibly appearing to be focused on titanic conflicts between costumed heroes and villains, effectively ask their readers to intellectually engage with a series of important moral issues relating to the concepts of criminality, justice, and the ethics of vigilantism.

Notes

[1] Although the term "graphic novel" can describe a stand-alone original narrative, it normally refers to a collection of narratives which had originally appeared as individual comics within a unifying story-arc. Both *Batman: The Dark Knight Returns* and *Batman: The Killing Joke* fall into this category.
[2] On the back cover of *Batman: The Killing Joke* is the warning "[s]uggested for mature readers."
[3] In his first appearance, in *Detective Comics* #27, the name of the character was hyphenated as the "Bat-Man"; by issue #30, although the hyphen was retained for the title panel it had been removed from references to the character's name within the main story panels.
[4] The Joker first appeared in *Batman* #1, 1940.
[5] *Batman: The Dark Knight Returns* was originally published in four single issues in 1986. The page numbers used in this chapter relate to the graphic novel published in 1996.

References

Aristotle. 1987. *The Nicomachean Ethics*. Trans. J. E. Cowell. New York: Prometheus Books.
Bakhtin, M. M. 1989. *The Dialogic Imagination*. M. Holquist. (ed.), Trans. C. Emerson and M. Holquist, Austin: University of Texas.

Blackburn, S. 2003. *Ethics: A Very Short Introduction*. Oxford: Oxford University Press.

Brubaker, E. 2008. *The Man Who Laughs*. New York: DC Comics.

Childs, Peter. 2008. *Modernism*. London: Routledge.

Dawkins, R. 1989. *The Selfish Gene*. Oxford: Oxford University Press.

Freud, S. 1990. *Art and Literature*. London: Penguin.

Garrett, G. *Holy Superheroes!* Colorado Springs: Pinon, 2005.

Gibran, K. 1988. *The Prophet*. London: William Heinemann.

Hardy, T. 1972. *Under the Greenwood Tree*. London: Macmillan.

Kant. I. 1997. *Groundwork on the Metaphysics of Morals*. Trans. M. Gregor. Cambridge: Cambridge University Press.

Kierkegaard, S. 1995. *Works of Love*. Trans. and edited by H. V. Hong. Princeton: Princeton University Press, 194.

King, S. 1974. *Salem's Lot*. London: New English Library.

Loeb, J. and Morris, T. 2005. "Heroes and Superheroes", in T. Morris and M. Morris (eds), *Superheroes and Philosophy*. Chicago: Open Court. 11-20.

Miller, F. 1996. *Batman: The Dark Knight Returns*. New York: DC Comics/Warner Books:

Moore, A. 1988. *Batman: The Killing Joke*. New York: DC Comics.

Morris, T. 2005. "What's Behind the Mask? The Secret of Secret Identities", in T. Morris and M. Morris (eds), *Superheroes and Philosophy*. Chicago: Open Court. 250-65.

Morris, T. and Morris, M. (eds) 2005. *Superheroes and Philosophy*. Chicago: Open Court.

Nietzsche, F. 1989. *Beyond Good and Evil.* New York: Vintage.

O'Neil, D. 2008. *Batman Unauthorized*. Dallas: BenBella Books.

Pearson, K. A. and Large, D. (eds), 2007. *The Nietzsche Reader*. Oxford: Blackwell Publishing.

Plato. 2008. *The Republic*. Trans. G. M. Grube. Indianapolis: Hackett.

Rand, A. 1964. *The Virtue of Selfishness*. New York: New American Library.

Reynolds, R. 1992. *Superheroes: A Modern Mythology*. London: Batsford.

Singer, P. (ed.) 1993. *A Companion to Ethics*. Oxford: Blackwell.

Wandtke, T. R. 2007. *The Amazing Transforming Superhero*. London: McFarland & Company.

CONTRIBUTORS

Steve Brie is a Senior Lecturer in English Literature at Liverpool Hope University. He has an MA and PhD from the University of Liverpool. He has published a monograph on the history of the King George and Queen Elizabeth Diamond Stakes, has edited two collections and published chapters and journal articles on poetry, film, television drama, theology, history, the graphic novel, comic books and popular music. His research interests include: the poetry of Charles Bukowski; British and American television drama and British and American popular music. (bries@hope.ac.uk)

Jim Casey is an Assistant Professor at High Point University in North Carolina. He has an MA from the University of North Texas, an MPhil from the University of Glasgow, and a PhD from the Hudson Strode Program in Renaissance Studies at the University of Alabama. He was the first Strode Exchange Scholar to study at The Shakespeare Institute in Stratford-upon-Avon. Although primarily a Shakespearean, he has published on such diverse topics as textual theory, performance theory, postmodern theory, comics, Shakespeare, Chaucer, and *Battlestar Galactica*.

Jim Daems teaches in the Department of English at the University of the Fraser Valley (British Columbia, Canada). He is the author of *Seventeenth-Century Literature and Culture* (Continuum, 2006) and co-editor (with Holly Nelson) of *Eikon Basilike* (Broadview, 2005). He has also published articles and reviews in *Milton Quarterly*, *Early Modern Literary Studies*, Men *and Masculinities: A Social, Cultural, and Historical Encyclopedia*, and *A Reader's Guide to Lesbian and Gay Studies*. (jim.daems@ufv.ca)

Susan Alice Fischer is Professor of English at Medgar Evers College of The City University of New York. She is Co-Editor of *Changing English: Studies in Culture and Education* and Book Reviews Editor for the online journal *Literary London: Interdisciplinary Studies in the Representation of London*. Recent essays and reviews have been published in *The Swarming Streets: Twentieth Century Representations of London*, *Tulsa Studies in Women's Literature*, *The Women's Review of Books*, *Critical Engagements* and elsewhere; forthcoming work on contemporary British literature is appearing in the *Blackwell Encyclopaedia of Twentieth-Century World Fiction* and in various journals and essay collections. She is completing a book about contemporary women's London narratives and editing a collection of essays about the changing notion of national identity in contemporary British literature and culture. (safischer@mec.cuny.edu)

Unhae Langis currently teaches at Slippery Rock University near Pittsburgh, Pennsylvania. Her work examines early modern literature from the perspectives of ethics, gender, and historical phenomenology. Her articles have appeared in *Comparative Drama, Literature Compass, Journal of the Wooden O Symposium, Ohio Valley Shakespeare Conference: Selected Papers,* and other journals. Forthcoming in 2011 are a monograph, *Passion, and Moderation, and Virtue in Shakespearean Drama* (Continuum) and an essay on usury, thrift/prodigality, and political friendship in *The Merchant of Venice* (Upstart Crow). (unhae.langis@sru.edu)

Louis Markos is Professor in English and Scholar in Residence at Houston Baptist University; he holds the Robert H. Ray Chair in Humanities. He is author of *Lewis Agonistes: How C.S. Lewis Can Train Us to Wrestle with the Modern and Postmodern World* (B & H Publishing, 2003), *From Achilles to Christ: Why Christians Should Read the Pagan Classics* (IVP Academic, 2007), and *Pressing Forward: Tennyson and the Victorian Age* (Ave Maria University Press, 2007). This essay is adapted from Chapter 8 of *The Eye of the Beholder: How to See the World like a Romantic Poet* (Winged Lion Press, 2010). (lmarkos@hbu.edu)

Becky McLaughlin is an Associate Professor of English at the University of South Alabama, where she teaches film studies and critical theory. She has published articles on perversion, paranoia, the gaze and modern poetry, as well as works of fiction and creative non-fiction. She has also co-edited *Everyday Theory*, a critical theory textbook, and is currently working on a book about the *Canterbury Tales* entitled *Chaucer's Cut*. (bmclaugh@jaguar1.usouthal.edu)

Robert McParland is Associate Professor of English at Felician College, NJ. He is the author of *Charles Dickens's American Audience* (Lexington, 2010), *Writing About Joseph Conrad* (Chelsea House, 2010), and the editor of *Music and Literary Modernism* (Cambridge Scholars Press, 2006). (mcparlandr@felician.edu)

Gillian (Jill) Rudd is a Senior Lecturer in the School of English at Liverpool University, England. She teaches and researches in the areas of late medieval English literature and nineteenth and twentieth-century women's writing. She has been interested in eco-criticism since 1998 and spoke at the first ASLE-UK conference in Swansea; she has published various green pieces, including her book *Greenery: Ecocritical Readings of Late Medieval English Literature* (Manchester University Press, 2007) and articles and chapters on mice (*Yearbook of English Studies*, 36:1, 2006) clouds (*Essays and Studies 2008: Literature and Science*) and most recently on various aspects of *Sir Gawain and the Green Knight* read from a 'green' perspective. She is the author of the sections on Ecocriticism and Medieval Literature for the *Oxford Handbook of Medieval Literature in English* (OUP, 2010) and the *Oxford Handbook of Ecocriticism* and is contemplating a book offering a green reading of *Sir Gawain and the Green Knight* alongside some other Middle English Gawain romances such as *Gawain and the Carl of Carlisle*.

Lawrence Phillips is Reader in English and Divisional Leader for Media, English and Culture at the University of Northampton. He is the editor of the peer-reviewed academic e-journal *Literary London: Interdisciplinary studies in the representation of London* (www.literarylondon.org), academic director of the annual international conference of the same name, and secretary of the UK Network for Modern Fiction Studies. A new collection co-edited with Anne Witchard, *London Gothic: Space, Place and the Gothic Imagination*, will be published by Continuum in 2010. His most recent book is an edited collection entitled *A Mighty Mass of Brick and Smoke: Victorian and Edwardian Representations of London* (Rodopi, 2007). He is also the author of *London Narratives: Post-war Fiction and the City* (Continuum, 2006), and the editor of a further collection entitled *The Swarming Streets: Twentieth-Century Literary Representations of London* (Rodopi, 2004). He has also published various essays on late Victorian and twentieth-century literature, and is currently working on a book on colonial culture in the South Pacific. (Lawrence.Phillips@northampton.ac.uk)

William T. Rossiter is Lecturer in English at Liverpool Hope University. He is the author of *Chaucer and Petrarch* (Brewer, 2010), and his research focuses mainly on late medieval and early modern literature, with a particular interest in Anglo-Italian literary and cultural relationships. He has written various articles on Chaucer, Petrarch, Boccaccio, John Lydgate and Sir Thomas Wyatt. He is currently co-editing (with Jason Powell) a volume entitled *Handle with Care: Authority and Diplomacy from Dante to Shakespeare*, and is carrying out research for a forthcoming monograph entitled *Wyatt Abroad*. (rossitw@hope.ac.uk)

Li-Hui Tsai received her PhD from Queen Mary, University of London, and is currently working as a postdoctoral research fellow, participating in a collaborative, interdisciplinary project of writing and science. Her article on Mary Robison, feminism and visual culture is due to appear in a scholarly edited collection on the subject of book illustration, and she is also currently preparing a new critical edition of Mary Wollstonecraft's letters. (dlhtsai@gamil.com)

INDEX

Page numbers in *italics* are bibliographic references. Page numbers in square brackets give the textual context for chapter notes.

DATE DUE